Palgrave Series in Asia and Pacific Studies

Series Editors
May Tan-Mullins
University of Nottingham Ningbo China
Ningbo, Zhejiang, China

Adam Knee
Lasalle College of the Arts
Singapore

Filippo Gilardi
University of Nottingham Ningbo China
Ningbo, China

The Asia and Pacific regions, with a population of nearly three billion people, are of critical importance to global observers, academics, and citizenry due to their rising influence in the global political economy as well as traditional and nontraditional security issues. Any changes to the domestic and regional political, social, economic, and environmental systems will inevitably have great impacts on global security and governance structures. At the same time, Asia and the Pacific have also emerged as a globally influential, trend-setting force in a range of cultural arenas. The remit of this book series is broadly defined, in terms of topics and academic disciplines. We invite research monographs on a wide range of topics focused on Asia and the Pacific. In addition, the series is also interested in manuscripts pertaining to pedagogies and research methods, for both undergraduate and postgraduate levels. Published by Palgrave Macmillan, in collaboration with the Institute of Asia and Pacific Studies, UNNC.

More information about this series at
http://www.palgrave.com/gp/series/14665

Bo Gao

China's Economic Engagement in North Korea

palgrave
macmillan

Bo Gao
Ningbo University of Finance and Economics
Ningbo, China

Palgrave Series in Asia and Pacific Studies
ISBN 978-981-13-0886-4   ISBN 978-981-13-0887-1   (eBook)
https://doi.org/10.1007/978-981-13-0887-1

Library of Congress Control Number: 2019930039

© The Editor(s) (if applicable) and The Author(s) 2019
This work is subject to copyright. All rights are solely and exclusively licensed by the Publisher, whether the whole or part of the material is concerned, specifically the rights of translation, reprinting, reuse of illustrations, recitation, broadcasting, reproduction on microfilms or in any other physical way, and transmission or information storage and retrieval, electronic adaptation, computer software, or by similar or dissimilar methodology now known or hereafter developed.
The use of general descriptive names, registered names, trademarks, service marks, etc. in this publication does not imply, even in the absence of a specific statement, that such names are exempt from the relevant protective laws and regulations and therefore free for general use.
The publisher, the authors, and the editors are safe to assume that the advice and information in this book are believed to be true and accurate at the date of publication. Neither the publisher nor the authors or the editors give a warranty, express or implied, with respect to the material contained herein or for any errors or omissions that may have been made. The publisher remains neutral with regard to jurisdictional claims in published maps and institutional affiliations.

Cover illustration: © [daboost]

This Palgrave Macmillan imprint is published by the registered company Springer Nature Singapore Pte Ltd.
The registered company address is: 152 Beach Road, #21-01/04 Gateway East, Singapore 189721, Singapore

ACKNOWLEDGEMENTS

I am grateful to Dr Ivaylo Gatev for his untiring support and guidance, and for funding my trip to Northeast China in 2014 without whom this project would have remained a pipe dream. I am also grateful to Dr Catherine Goetze, Dr Christopher Pierson, Dr Miwa Hirono, Dr Jonathan Sullivan, and Dr Gregory Moore from the University of Nottingham for their help during different periods of my research. Thanks to the financial support from the Institute of Asia Pacific Studies and the Graduate School of the University of Nottingham, Ningbo, China, to my travel for presenting my research at conferences in Nottingham, Shenzhen, Seoul, and Beijing was made possible.

Finally, my family, especially my parents, gave me a reason to believe; their financial and emotional support made this job more than worthwhile.

PUBLISHED TITLES IN PSAPS

China's Economic Engagement in North Korea
By Bo Gao

China as a Global Clean Energy Champion: Lifting the Veil
By Philip Andrews-Speed and Sufang Zhang

World Heritage Conservation in the Pacific: The Case of Solomon Islands
By Stephanie Clair Price

Eco-development in China: Cities, Communities and Buildings
By Wu Deng and Ali Cheshmehzangi

Designing Cooler Cities: Energy, Cooling and Urban Form: The Asian Perspective
Edited by Ali Cheshmehzangi and Chris Butters

Mediatized China-Africa Relations: How Media Discourses Negotiate the Shifting of Global Order
By Shubo Li

Assessing Intellectual Property Compliance in Contemporary China: The World Trade Organisation TRIPS Agreement
By Kristie Thomas

Chinese War Correspondents: Covering Wars and Conflicts in the Twenty-First Century
By Shixin Ivy Zhang

China's Media and Soft Power in Africa: Promotion and Perceptions
Edited by Xiaoling Zhang, Herman Wasserman, and Winston Mano

CONTENTS

1 Introduction   1

2 China's Economic Activities in the North Korean Mineral Resource Sector   23

3 China's Economic Activities in the North Korean Fishing Industry   47

4 Chinese Cross-Border Economic Activities in North Korea   73

5 The Regional Impact of Chinese Economic Activity in North Korea   111

6 Conclusion   143

Appendix A: Introduction   155

Appendix B: China's Economic Activities in the North Korean Mineral Resource Sector   157

CONTENTS

Appendix C: China's Economic Activities in the North Korean Fishing Industry   159

Appendix D: Chinese Cross-Border Economic Activities in North Korea   163

Index   169

LIST OF TABLES

Table 2.1	Details of Chinese economic activities in North Korea in the mineral and energy sector	30
Table 3.1	Chinese economic activities in North Korea on fishery industry	50
Table 4.1	Comparison of geographical condition of Shenzhen and Rason	95
Table 5.1	South Korean aid to North Korea, 2003–2007	131
Table 5.2	South Korea official strategic products aid, 2003–2007 (food amount: 1000 tons; value amount: billion won)	133
Table 5.3	South Korean aid to North Korea, 2008–2012	133
Table 5.4	US aid to North Korea, 1996–2009	134

CHAPTER 1

Introduction

BACKGROUND

China and North Korea had become blood allies since the beginning of the Cold War, in particular following the friendship built during the Korean War against US-led UN troops from 25 June 1950 to 27 July 1953 (Haruki, 2014; Seth, 2010). The physical conflict ended though the war did not. Since then, China has offered large amounts of funds and material aid to North Korea according to the Treaty of Friendship, Cooperation and Mutual Assistance between the People's Republic of China (PRC) and the Democratic People's Republic of Korea (DPRK) signed on 10 September 1961 (Cornell, 2002; Beal, 2005). During the Cultural Revolution from 1966 to 1976, there were harsh ideological disputes about North Korea's orthodox schooling and China's revisionism of socialism especially when Beijing started to get in touch with Washington, DC, in 1972 (Harrold, 2004; Adrian, 2018: 78–79). After that, China's establishment of a diplomatic relationship with South Korea in 1992 also seriously influenced the top-level interaction between Beijing and Pyongyang (Liu Jin-zhi et al., 2006; Cha, 2013: 325–327). Yet these two issues have not halted the aid from Beijing to North Korea, which maintains the survival of China's strategic buffer zone against the US and its allies.

In the post-Cold War era, especially since the early 2000s, the Sino-DPRK relationship has become commercialised. It started with the entry of a small number of Chinese companies into North Korea in the early 2000s

© The Author(s) 2019
B. Gao, *China's Economic Engagement in North Korea*,
Palgrave Series in Asia and Pacific Studies,
https://doi.org/10.1007/978-981-13-0887-1_1

1

and officially began with the signing in 2005 of the Agreement between the Government of the PRC and the Government of the DPRK for the Promotion and Protection of Investment. Chinese economic activities in North Korea expanded rapidly in several fields such as mineral resources, the fishing industry, physical infrastructure, tourism, and labour cooperation. The commercialisation of the Sino-DPRK relationship can be observed from three specific changes. The first change is the reduction of official economic assistance and rapid increase of investment. The number of Chinese investment projects in the DPRK increased rapidly since 2002 (Choo, 2008: 343–350; Ford and Kwan, 2008). The second change concerns multiple economic actors. The new Chinese economic activities have been implemented by not only the central government but also the sub-state-level economic actors. The latter, such as local companies and regional governments (city and province), are also more active than the central government in the huge field of investment in North Korea. Such investment includes those made in the marketplace, the construction of social infrastructure (such as roads and railways), mineral extraction, computer production, marine production, and fishing licensing. The third change relates to the measures taken to support North Korea, which has been transformed from direct official assistance to a mixture of official assistance and investment in order to help Pyongyang develop its own economic strength. The Chinese government aims to encourage Pyongyang to follow the Chinese style of economic reform and achieve integration into the international economy. This idea, however, is rejected, or at least resisted, by Pyongyang. The response from China has been to promote and encourage investment in North Korea and to use technical assistance in exchange for natural resources with a view to improving North Korea's technological capability in the short term and building the long-term comprehensive economic self-development abilities of North Korea rather than directly aid.

DEFINING THE GAP

In the current research on the Sino-DPRK economic relationship, there are two major research strands. The first, mainly researched by Chinese scholars, is dominated by discussions of the status quo and existing problems in Sino-North Korea trade and measures taken to address them. The main problems include huge difficulties in, and risks of, trade settlement, currency problem (use of RMB) the increase in North Korea's outstanding payments, and the negative influences of political issues, such as the nuclear crisis in North Korea. Relevant measures include the promotion of inter-government cooperation and the institutionalisation of trade, providing aid for the construction of infrastructure, and the resolution of North Korea's nuclear problems (Sun, 2004: 67–71; Yu, 2008: 32–34; Lin and Jin, 2009: 37–43; Wang, 2008: 48–50; Zhang, 2006: 3–8; Zhang, 2007: 38–41; Zhang et al., 2009: 36–37; Yu, 2010: 121–123; Han, 2011: 12–23; Zhang, 2011: 13–21; Xu, 2011; Li, 2012: 35–39; Piao, 2012: 44–53; Bai, 2013; Wang, 2013: 62–63; Wang and Zhang, 2014: 451–470; Du, 2014). Man (2011) uses the case of Dandong-Sinuiju economic cooperation to explain a top-down model of the Sino-DPRK economic relationship and predicts future developments. Li (2011: 58–61), Sun (2015: 64–68), Piao and Li (2012: 3–10) and Huang and Hu (2014: 3–10) also discusses the problem of North Korean escapees to Northeast China, their negative impact on China's diplomacy and how to deal with North Korean escapees by pushing economic reform in North Korea and achieving cooperation with the UN. Lin and Hao (2011: 11–18), Zhang and Ru (2012), and Ge (2015: 111–115) also discuss the significance of Sino-DPRK economic cooperation to the access of the Sea of Japan through Tumen River. Liu (2008: 83–89) evaluates the attempt of Beijing in pushing economic reform in North Korea through economic participation.

The second research strand provides explanations for China's economic policy regarding North Korea, especially from the general state level, and in the traditional area of security, such as the aim of maintaining regional stability and peace and avoiding the collapse of North Korea (Russell, 2000: 47–64; Shambaugh, 2003: 43–56; O'Hanlon and Mike, 2003; Fuqua, 2007; Lee, 2009; Lim, 2009; Stares and Wit Joel, 2009; Moore, 2014: 77–80). Rozman (2007), Moore (2008: 1–29), Hundt (2010: 132–142), and Nanto and Chanlett Avery (2010) claim that Beijing's ultimate objective in pushing Chinese economic activities in North Korea is in order to sustain regional stability, thereby persuading Pyongyang to restrain itself and attempting to lower the possibility of a US attack on North Korea. Goldstein (2006), Hagstrom and Soderbeg (2006), Ikenberry and Moon (2008: 45–59, 140–150), Park and Scott (2013), Huang and Shih (2014) point out that China aims to use North Korea as a tool to increase its regional influence and ensure security by balancing the US military influence in Northeast Asia. French (2007) and Haggard and Noland (2009: 10–12) recognise that Beijing plays a key role in the encouragement of investments in North Korea because it aims to promote regional economic integration of Russia's Far East, Northeast China, and the Korean Peninsula, in particular the Great

Tumen River Initiative. Many South Korean scholars, such as Lee (2003: 1–8), Kim (2006: 898–916), Joo and Kwak (2007), Choo (2008: 360–370), and Yoon and Lee (2013: 19–31) see the rapid increase of Chinese investment as Beijing's strategic objective of leading North Korea towards economic reform, increasing its dependence on China and finally achieving denuclearisation of North Korea. Kim (2011: 257–271) also takes the example of Sinuiju, a North Korean city on the Sino-DPRK border, as an indication that the intention of Chinese economic investment in North Korea is to develop Northeast China.

Indeed, the previous research outlined above is helpful in understanding the Sino-DPRK economic relationship. However, little work has been done on the specific activities in the field of China's economic activities in North Korea from the non-military security drivers and actors below the state level. This research is not about the structural change of Chinese economic activities; rather, it considers Beijing as the one who controls and orchestrates the actions of the other Chinese actors and recognises traditional security as the main motivation of Beijing. Even though they contributed to the non-traditional security problems, the major impact is still discussed around the central government with two major weaknesses.

Firstly, Chinese economic activities have changed with the rapid increase of Chinese investment and the reduction of official assistance. Its role has been weakened as a result of domestic decentralisation of the economy (because Beijing has recentralised political power since Xi became President) and active engagement of actors below the state level with North Korea. Meanwhile, the requirement of developing Northeast China is both too wide and too partial for two reasons. On the one hand, compared to the northeast provinces of Jilin and Liaoning, Heilongjiang province (also in Northeast China) is almost irrelevant to the border economy with North Korea except the oil transportation from Daqing to North Korea. However, it has benefited from developing a cross-border economy with the Russian Far East. On the other hand, Chinese economic actors in the DPRK are not only from Northeast China but also from other coastal provinces. The spread of ethnic Korean businesses towards other coastal areas of China has created multiple identities for these businessmen and expanded the relationship between North Korea and different provinces outside Northeast China. For instance, Zhejiang province in Southeast China encourages ethnic Korean businesses to join the local chamber of commerce. Thus, the requirement of developing Northeast China is only one reason for Chinese economic engagement with DPRK.

INTRODUCTION 5

Secondly, the idea of traditional security-oriented motivation could explain Beijing's active organisation of the Six Party Talks and other mediation between North Korea and the US in order to avoid potential military invasion by the US of North Korea and protract a complete resolution of the North Korean nuclear problem through diplomatic negotiation. However, it is not appropriate to explain Beijing's intention to implement economic activities in North Korea from both general strategic and specific details. From the general strategy and the military point of view, Beijing has avoided a potential short-term regional war on the Korean Peninsula through its mediation. It successfully sustained the regional peace and fundamental order even it was a cold peace on the brink of military conflict. Its encouragement to invest in North Korea aims to strengthen its influence over the country, to push through economic reform, and to raise expectations that the investments of actors below the state level could help the construction of independent developing abilities of North Korea in non-military areas to reduce the burden of offering economic assistance.

From the specific areas of investment, even if the official assistance could be seen as a tool for sustaining the survival of the Pyongyang regime, it could be very difficult to connect the investments motivated by resolving local socio-economic problems with the grand strategy of the central government, especially as there is divergence between local requirements and national strategy.

This book attempts to close the gaps above by answering the four questions below:

1. What is the relationship between Beijing and actors below the state level in their economic activities in North Korea since 2002?
2. What are the drivers of actors below the state level to implement economic activities in North Korea and what are their differences from the national interests?
3. What is the impact of Chinese economic activity in North Korea on regional security and China's grand strategy in Northeast Asia?
4. What does this mean to the making of China's foreign policy?

The first question aims to make clear the specific activities of the central government and actors below the state in North Korea first. Then the relationship between Beijing and actors below the state is described by outlining and comparing the amount, the types, and the funding of economic activities implemented by actors at the state level (central government and central state-owned companies) and at the level below the state (governments on the province and city levels, local state-owned companies, and private enterprises) in North Korea since 2002. After that, in contrast to the (Beijing-dominant) relationship of central-local/sub-level actors in economic interaction with North Korea in the Cold War era, the (bottom-up) characteristic of this central-region relationship is discussed specifically.

The second question attempts to highlight three points. The first concerns the drivers of actors below the state level in the implementation of economic activities in North Korea. The point after that is how effective these activities are in helping resolve such local problems faced by China as environmental pollution, population outflow, local industrial development, and the loss of traditional fishing areas. The final point is to demonstrate that these activities are mainly driven by the desire to protect local interests. This can be examined by making comparisons between the local and national data related to these economic activities. Usually these economic activities focus on the local interests because their product outputs are relatively significant to the local level but very small at the national level.

The third question mainly evaluates the general impact of Chinese activities in North Korea on the regional security of Northeast Asia, especially the Korean Peninsula, at three levels. The first level is the domestic level of the Korean Peninsula, in particular the economic reform and opening up of North Korea. This section discusses how Chinese economic activities push North Korea to broaden its economic 'opening up' to the world and avoid regime collapse by attracting funding. The second level is the relationship between China and South Korea. This reveals that the rapid increase of Chinese economic activities in North Korea has led to concerns in South Korea about the economic overdependence of North Korea on China and created further negative impact on Sino-Republic of Korea (Sino-ROK) relations, especially the resolution of historical disputes. The third level is the general regional security problem, especially the denuclearisation of North Korea through Six Party Talks. This level illustrates how Chinese economic activities offer the fundamental conditions of Six Party Talks by avoiding the collapse of the North Korean regime. However, in general, the huge amount of funding brought about by these activities weakens the weight of US economic leverage to engage the denuclearisation of North Korea and almost makes it impossible to denuclearise North Korea through dialogue and economic pressure.

The final question focuses attention on the process of China's foreign policymaking as it becomes more pluralistic with the decentralisation of power from Beijing. The central government is not the only, nor the ultimate, policy-implementing body on foreign economic policy. Multiple actors below the state level, such as provincial and city-level governments, local state-owned companies and private enterprises, and even social associations and the general public, can play a role in China's foreign policymaking, especially at the implementation stage, allowing their own voices to be heard and protecting their interests.

This book aims to examine that the commercialisation of the Sino-DPRK relationship is driven by a multiplicity of actors below the state level, which include governments at the provincial and city levels, local state-owned companies and private enterprises, as well as social associations. These actors have become economically engaged in North Korea at a deep level. Their activities both contribute and occasionally run counter to Beijing's overall objectives of keeping regional peace and stability in Northeast Asia and sustaining positive relationships with neighbouring countries. At a higher level, the implementation of China's foreign economic policy is pluralistic with the decentralisation of Beijing's authority and active engagement of actors below the state level. Even the decision-making of China's foreign economic policy is pluralistic in special cases such as Chang-Ji-Tu National Strategy, which will be introduced later in the empirical chapters.

This book contributes to the existing literature by adding new ideas. First of all, a comprehensive picture is drawn of Chinese economic activities in North Korea. It includes activities implemented by actors in different provinces (Zhejiang, Shandong, Henan, and Chongqing) rather than focusing only on Jilin and Liaoning provinces in Northeast China as much previous research has done. This is followed by an illustration of the changed relationship between Beijing and actors below the state level (the majority of Chinese actors in North Korea) in the implementation stage of foreign economic policy which concerns economic participation in North Korea. The traditional hierarchical central-local relationship during the Cold War is being replaced by a bottom-up model with the decentralisation of Beijing's power over the economy. Furthermore, with the increased distance of Beijing from the administration of local affairs, Chinese economic activities, participated in mainly by actors below the state level in North Korea, are driven by reasons of developing the local economy and resolving non-traditional security problems. They are less limited by the concerns of national interests at the strategic level and even run counter to

8   B. GAO

the national interests in some cases. This book aims to improve new insights from the sub-state view but does not attempt to trivialise the military factors behind Beijing's motivations of promoting and encouraging Chinese economic activities in North Korea. These significant military factors include consolidating North Korea's domestic stability and avoiding a refugee wave led by the regime collapse, which have been frequently discussed and mentioned in the previous scholarships. Before presenting the methods and organisation of this book, a few important concepts used in the empirical chapters need to be outlined first in the section below.

Significant Concepts

Decentralisation in China

China is a single party system country with several decades of decentralisation since its economic reform in the 1980s. During the last thirty years, the Central Committee of the Chinese Communist Party (CCP) and the State Council in Beijing have introduced a number of documents to implement the gradual decentralisation of power. Jiang (2008: 58–59) and Cao (2013: 122) outline relevant documents which include 'Notice about the problems in the party and political organisation reforms of province, city and autonomous region' in December 1982; 'Notice about the problems in the local, city and distinction party and political organisation reform' in February 1983; 'Notice about the problems in the town level party and government organisation reform' in December 1983; 'The advice of Central Committee of CCP (Chinese Communist Party) and the State Council to the local government organisation reform' in January 1991; 'Plans for Party and government organisation reform' and 'The notice about the implementation of party and government organisation reform plans' in July 1993; and finally, 'The decision of Central Committee of CCP about problems in improving socialist market economic institution' in 2003 (Translated by author; see original names in Mandarin and pinyin in Appendix A, point 1).

In particular, the decision of 2003 clearly pointed out 'a reasonable division of rights and responsibilities of central government and local governments on managing socio-economic affairs' and 'the national and cross-province (as well as autonomous regions and municipalities) affairs will be managed by central government in order to ensure the national unification of legal system, political order and market. The regional affairs belonging to the local administrative region will be managed by local gov-

INTRODUCTION 9

ernments in order to promote the working efficiency, reducing managing cost and promoting administrative dynamics' (Cao, 2013: 122–125) (translated by author; see original names in Mandarin and pinyin in Appendix A, point 1).

Thus, it can be seen that the decentralisation that has taken place in China over the last three decades and the core themes that run through these documents are the decentralisation of Beijing and the increasing independence of local authorities from Beijing when dealing with the affairs within their administrative scope.

From the structure of government, the central government does not have its own department for implementing policies. The ministries, committees, bureaux, and offices under the State Council are a fundamental administrative part of government. However, these departments mainly take responsibility for policymaking, macroeconomic control, and the provision of guidelines, but not the implementation of policy. Thus, Beijing depends only on the regional governments for policy implementation (Shen and Song, 2009: 15). The central government usually represents social public interest in general and aims to maximise its own interests. There are dual levels of regional governments' interests. On the one hand, their interests align with those of the central government, which aims to maximise public interest and promote social development by organising industrial production. On the other hand, the interests of regional governments are in the socio-economic development of their own regions, which is clearly independent from the interests of the central government (Shen and Song, 2009: 16–18). Under the traditional planned economy, the regional governments were restrained by the administrative and financial control of the central government and their independence from the central government is not very clear. The regional governments are the only agents of the central government and passively accept and implement policy under direct control from the top without independence, flexibility, or subjectivity. After the economic reform, with the decentralisation of economic power (especially the devolution of power of regional state-owned companies, in terms of supervision and management, from central government to regional governments), and new economic development-oriented evaluation systems to officials in the sub-level governments, the motivation for self-development by regional governments existed and increased rapidly. Regional government began to strengthen control of local state-owned companies, who are regionally the most powerful business

10   B. GAO

actors, and to develop their own flexibilities on understanding central government policies in order to make regional development effective (Jiang, 2008: 57).

Non-traditional Security

This section aims firstly to define traditional security and non-traditional security (NTS), and then to outline the types of NTS problems which exist in the current context and connect them to the research topic. Traditional security threats are those factors that could threaten the security of sovereign states. Normally these are military threats, but the concept also includes political and diplomatic conflicts (Burgess, 2010: 1–5). Depending on the differences in the level of threat, traditional threats may be divided into three types: military competition, military deterrence, and war. War may be categorised by different levels, such as world war, regional war, and civil war, and by different types such as conventional war and nuclear war (Burgess, 2010: 1–5). In contrast to traditional security, the NTS threats refer to the non-military, non-political, and non-diplomatic factors, which could threaten the general survival and development of human beings and sovereign states (Tsuneo Akaha, 2002: 1–2). NTS threats cover a wider and more complex range of threats than do traditional ones. They could be economic security, financial security, environmental security (pollution, collapse of natural systems and diversity), information security (hacker, virus, and other illegal activities of transporting and stealing information), resource and energy security, terrorism, proliferation of weapons (especially weapons of mass destruction), spread of disease, cross-border crime, smuggling and drug problems, illegal immigration, piracy attacks, or money laundering (Tsuneo Akaha, 2002: 1–2).

According to Lou and Teng (2007: 15), NTS problems normally include five important characteristics: firstly, both causes of and solutions to NTS problems are normally transnational; they may appear not only in one country but in one region and then create negative influences at the regional or even the global level; secondly, the creators of NTS problems are uncertain, they could be state or non-state actors such as individuals, organisations, or groups; thirdly, once NTS problems intensify, they may transform into traditional security problems which may then be resolved by military means, such as violent conflict or even regional war; fourthly, the state remains the main actor in the resolution of NTS problems and has the autonomous right to resolve the problem; finally, the settlement of

INTRODUCTION   11

NTS problems requires international cooperation in order to reduce the negative impact of threats and achieve a complete resolution.

Recently, China has faced many NTS threats, especially in six main areas. The first threat is the environmental security problem which includes four parts: water loss and soil erosion; large-scale environmental pollution (air pollution and acid rain, water pollution); shortage of energy and mineral resources; and decrease in biological diversity (Li Xiang-lan, 2002: 1–3). The second threat is the information security problem, especially the loss of information under attacks from external hackers and from viruses (Wang and Liu, 2011: 30–33). The third threat is the possible spread of an epidemic with rapid changes in DNA and improved counter-medical abilities (Li, 2002: 1–3). The fourth threat is due to China's huge population, which increases pressure on the limited resources and deepens the welfare burden on an ageing society (Yu, 2015). The fifth one concerns border control problems, which include the drug trade in Northwest, Northeast, and Southwest China, and illegal immigration from North Korea (Liu and Wang, 2010: 45–50; Cui, 2010: 55–58). The final threat is that of financial security. During the period of deepening reform, the imperfect Chinese financial system may be easily manipulated by external hot money and other financial risks (Wang and Liu, 2011: 30–33).

Among the six types of NTS threats discussed above, three are relevant to the research topic. The first of these is resource scarcity. Currently, due to the rapid increase in population and modernisation, China relies heavily on the import of oil and many other resources. However, most transportation lines by sea from the Middle East are not safe because the Chinese navy is not strong enough to protect them in the case of war. China is in the process of adjusting its status as an oil-import country (Yu, 2015). On the one hand, China is pushing its technical project of coal liquefaction to produce oil; therefore, the importation of coal from North Korea is important (Yin and Ding, 2006: 1–6). On the other hand, as the largest owner and exporter of rare earth minerals in the world, China plans to improve the status of these as a strategic resource in order to increase the dependence of the world on China for rare earth minerals, thereby balancing Chinese dependence on the import of oil (Yu, 2015).

The second NTS threat relevant here is environmental pollution which led to food safety problem and seafood resource scarcity. China is bordered by four seas: Bohai Sea, Yellow Sea, East China Sea, and South China Sea. However, apart from the South China Sea, which is relatively further away from the Chinese mainland than the others, these seas have

12   B. GAO

been seriously polluted resulting in an underproduction of seafood (Dai, 2007: 255–260). Chinese traditional fishing areas also reduced dramatically due to the fishery agreement signed between China and South Korea in the early 2000s because the number of Chinese fishing boats working in the South Korean Exclusive Economic Zone significantly reduced under the quota restrictions imposed by South Korea according to the agreement. The social concerns about the negative impact of Japan's nuclear accident also created a need for alternative sources for those fishery products traditionally imported from Japan. Thus, Chinese economic activities in the North Korean marine field could sustain the supply of seafood and make up for the loss caused by reduced fishing areas, sea pollution, and overfishing.

The third threat comes from the cross-border problem. Northeast China suffers from two main cross-border problems. One is social instability caused by illegal immigration from North Korea. Chinese economic activities in North Korea may also be helpful in strengthening border control in order to reduce the extent of illegal immigration by improving local living conditions and decreasing unemployment. In addition, Jilin and Liaoning provinces, especially the Yanbian Ethnic Korean Autonomous Prefecture, face the problem of population outflow to South Korea, which directly leads to a reduction in terms of local culture and labour shortages. Chinese economic activities in North Korea which focus on cooperation in tourism, physical infrastructure construction, and mutual management of the Special Economic Zone in North Korea create conditions for the resolution of these problems.

METHODS

This book uses qualitative research methodology to study how the Chinese economic activities in North Korea are motivated by the NTS concerns of actors below the state, the relative central-local relations, and their regional impacts. Triangulation occurs through documentary analysis, media information, and elite interview techniques, which draw a full picture of Chinese economic activities in North Korea. In telling the story of how the NTS concerns of actors below the state drive the commercialisation of China-North Korea relations, this book is guided by a certain investigative empiricism that seeks to take it beyond what is already known about China-North Korea relations around the Six Party Talks and North Korea's nuclear weapons.

The main evidence of Chinese economic activities is presented in three empirical chapters that deal with the relations between Beijing and actors below the state, which are motivated by specific NTS problems. Each empirical chapter begins with an introduction of core NTS threats and the specific information of Chinese economic activities in North Korea which were implemented to resolve them. In doing so, it draws on reports mainly from Chinese media, but also from South Korea news agencies, about local economic activities in North Korea. It also uses evidence from the academic literature which presents the NTS problems of regions which conduct economic activities in North Korea and suggests possible solutions that include specific economic activities from the media reports. These secondary sources are covered separately under different types of NTS problems in each empirical chapter and may concern mineral resource scarcity, food safety (environmental pollution), and cross-border security on illegal immigration and cultural decline.

Apart from news reported in the media, each evidential chapter also contains an analysis of central-local relations in China on the policymaking and implementation of economic activities in North Korea. The Chinese economic activities in North Korea from the early 2000s are conducted mainly by actors below the state, especially local governments, local state-owned enterprises, and non-state actors, which include private enterprises and non-governmental organisations. The evidence presented in these sections derives from official speeches, announcements, and documents, especially the annual reports of local governments, which are available on their official websites, as well as the policy-cum-strategy collections stored in local libraries and archives. Apart from the official documents and other publications concerning China-North Korea engagement, this book also includes a number of annual reports from the companies who have developed business relations in North Korea in order to show their subjectivities and enthusiasm beyond the central government.

The third source of information derives from over twenty confidential elite interviews conducted by the author during several research trips in China and South Korea between the autumn of 2012 and the winter of 2014. The interviewees include scholars and academics from universities and think tanks in Beijing and other regions who have business relations with North Korea, officials in the central government of Beijing and different departments of local authorities at both provincial and city levels, businessmen whose companies have business partners in North Korea, and journalists who wrote relevant reports on Sino-DPRK economic

14   B. GAO

engagement. Interviewees were selected on the basis of their knowledge and expertise in the programmes and policy areas that fall within the scope of this research. The method of selection consisted of going through the organisational charts of target institutions in order to identify suitable individuals for interview. The first interview in China was conducted by the author from the contact information shown on the website of one local state-owned company in a neighbouring city and then developed through the business and academic network under the snowball effect. The interviews in South Korea were designed with, and supported by, Dr. Ivaylo Gatev. Interviewees were usually contacted by telephone or text message to see if, and when, they may be available for an interview. All interview material used in the writing of this project is referenced by citing the date and the location of the interview. No individuals responsible for the information quoted in the chapters are named as all interviewees have been assured of strict confidentiality. Additionally, the interviews were not taped but notes were made with the permission of the interviewees. The specifics of each interview were memorised and written down after the interviews. The questions to interviewees are also outlined in the Appendix. Meanwhile, because most of the questions are open-ended and relevant to the varied personal experience and understanding to the different fields of Sino-DPRK economic cooperation, the answers are not quantified.

Most of the interviews were face-to-face, semi-structured, and guided by open-ended questions to allow reasonable scope for discussion. Depending on the availability of interviewees and the personal rapport established, the length of each interview was between forty-five minutes and two hours. The language used in the interview was Mandarin for Chinese scholars and English for South Korean scholars. Only one interview was made by an agent of the author who was close to a respondent in a relatively high government position in order to avoid difficulties of a direct interview by the author.

The information collected from the elite interviews added flesh to the bones of the data obtained through documentary analysis and continued the stories from the media which tend to focus only on the beginning of economic cooperation, especially the launch events of cooperative projects and the ceremony of signing treaties. The interviews have four major functions: clarifying the questions arising from the documents and policy papers, getting additional documentary material that was not easily accessible, learning the evaluation of events from the personal and professional perspective of interviewees, and receiving expert commentary on specialist

INTRODUCTION 15

topics relevant to the book. It should be mentioned that in China the identity of academics and researchers in the universities and think tanks is similar to government officials because in China most universities and think tanks are in the official system. These academics and scholars are very familiar with government policymaking progress, especially the bargaining between the central government and local actors.

The need for triangulation is demonstrated by Walliman (2011: 73) who states that 'qualitative data rely on human interpretation and evaluation and cannot be dispassionately measured in a standard way. Checks on the reliability and completeness of qualitative data can be made by consulting a variety of sources of data relating to the same event—this is called triangulation.' Each one of the three data collection methods used here, documentary analysis, media news, and elite interviews, only addresses one part of Chinese economic activities in North Korea. Their combination is suitable for the empirical investigation into Chinese economic activities in North Korea undertaken here. It benefits the researcher to establish the facts of what is happening on the ground in sufficient detail, which is a fuller picture of Chinese economic activities in North Korea beyond the general description in the official documents and incoherent reports of media.

ORGANISATION

Following this introductory chapter, there are three empirical chapters. The first of these, Chap. 2, discusses activities in the sector of mineral resources, for example, direct investment and the foundation of joint ventures, the drivers here being the prevention of environmental pollution, the development requirements of local industry, and the reduction of economic costs. In this section, actors below the state level are the major actors in Chinese economic activities in North Korea whereas the central government in Beijing remains directly involved in a few economic activities in North Korea relevant to central state-owned companies. Meanwhile, Beijing also provides aid to North Korea in order to help the achievement of economic activities of several local Chinese state-owned companies.

Chapter 3 discusses activities in the fishing industry, such as the civil cooperation programme, direct investment, and buying fishing licences, the drivers being the foundation of alternative fishing areas to combat reduced traditional fishing fields, seeking a cleaner environment, and the impact of the Japanese Fukushima nuclear accident in 2011. Actors below the state level are the major actors of Chinese economic activities in North Korea while Beijing plays the role of opportunities supplier and diplomatic emergency mediator.

Chapter 4 discusses activities in the sector of cross-border movements, including physical infrastructure, tourism, and light industry, with the drivers being improvement of the local economic conditions, reduction of population outflow, and border controls. Actors below the state level are the major actors of Chinese economic activities in North Korea whilst Beijing plays the role of the agent who builds the connection between North Korea and governments at the province and city level. Beijing also offers assistance to increase the attractiveness of the 'Chang-Ji-Tu project' in Jilin province to the national strategy in name only, that is, without any other practical support.

Chapter 5 is a discussion of the impact of China's economic activities in North Korea on the regional security order of Northeast Asia, with a focus on the Korean Peninsula. The chapter follows the previous logic that the impact of China's economic activities has more divergence than consistency with the national strategy of Beijing in maintaining regional peace and stability as well as in sustaining positive relationships with neighbouring countries. On the one hand, the positive impact is pushing North Korea's economic 'opening up' and avoiding regime collapse in Pyongyang. China's economic activities offer enough funding to North Korea to improve its attractiveness in terms of physical infrastructure to external funding from other countries, and, at the same time, because of Pyongyang's concern of economic overdependence on China to push it to enlarge its scale of use of non-Chinese foreign investments. On the other hand, China's rapid increase of economic engagement in North Korea has made South Korea increasingly anxious about the weakened sovereignty of North Korea and even the practical status of a fourth province of Northeast China. Meanwhile, China's increasing control of North Korea fishery resources also reduces South Korea's opportunities to develop its fishery industry in North Korea. Thus, the dispute between China and South Korea over oceanic economic zones has intensified and caused several rounds of negotiations to fail. Furthermore, Chinese economic activities reduce the effectiveness of US economic aid and subsequently delay the denuclearisation of North Korea through dialogue in the Six Party Talks. China's economic programmes in North Korea, backed by large amounts of funding, actually increase the expectation of North Korea for aid from the US. This aid is used to exchange the denuclearisation of North Korea so that the national security and survival of Kim's family (Kim Jung-Il, the second generation of North Korean leader who succeeded the leadership from his Father Kim Il-Sung) is assured. However, the aid from the US has always been extremely small in contrast to Chinese economic funding. This book concludes with some thoughts on the drivers of economic activities in North Korea, central-local relationships in China, and the regional impacts of Chinese economic participation in North Korea as well.

REFERENCES

Adrian, Buzo (2018) *Politics and leadership in North Korea: the guerrilla dynasty* (2nd ed.). London; New York: Routledge.

Akaha, Tsuneo. Non-traditional Security Issues in Northeast Asia and Prospects for International Cooperation. *Prepared for UN University Seminar 'Thinking Outside the Security Box: Non-traditional Security in Asia: Governance, Globalization and the Environment'*. March 15, 2002, 1–2.

Akaha, Tsuneo (ed.) (2002) *A Future of North Korea.* London and New York: Routledge.

Bai, Jie (2013) *North Korea Observation Notes (朝鲜半岛观察笔记 Chaoxian Bandao Guancha biji).* Beijing: World Knowledge Publishing House.

Beal, Tim (2005) *North Korea: The Struggle Against American Power.* London and Ann Arbor, MI: Pluto Press.

Burgess, J. P. (ed.) (2010) *The Routledge handbook of new security studies.* London; New York: Routledge.

Cao Guiquan. The distribution mode of multi-government and the systemic reform of China's administrative and management. *Theory and Modernization,* Vol. 103, No. 3 (May, 2013), pp. 121–127.

Cha, Victor (2013) *The Impossible state: North Korea, past and future.* New York: Ecco.

Choo, Jaewoo. Mirroring North Korea's Growing Economic Dependence on China: Political Ramifications. *Asian Survey,* Vol. 48, No. 2 (2008), pp. 343–372.

Cornell, Erik (2002) *North Korea under Communism: Report of An Envoy to Paradise.* London and New York: Routledge Curzon, Taylor and Francis Group.

Cui Junyong. Research about strategy to the drug trafficking in Yanbian area related to South Korea. *Academic Communication (学术交流 Xue Shu Jiao Liu),* Vol. 191, No. 2 (February 2010), pp. 55–58.

Dai Xiao-song. Developing Sea Circular Economy, Improving the Sustainable Development of Liaoning Sea Economy. *Territory and Natural Resource,* Vol. 2 (2007), pp. 255–260. 发展海洋循环经济，促进辽宁海洋经济可持续发展，国土和自然资源，2007 年02 期，255–260.

Du, Bai-yu (2014) *My Story in Pyongyang: A Journalist of Xinhua News in North Korea* (我的平壤故事:一个新华社记者@朝鲜, *Wo de Ping Rang Gushi: Yige Xinhuashe Jizhe zai Chaoxian*). Beijing: Huaxia Publishing House.

Ford, Glyn and Kwan Soyoung (2008) *North Korea on the Brink: Struggle for Survival.* London: Pluto Press.

French, Paul (2007) *North Korea, The Paranoid Peninsular: A Modern History.* London and New York: Zed Books.

Fuqua, Jacques (2007) *Nuclear Endgame: The Need for Engagement with North Korea.* Westport and London: Praeger Security International.

Ge, Zheng-ying. China's Dilemma in the Ocean Access of Tumen River and its Countermeasure. *Journal of Leshan Normal University,* 乐山师范学院学报 *(Leshan Shi Fan Xue Yuan Xue Bao),* No. 05 (2015), pp. 111–115.

Goldstein, Avery (2006) China's Interests and the Korean Peninsula. In Alastair Iain Johnston and Robert S. Ross, eds., *New Directions in the Study of China's Foreign Policy.* Stanford, CA: Stanford University Press, p. 145.

Haggard, S and Noland, M. The Political Economy of North Korea: Implications for Denuclearization and Proliferation. *East-West Center Economy Series,* No. 104 (June 2009).

Hagstrom, Linus and Marie Soderbeg (eds.) (2006) *North Korea Policy: Japan and the Great Powers.* London and New York: Routledge, Taylor and Francis Group.

Han, Jing-yu. Discussing Sino-DPRK economic & trade cooperation. *Science & Technology Information,* 科技信息*(Keji Xin-xi),* Vol. 30 (2011), pp. 12–23.

Harrold, Michael (2004) *Comrades and Strangers: Behind the Closed Doors of North Korea.* West Sussex: John Wiley& Sons Ltd.

Haruki Wada (2014) *The Korean War: an international history (translated by Frank Baldwin).* Lanham, Maryland: Rowman & Littlefield.

Huang, Chiung-Chiu and Shih Chih-yu (2014) *Harmonious Intervention: China's Quest for Relational Security.* Farnham, Surrey, England; Burlington, Vermont: Ashgate Publishing Limited. Hardcover.

Huang, Zhi-xiong and Hu Jian-sheng. The International Legal Status of North Korean Escapees and China's Relevant Policies. *Present day Law Science (*时代法学 *Shi Dai Fa Xue),* Vol. 12, No. 5 (Oct. 2014), pp. 3–10.

Hundt, D. China's Two Koreas Policy: Achievements and Contradictions. *Political Science,* Vol. 62 (2010), pp. 132–142.

Ikenberry, G. John and Moon Chung-in (eds.) (2008) *The United States and Northeast Asia: debates, issues, and new order.* Lanham, MD: Rowman & Littlefield.

Jiang Guobing. The Strategic Choice of China's Devolution of Government Power. *Journal of Changsha University,* (长沙大学学报 *Changsha daxue xuebao),* Vol. 22, No. 1 (Jan 2008), pp. 57–59.

Joo, Seung-Ho and Kwak Tae-Hwan (eds.) (2007) *North Korea's Second Nuclear Crisis and Northeast Asian Security.* Aldershot: Ashgate.

Kim Jae-Cheol. The Political Economy of Chinese Investment in North Korea: A Preliminary Assessment. *Asian Survey*, Vol. 46, No. 6 (2006), pp. 898–916.

Kim Jin Moo. North Korea's Reliance on China and China's Influence on North Korea. *The Korean Journal of Defense Analysis*, Vol. 23, No. 2 (2011), pp. 257–271.

Kim, Sung-Chull (2006) *North Korea under Kim Jong-Il: From Consolidation to Systemic Dissonance*. Albany: State University of New York Press.

Lee Chang Jae. Trade and Investment in North Korea. *Korea Institute for International Economic Policy*, Vol. 1 (2003), pp. 1–8.

Lee, Joo-A. To Fuel or Not to Fuel: China's Energy Assistance to North Korea. *Asian Security*, Vol. 5, No. 1 (2009), pp. 45–72.

Li, Qi. On the "3-illegal" Phenomena in the Area Bordering North Korea in Jilin Province. *Journal of Henan Police College (河南警察学院学报, Henan Jing Cha Xue Yuan Xue Bao)*, Vol. 20, No. 2 (Apr. 2011), pp. 58–61.

Li, Chun-hua. The Research on the Problem of the Trade between China and North Korea and Cross-border RMB Settlement. *Journal of Jilin Financial Research, 吉林金融研究 (Jilin Jin-Rong Yan Jiu)* (Dec 2012), pp. 35–39.

Li Xiang-lan. The new sight of the environment around China: untraditional safe problem', *Territory and Natural Resource Study*, Vol. 2 (2002), pp. 1–3. 周边环境新视角: 非传统安全问题, *国土与自然资源研究*, 2002 年 02 期, 1–3.

Lim, Jae-cheon (2009) *Kim Jong-Il's Leadership to North Korea*. New York: Routledge.

Lin, Jin-shu and Hao Fang-long. Economic Cooperation Between Changchun-Jilin-Tumen Pilot Zone and Rajin-Sonbong. *Journal of Yanbian University (Social Sciences) (延边大学学报社会科学版, Yanbian Da Xue Xue Bao, She Hui Ke Xue Ban)*, No. 02 (2011), pp. 12–18.

Lin, Jin-shu and Jin Mei-hua. Present Situation and Countermeasures of Jilin-North Korean Trade. *Journal of Yanbian University (Social Sciences) (延边大学学报 (社会科学版) Yanbian Da Xue Xue Bao, She Hui Ke Xue Ban)*, No. 03 (2009), pp. 43–48.

Liu, Ming. North Korean Economic Reform: Exploring a Third Way and its Uncertain Future. *World Economy Research (世界经济研究 Shijie Jingji Yanjiu)*, No. 07 (2008), pp. 83–89.

Liu Jin-zhi, Pan Jing-chu, Pan Rong-ying and Li Xi-yu (2006) *The Relationship between China and Korean Peninsula Countries: The Collection of Documents, 1991–2006*. Beijing: World Knowledge Publish, Inc. 中国同朝鲜半岛国家关系文件资料汇编 1991–2006. 北京: 世界知识出版社.

Liu Ting and Wang Haijun. Drug issue from the Perspective of Non-Traditional Security. *Journal of Yunnan Police Officer Academy*, Vol. 2 (2010), pp. 45–50. '非传统安全视野下的毒品问题研究', 云南警官学院学报, 编辑部邮箱 2010 年 02 期, 45–50.

Lou Wei and Teng Song-yan. Non-traditional security threats of Northeast China and regional Cooperation. *Journal of Tonghua Teachers College*, Vol. 28, No. 5

(2007), pp. 15–19. 东北亚地区非传统安全威胁与地区合作，*通化师范学院学报*, 2007 年 05 期, 15–19.

Man Haifeng. Open Regionalism and Development Trend of Boundary Economic and Trade Cooperation between China and North Korea: A Case Study of Economic and Trade Cooperation between Dandong and Sinuiju. *Journal of Eastern Liaoning University (Social Science)*, Vol. 13, No. 2 (2011), pp. 131–136. '开放的地区主义与中朝边境经贸合作发展方向——以丹东—新义州两市开展经贸合作为研究视角'，*辽东学院学报(社会科学版)*, 2011 年 02 期, 131–136.

Moore, G. (2014) *North Korean nuclear operationality: regional security & non-proliferation.* Baltimore: John Hopkins University.

Moore, Gregory J. How North Korea Threatens China's Interests: Understanding Chinese 'Duplicity' on the North Korean Nuclear Issue. *International Relations of the Asia-Pacific*, Vol. 8 (2008), pp. 1–29.

Nanto, Dick K and Emma Chanlett-Avery (2010) *North Korea: Economic Leverage and Policy Analysis.* Congress Report Service.

O'Hanlon, Michael and Mochizuki Mike (2003) *Crisis on the Korean Peninsula: How to deal with a Nuclear North Korea.* McGraw-Hill:The Brookings Institution.

Park, Kyung-Ae and Snyder Scott (eds.) (2013) *North Korea in transition: Politics, Economy and Society.* New York: Roman and Littlefield Publisher, INC.

Piao, Guang-ji. The Transformation Dilemma of Sino - DPRK Economic and Trade Relations and Its Countermeasures. *Northeast Asia Forum (东北亚论坛 Dong Bei Ya Lun Tan)*, No. 03 (2012), pp. 44–53.

Piao, Jian-yi and Li Zhi-fei. The internationalization of North Korea escapees and its impacts to China. *Modern International Relations (现代国际关系, Xian Dai Guo Ji Guan Xi)*, No. 07 (2012), pp. 3–10.

Rozman, Gilbert (2007) *Strategic Thinking about the Korean Nuclear Crisis: Four Parties Caught Between North Korea and the United States.* New York: Palgrave Macmillan.

Russell Ong. North Korea's enduring importance to China's security interests in the post-Cold War era. *Asian Journal of Political Science*, Vol. 8, No. 1 (2000), pp. 47–64.

Seth, M. J. (2010) *A Concise History of Modern Korea: From the Nineteenth Century to the Present.* Plymouth: The Rowman & Littlefield Publisher Inc.

Shambaugh David. China and the Korean peninsula: Playing for the long term. *The Washington Quarterly*, Vol. 26, No. 2 (2003), pp. 43–56.

Shen Rong-hua and Song Yu-ping. Rethinking China's Local government systemic reform. *Theoretical Investigation*, Vol. 149, No. 4 (Nov. 2009), pp. 15–19.

Stares, Paul B and Wit Joel S. *Preparing for Sudden Change in North Korea.* Council Special Report No. 24, January 2009, Council of Foreign Relations.

Sun Lin. Public Security Management and Legal Measures of Illegal Immigration Problem—Based on the case study of North Korean citizen criminal in Jilin province. *Journal of Changsha University (长沙大学学报, Changsha Da Xue Xue Bao)*, Vol. 29, No. 6 (Nov. 2015), pp. 64–68.

Sun Yong. The Economic Cooperation between Northeast China and North Korea and its outlook. *The Border Economy and Culture*, Vol. 4 (2004), pp. 67–71. '东北地区和朝鲜经济合作及其展望. 边境经济和文化', 2004 年 04 期, 67–71.

Walliman, N. (2011) *Research Methods: The Basics*. London and New York: Routledge, p. 73.

Wang, Chun-sheng. The status-quo of Sino-Russia and Sino-North Korea border trade development and its countermeasures. *China Forex (中国外汇, Zhong Guo Wai Hui)*, No. 23 (2013), pp. 62–63.

Wang Qi and Liu Lian. Chinese Non-Traditional Security Problem and Countermeasure. *Journal of Shandong Academy of Governance*, Vol. 2 (2011), pp. 30–33. '我国目前面临的非传统安全问题及对策', 山东行政学院学报, 2011 年 02 期, 30–33.

Wang Run-bo. The Existed Problems and Advices of China-North Korea Trade Settlement. *Jilin Finance Research. (吉林金融研究 Jilin Jinrong Yanjiu)*, Vol. 6 (2008), pp. 48–50.

Wang, Yuan and Zhang Yu-shan. Analyzing status-quo of Jilin province's economic and trade cooperation with North Korea and its countermeasures. *North Korea and South Korea History Research (朝鲜·韩国历史研究, Chao Xian he Han Guo Li Shi Yan Jiu)*, No. 00 (2014), pp. 451–470.

Xu, Hongshui. Discussing about the problems in the cross-border use of RMB in the Sino-DPRK border areas. *China Money, 中国货币市场 (Zhong-guo Huo Bi Shi Chang)*, No. 11 (2011), pp. 51–54.

Yin Jian-ping and Ding Qi. Adhering to the Principia of Steady Progress for Developing Coal Liquefaction Industry. *Journal of China University of Petroleum*, Vol. 22, No. 5 (2006), pp. 1–6. '发展煤炭液化产业必须坚持稳步推进的原则', 中国石油大学学报(社会科学版), 2006 年 05 期, 1–6.

Yoon, Seung-hyun and Lee Seung-ook. From old comrades to new partnerships: dynamic development of economic relations between China and North Korea. *The Geographical Journal*, Vol. 179, No. 1 (March 2013), pp. 19–31.

Yu, Guang-yi. The status-quo, problems of Sino-DPRK economic condition and strategy. *Journal for Party and Administrative Cadres, 党政干部学刊 (Dang Zheng Gan-bu Xue Kan)* (May 2008), pp. 32–34.

Yu Xiaofeng (2015) *A General Book of Non-traditional Security*. 非传统安全概论 Feichuantong Anquan Gailun. Beijing: Beijing University.

Yu, Zai-Xia. Discussing North Korean Economy. *CangSang (沧桑)*, No. 01 (2010), pp. 121–123.

Zhang, Dong-ming. A Study on Industrial Development and Cooperation Between China and DPRK. *Northeast Asia Forum (东北亚论坛 Dong Bei Ya Lun Tan)*, No. 5 (2011), pp. 30–42.

Zhang, Feng. Win-Win in the cooperation and complementation: Analyze the exploring condition of China-North Korean mineral resource. *Korean Studies*, Vol. 3 (2006), pp. 188–192.

Zhang, Hui-zhi. Opening Practice during the Process of Revitalization in Northeast China: The cooperation Between China and North Korea. *Northeast Asia Forum (东北亚论坛 Dong Bei Ya Lun Tan)*, No. 05 (2007), pp. 38–41.

Zhang, Jia-xin and Miao Ru. The Analysis of the Logistics Economic Benefits of the Transport Construction of Changchun - Jilin - Tumen Pilot Zone: A Case Study of Sino - DPRK Channel. *Northeast Asia Forum (东北亚论坛 Dong Bei Ya Lun Tan)*, No. 05 (2012), pp. 96–106.

Zhang, Ying, Lu Yu-duo and Sun Xiu-ying. Exploring Sino-DPRK economic cooperation under the Nuclear Crisis of North Korea. *Liaoning Economy, 辽宁经济 (Liaoning Jing-ji)*, Vol. 11 (2009), pp. 36–37.

CHAPTER 2

China's Economic Activities in the North Korean Mineral Resource Sector

INTRODUCTION

The previous chapter outlined the historical background, potential academic contribution, important concepts, and methodology of this project. What follows are three empirical chapters about China's economic activities in the North Korean sectors of mineral resources, the fishery industry, and cross-border activities. They show that Chinese economic activities in North Korea, in the sector of mineral resources, were implemented mainly by actors below the state, such as provincial and city-level governments, local state-owned companies, and private enterprises. These activities were driven by non-traditional security (NTS) concerns, such as resource scarcity and environmental considerations, as well as other reasons, such as reduction of economic costs, improvement of social welfare, and local industrial transition. This chapter focuses on Chinese economic activities in the North Korean mineral resource sector.

Chinese general perception of NTS with respect to mineral resources concerns both imports and exports. For mineral resources, which China needs to import from other countries, this security means the assurance of

---

This chapter has been previously published and includes the complete source citation as follows: Gao Bo (2014) 'China's economic activities in the North Korean mineral sector: motivations and implications'. *International Journal of Energy Security and Environmental Research*. Vol. 1(2) 17–28.

© The Author(s) 2019
B. Gao, *China's Economic Engagement in North Korea*,
Palgrave Series in Asia and Pacific Studies,
https://doi.org/10.1007/978-981-13-0887-1_2

supply, attempts to reduce dependence on other countries, or to at least diversify import origins. Such security has been threatened in two ways. Firstly, the international sea lanes are not secure for Chinese shipping due to the distance between numerous US overseas military bases and China's relatively weak naval strength; therefore, China needs to develop sources closer to home in order to keep the Chinese pipeline away from the control of the US navy (H. Wu, 2011: 330–331; Fan, 2012: 26–28). Secondly, external political sensitivities, especially local protectionism, have weakened the possibility for Chinese companies to purchase foreign enterprises (Lan, 2011: 152–165). While China imported energy from other countries, it also exported certain types of mineral and seeks to maintain the competitiveness of these products in the global market. In China, a country as large as Europe, different conditions predominate in different provinces, each of which has its own interests and motivations. This chapter aims to explore the different interests towards economic cooperation with North Korea found at the level of the central government, and that of actors below the state. From the perspective of the central government, the main motivation is to secure access to mineral resources. This should be understood in the context of the general perception of resource security discussed above. However, for actors below the state, mainly regional governments, local state-owned companies, and private enterprises, the reason for engaging with North Korea is to do with factors such as environmental pollution and the survival of small and medium enterprises (SMEs), which impose an economic cost on them. It also analyses how their activities in North Korea can reduce these problems. In doing so, it distinguishes between the objectives of the central government in Beijing and those of actors below the state, mainly regional governments and private enterprises. The chapter also argues that the actors driving the policies behind these activities are mainly actors below the state, such as the local government, private, and state-owned companies. Except for providing aid and engaging in dialogue with the North Korean authorities for the participation of central state-owned companies, the central government rarely plays an essential or active role in these activities. During the Cold War era it relinquished its unchallenged role of conducting negotiations on economic cooperation, signing all the agreements (as a part of the general treaty) with North Korea on energy supply, especially the construction of the oil pipeline connecting Northeast China (Dandong) and North Korea.

The following paragraphs begin with a short introduction about the similarities and differences between central state-owned companies and local state-owned companies. Central state-owned companies rarely participate in the North Korean economy, except in the mineral resource sector where they play a relatively important role. Then the chapter outlines the specifics of China's economic activities in the North Korean mineral resource sectors, that is, in three fields: coal, rare earth, and iron, in the post-2003 era. This information includes direct investments, technology transfer, joint ventures, and the construction of physical infrastructure. It explores the motivations and significance of these activities found at the level of both state and non-state actors. The motivations and significance include the requirement for industrial system upgrades, reduction of environmental pollution, control of external resources, and the use of advanced technology. Lastly, the chapter examines the role of the central government and that of sub-state actors in China's economic engagement with DPRK. Actors below the state—either the regional government, with their local state-owned companies at the provincial level, or small-scale private enterprises at the city level—have played a major role in the implementation of China's economic strategy towards North Korea. By contrast, the Chinese central government rarely plays a direct role. It mainly provides assistance during the process of negotiation with the North Korean side.

CHINESE ENTERPRISES: DIFFERENT TYPES OF SOEs AND ECONOMIC ACTIVITIES IN DPRK

This section outlines two types of Chinese state-owned enterprises (SOEs) and their differences, and points out the economic activities of both SOEs and SMEs in DPRK. Firstly, concerning ownership, Chinese companies are divided into three types: central SOEs (in Chinese 中央企业 zhong yang qi ye), regional SOEs (in Chinese 地方国企 di fang guo qi), and private companies. Even though regional SOEs have experienced the structural transformation from public to private ownership that has taken place in China in recent decades, to some extent they still maintain close ties with regional governments at the provincial and city levels. Governments at the provincial level always supervise the SOEs at both provincial and city levels (Montinola, Qian and Weingast, 1996: 61–65). Thus, they pay more attention to the interests of local authorities than to those of the central government.

26   B. GAO

The central SOEs are directly supervised and managed by the Assets Supervision and Administration Commission of the State Council (SASAC), which was founded in 2003 by the central government in Beijing (SASAC, 2008). Currently, there are 117 central SOEs in China which are active in public procurement, for example, the military industry and the State Grid; the exploration and sale of strategic resources, such as oil; and the supply of consumer goods and services, such as the construction industry (SASAC, 2008). These central SOEs are connected to the central government and represent the national strategic interests of China.

CHINA'S ECONOMIC ACTIVITIES IN NORTH KOREA IN THE SECTOR OF MINERAL RESOURCES

After discussing the similarities and distinctions between central SOEs and regional/local SOEs above, this section firstly reviews the history of Sino-DPRK mineral resource cooperation. Then it outlines the details of Chinese economic activities in North Korea at two levels: state and sub-state (regional). Firstly, state-level economic activities include initiating potential investment and cooperative programmes between the PRC and the DPRK and acting as a broker between Chinese companies, especially provincial and city-level state-owned companies, and the North Korean side.

Before 2003, the mineral resource cooperation between China and North Korea was directly controlled by the central governments of the two countries in the form of the provision of aid from China to North Korea. The first agreement to include mineral resources was the Sino-DPRK 1971–1976 Agreement on the Mutual Supply of Important Products, signed in 1970. During these five years, China provided 500,000 tons of oil to North Korea. The renewed agreement in 1975 ensured the supply of 100–150 tons of oil per year between 1976 and 1979 from China to North Korea at a special reduced price. This amount achieved 30 per cent of North Korean annual oil consumption at that time. On 20 December 1975, as China's first and only oil pipeline for export, the construction of the Sino-DPRK Friendship Oil Pipeline in Dandong was finished and began to operate (see Appendix B, point 1). In the following three decades since 1980, China continued its supply to North Korea at a rate of 500,000 tons of oil and 40 million dollars of coke annually except for a six-month suspension from January to June 2014 in response to North Korea's third nuclear test. Furthermore, in 1982, China also assisted North Korea to build the Oil Processing Refinery in Sinuiju with an expected output of 2 million tons of oil (see Appendix B, point 1).

Since 2003, China's economic activities in the sector of mineral resources switched from the aid-dominant mode to the trade-dominant mode with a rapid increase of import among all the sectors of mineral resources in North Korea. In 2003, the import of mineral resources from North Korea achieved over 17 per cent of China's import from North Korea. Since 2005, the mineral resource import achieved 61 per cent and occupied the status of largest import sector from North Korea for one decade (Lin, 2009: 39–40). Different levels of Chinese participants in North Korea invested in coal, rare earth, and iron ore through direct investments, technology transfer, and the foundation of joint ventures. Specific information about these economic activities is discussed below.

Economic Activities at the State Level

Concerning investments in coal, the Ministry of Commerce in Beijing has provided assistance on contacting the North Korean side for the Wu Kuang Group Company, one of the central state-owned companies in China. Meanwhile, Zhou Zhongshu, Wu Kuang's General Manager and Chairman of the Chinese Communist Party (CCP) branch in Wu Kuang, also gained permission from the central government and joined the official Beijing delegation to North Korea in early October 2005 (China Minmental Corp, 2005a). This delegation successfully completed a difficult one-year negotiation between Wu Kuang and its North Korean partner over the investment in the Long-deng coal mine (China Minmental Corp, 2005b). On 20 October 2005, Zhou Zhongshu signed an agreement to set up a joint venture in the North Korean coal field with Lee Ryong-nam, the deputy minister of the North Korean Business Department. This agreement was the first cooperative programme between North Korea and a foreign country outside its Special Economic Zone (SEZ), and shows the opening of the North Korean resource sector to the outside world (China Minmental Corp, 2005a). This delegation represents a high-level interaction with the involvement of the central government.

In addition to providing assistance to central state-owned companies, in special cases the central government also directly intervenes to finalise economic negotiations. For example, in 2011, in order to help Liaoning Machine (LIMAC) Corp, a local state-owned company, to succeed in negotiating with the North Korean side on an investment in a rare earth mine, Beijing provided economic aid to North Korea. The aid comprised

28 B. GAO

300,000 tons of fertiliser and 500,000 tons of corn (Cheminfo, 2011). This demonstrates the direct and indirect support from the central government to Chinese economic activities in North Korea.

Economic Activities at the Level Below the State

At the level below the state, different actors at the provincial and city level, such as regional governments, local SOEs, and private SMEs, formed groups to negotiate joint ventures with North Korea in order to provide technical support, manpower, and the construction of infrastructure, such as railways and electrical support. They became involved in this type of aid as a form of investment.

In the area of coal extraction and processing, YiMa Coal Corp, the third-largest local state-owned company in Henan province, succeeded in reaching cooperation on two projects in North Korea. These projects involve the opening of a 10 million ton coal mine and a 1.2 million ton coal chemical project, and the construction of physical infrastructure, including electrical power plants, coal-separating plants, and a project for the comprehensive utilisation of coal gangue (YiMa Corp, 2008). YiMa Coal Corp's North Korean partner, Anju Coal's joint companies are the largest developer of coal products in North Korea. On 12 December 2008, the vice top manager of Yimei Corp. Ltd. and the CEO of Anju Coal's joint companies institution, together with the leader of the North Korean delegation, signed a letter of intent between the two companies (YiMa Corp, 2008).

In contrast to the individual activities of central state-owned companies and Beijing, the regional/local SOEs and private SMEs chose to form cooperative groups in order to jointly invest in the coal mines of North Korea. In 2008, from Shandong province, three private enterprises from two cities, Ruiyu Mineral Corp from Rizhao, Diyuan Industry Corp and Yide Industry Corp from Weihai, formed a group and invested in a North Korean coal mine. From Liaoning province, another domestic cooperative group was formed between a local SOE from Dandong, Datongjiang trade, and two private companies from Dalian, Zanhua trade and Hongyang trade. This cooperative group also formed a joint venture with a North Korean partner and gained the exploration rights to a coal mine in North Korea (Anonymous Interviewee, 2011).

Similar to coal mining discussed above, Chinese central governments and regional SOEs are still motivated by different reasons in the sector of rare earth and iron ore. Rare earth is the collective name of thirty-two special chemical materials. In fact, deposits of these minerals are actually very large. They are called rare earths because they are very difficult to obtain due to the extremely complicated purification process accompanying their extraction. With the development of scientific technology, the strategic value of rare earth minerals has increased. They are irreplaceable in the production of electronic components for the military industry, among others. Similar to coal mining discussed above, Chinese central governments and regional SOEs are still motivated by different reasons. According to China's Ministry of Commerce (2008) and another interview (Anonymous Interviewee 3, 12 September 2012), on 17 August 2012, Liaoning Equipment Co Ltd., a local state-owned company, formed a joint venture called 'North Korea Liaofeng Non-ferrous Metals Joint Venture' with the North Korea Lianfeng Group. With a registered investment portfolio of 23.16 million dollars and a twenty-year operating lease to develop a 20 million ton rare earth mine in Musan, Liaoning Equipment Co Ltd. used 9.2 million dollars (8 million euros) to acquire 51 per cent of the shares of the joint venture. The North Korean partner used its facilities, such as the land, the coal mine, and the company buildings, as its funding for the remaining 49 per cent share (7.6 million euros) (LIMAC, 2008).

In the iron ore mining sector, some regional SOEs founded joint ventures with North Korean enterprises. According to the records of the ChangBai Ethnic Korean Autonomous Town Environment Protection Bureau (2007), on 11 May 2007, Shuguang Industrial Trade Co, a local state-owned company based in Jilin City, spent 51.8 million RMB on acquiring fifty years' exploration rights for an iron mine in North Korean Kabsan. Ren (2006: 11–12), Zhang (2006), and SINA (2005) describe how, in 2005, three local state-owned companies, Jilin Tonggang Co Ltd. and China Steel Co Ltd. from Changchun, and Tianchi Industrial Trade Co Ltd. from Yanbian, achieved a cooperative programme by way of compensatory trade with North Korean Musan iron mine, providing funds to the tune of 7 billion RMB, technical support in the form of training personnel on relevant knowledge and skills, and infrastructure by building an electrical power station and roads from Musan to Yanbian, in exchange for iron ore and mining rights for fifty years. In order to ensure the success of the projects described above, the Jilin Department of Commerce provided 110 million RMB of economic aid to North Korea. Thus, in contrast to several different types of activities of regional SOEs and private enterprises, the engagement of one central state-owned company, that of Wu Kuang, is fairly limited (see Table 2.1).

30 B. GAO

Table 2.1 Details of Chinese economic activities in North Korea in the mineral and energy sector

Name of sector	Chinese actor	North Korean partner	Type
Coal	Wu Kuang Group	Ryongdong Coal Mine	Agreement for joint venture in 2005
Coal	Ruiyu Mineral Corp, Diyuan Industry Corp, and Yide Industry	N/A	Joint venture in 2008
Coal	Datongjiang trade, Zanhua trade, and Hongyang trade	N/A	Joint venture in 2010
Coal	YiMa Coal Corp	Anju Coal	Opening of a 10 million ton coal mine and a 1.2 million ton coal chemical project and the construction of physical infrastructure, including electrical power plant, coal-separating plant, and a project of comprehensive utilisation of coal gangue
Rare earth	Liaoning Equipment Co Ltd.	North Korea Lianfeng Group	Foundation of North Korea Liaofeng Non-ferrous Metals Joint Venture (23.16 million USD) for a twenty-year operating lease to develop a 20 million ton rare earth mine: 6.3 million USD for mining rights; Liaoning Equipment Co Ltd. used 9.2 million dollars (8 million euros) funds to acquire 51 per cent of the shares of the joint venture. The North Korean partner used the real facilities, such as land, the coal mine, and company buildings, as funding of the remaining 49 per cent share (7.6 million euros)
Iron ore	Shuguang Industrial Trade	North Korea Kabsan Iron Mine	51.8 million RMB on acquiring fifty years' exploration rights
Iron ore	Jilin Tonghua Steel, China Steel, and Tianchi Industrial Trade	North Korea Musan Iron Mine	Providing funds to the tune of 7 billion RMB, technical support in the form of training personnel in relevant knowledge and skills, and infrastructure by building an electrical power station and roads from Musan to Yanbian. This programme is assisted by 110 million RMB aid from the Jilin provincial government

According to the information provided in Table 2.1, it is clear that in the first decade after 2002, there have been multiple channels of interaction both at the state level and at the level below the state, between China and North Korea. Even though the traditional oil supply from China to North Korea still continued during these years, Beijing' role remained weakened from its dominant control of affairs concerning Sino-DPRK mineral resources during the Cold War era, to be the broker of any cooperation deadlocks for Chinese companies facing difficulties with their development programmes in North Korea. This can be seen from the limited extent of Beijing's engagement in contrast to the relatively large number of economic activities from diversified regions. At the level below the state, there were cases about cooperation between Chinese companies and the North Korean side on technology transfer, construction of physical infrastructure, and the foundation of transnational joint ventures. In other words, from the view of multi-level governance, Chinese actors have only two levels of jurisdiction in their economic interaction with North Korea. The central government mainly provides a framework and assistance to the cooperation with North Korea, while the companies, both local SOEs and SMEs, only participate in specific economic activities. These two levels of jurisdiction do not overlap. However, although the levels of jurisdiction are limited, the ways of jurisdiction remain varied. The central government assists the negotiations and provides framework support, while the SOEs and SMEs participate through joint ventures, technology transfer, and direct investments.

Chinese economic actors in the North Korean sector of mineral resources are driven by particular concerns. In the coal industry, they are driven by the national strategy of coal liquefaction technology development at the state level and the lower cost of exploration and avoidance of purchase by local state-owned companies at the sub-state level for SMEs. In the rare earth sector, compensation of rare earth outflow for long-term control by the international rare earth market is the driver at the state level. In contrast, pollution dumping, or, in other words, keeping the pollution for processing rare earth outside China, is the major reason at the level below the state. In the sector of iron ore, Jilin province's plan of developing its vehicle industry and the requirement for railways are the major motivations.

32   B. GAO

Drivers and Consequences of China's Economic Activities in North Korean Coal Mines

China's industrial and economic development has close ties to the mineral resource industry, especially coal. In 2013, as the country with the third-largest coal deposit in the world, China consumed 402 million tons of coal (half of the world's total coal consumption), produced 370 million tons of coal, and also imported 32.7 million tons of coal from other countries (China's Ministry of Commerce, 2014). The paragraphs in the section below show the absence of the relationship between the national strategy of China on coal liquefaction (to turn coal into a relatively cleaner fuel oil and remove the dust and sulphur) and economic activities in North Korea, and then discuss the motivations of actors below the state, such as regional SOEs and SMEs.

State Level: China's National Strategy for Oil Production Through Coal Liquefaction

Coal liquefaction has been an effective way to reduce dependence on oil imports from other countries and is projected to reach 60 per cent of China's comprehensive oil consumption in 2020 (Shu, 2008: 106–109; H. Wu, 2011). Since 2000, China has invested significant resources in developing the technology necessary for oil liquefaction (Yin and Ding, 2006: 1–5; Li et al., 2007). In Shandong, Henan, and Shanxi provinces, which are rich in coal, liquefaction was heavily promoted through a cooperative programme between research centres and central coal companies. The programme was funded by Beijing (Wang, 2007). With the improvement of advanced technology, the expected production of coal liquefaction also increased significantly. In 2007, the China Shenhua Group developed the most advanced oil liquefaction technology in the world by using 1000 tons of coal to produce over 300 tons of fuel oil through direct liquefaction. The Group then tried to expand this technology to the whole of China (Shenhua Group, 2012). This technology reduces the environmental impact of liquefaction by draining pollution through the cyclic utilisation of wasted water, the use of oil sludge in the production of electricity, and the store of carbon dioxide 1500–2500 metres underground (Shenhua Group, 2012).

Although a few Chinese coal SOEs have developed the advanced technology for coal liquefaction, these SOEs are mainly from Shanxi and Shandong provinces. There is rarely relevant information about the coal liquefaction technology of central SOEs. Thus, the involvement of Beijing in the investment of Wu Kuang was a result of its ownership of central SOEs, rather than the coal liquefaction strategy. Meanwhile, Chinese central SOEs, as well as the regional SOEs, such as YiMa from Henan, rarely developed businesses in North Korea. Thus, they lacked experience in negotiating with North Korea, especially as the Long-deng coal mine is a significant source of coal in North Korea. The assistance provided by Beijing was helpful to resolve the deadlock in the negotiations. It can also be explained as a result of inter-provincial economic blockades in China. The regional SOEs from Henan province could only invest in North Korea after failing to gain inter-provincial cooperation.

The Drivers of Actors Below the State and Consequences

After showing the absence of links between the national strategy of coal liquefaction and Wu Kuang, this section discusses the drivers of actors below the state level. Firstly, ensuring the survival of SMEs is an important reason. In Shandong province, SMEs, rather than local state-owned companies, play a major role in coal-related economic activities. This is the result of the unsuccessful integration of seven large coal SOEs inside Shandong due to the lack of agreement over the distribution of power and future interests (Ding, 2011) (see Appendix B, point 2). This extended the survival of private SMEs in Shandong province and provided opportunities for them to invest in North Korea. They were not immediately swept out of the local market by the seven large companies due to their failed integration. To these companies, which are presently unable to develop local coal deposits because of financial difficulties, North Korea is a passive choice, but still a good place for investment because North Korea needs external investment to attract foreign currency. The SMEs' major target is survival, in contrast to the huge overseas strategic purchases implemented by powerful large companies which already monopolise much of the domestic market and have started to expand into overseas markets. Thus, it can be argued that these Shandong SMEs invested in North Korea with a different motivation to the national strategy on coal liquefaction and resource control. Meanwhile, the provincial government also benefited from the successful removal of Shandong SMEs from the local market because only the consortium of the seven city-level SOEs in Shandong province could pay full attention to provincial coal resources.

The strategy of investing in North Korea left room for the survival of SMEs in Shandong province. This can be seen from the slow steps taken towards coal company integration in Shandong. In 2008 and 2012,

Shandong province made the decision to reorganise its coal industry by closing the underdeveloped small-scale companies and encouraging large local state-owned companies to purchase private SMEs. However, with the increase of participation in North Korean coal mines, private SMEs promoted their own strengths and survived by keeping their scale of operation beyond the minimum official standard of company scale (300,000 RMB). Even in recent years, the majority (90 per cent) of Shandong coal companies met financial difficulties due to the rapid drop in coal prices. This resulted in widespread bankruptcy of SMEs in Shandong. For example, in the Shandong city of Zaozhuang, six other private SMEs closed in 2013 (ChinaIRN.com, 2013). However, the three private SMEs with investments in North Korea still survived without being purchased and bankruptcy.

Another driver of expansion into the North Korean coal mining sector is to do with the high casualty rate among workers in Chinese coal mines. The low security risk of coal mine death due to a positive geographical condition in North Korea is a further motivation. In 2002, the overall number of casualties in Chinese coal mines was between 7000 and 8000 (Xinhua Net, 2008). Although that number has reduced to less than 2000, in 2011 the death rate for every million tons of coal in China was still thirty times higher than that of the US (Xinhua Net, 2008; Central Government of PRC, 2012). The low education level of workers and the dangerous working conditions of coal mines (both naturally deep underground and culpability of mine owners in the failure of offering security guarantee) are recognised as two key reasons for such high casualty rates in China's coal production (Hao, 2007; Chen, 2009). In the latter case, 95 per cent of coal mines in China are underground mines. They are easily threatened by gas explosion, natural fire, heavy earth pressure, and flooding (Xinhua Net, 2008). In the past, the high casualty rates in China's coal production did not result in heavy economic losses nor in any moral pressure on companies and local governments because of media control, but now conditions have changed (Chen, 2006). With the spread of modern information technology, the effort of hiding coal mine accidents is increasingly difficult. The central authorities are determined to be involved in the supervision of coal mine production and have allowed China Central Television (CCTV) to broadcast live the rescue of miners during coal mine accidents (Cai and Xu, 2010). Compensation claims cannot be denied or dealt with in secrecy by the owners of the coal mines.

The conditions in North Korean mines are comparatively better. As explained by one interviewee, coal deposits in North Korea are shallower than those in China. In some places, the use of surface mining is sufficient. The interviewees (Anonymous Interviewees 1 and 2, 3–5 July 2011) said: 'The conditions in North Korean coal mines are so good that you can even use a hammer to ascertain the depth of a coal mine. That's why Chinese companies are willing to build roads in North Korea in exchange for exploration rights. Nobody will die in that kind of open-cast mine unless you dig a hole and jump into it.' Thus, to the private enterprises and other local SOEs, who either lack advanced security facilities or are very sensitive to the potential economic cost and weak moral reputation, North Korea is a suitable choice for the development of coal mines. In short, the economic concerns, both the survival of SMEs and the potentially reduced costs as a result of better mining conditions, motivated Chinese economic activities in coal mining in North Korea. These economic concerns are relevant to the national strategy of coal liquefaction, a high economic cost project.

Divergence Between Actors Below the State and Central Government
From the analysis of different motivations to the economic activities in North Korea in the sector of coal mining, discussed above, and the view of multi-level governance, at the two different levels of jurisdiction (state level and the level below the state), the general target of jurisdiction at the state level about promoting coal liquefaction is not represented. In contrast, for the specific target of jurisdictions at the level below the state, the main drivers are the survival of the SMEs and the reduction of costs from better geographical conditions. It is clear that the specific activities in the field of coal mainly represent the will and interests of actors below the state.

Firstly, the activities are significant to the survival of a few companies, either the regional local state-owned companies or private companies. To the local state-owned companies who develop the coal liquefaction technology, their expansion into the control of coal mines is important for their survival in the future for two reasons. For one thing, the local state-owned companies cannot compete with central state-owned companies for the ultimate priorities of policymaking from the central government. Although coal liquefaction is a national strategy with a long history, it is no longer the core of the grand national strategy because coal is no longer the most essential resource for China. The oil produced from coal liquefaction is an alternative step to diversify the sources of oil supply. The central state-owned companies, such as China Petrochemical Corporation (SINO PEC), are following the will of the central government and playing the most crucial role of securing the oil supply through practical implementation of the inter-government agreement on oil, and also gas, cooperation between China and DPRK. The national strategy of coal liquefaction benefited the regional SOEs, who followed the central SOEs, to gain the policy priorities. To the private enterprises from Shandong province, it has been noted that their activities are actually an active response to the prospective reduction of their share of local coal mines due to the integration of several big coal companies. In other words, these activities represented a relatively weak position of local state-owned companies and private enterprises because the difficulties created which threaten their survival are from the top rather than from the bottom. They did not benefit from the decision-making of the central government, while their interests were more or less harmed so that they responded by way of implementing economic activities in North Korea.

Secondly, the motivation of economic interest shows the self-motivated, rather than top-commanded, characteristic of actors below the state. For one thing, the price reform of coal-fired power stations is recognised by the coal companies as a chance to increase profits by promoting the price of coal. That is the reason for some companies to go to North Korea, for the prospectively larger gap between costs in North Korea and the domestic price of coal. However, in recent years many coal companies came to the edge of collapse under a relatively free-market-price-decision domestic situation. For another, the better geological conditions for coal mining in North Korea is a clear motivation in meeting the intention of lowering economic costs by reducing, and even avoiding, casualties during the exploration for coal. The central government in China is always concerned about the security of working conditions. The law of safe production was also approved in 2002. However, the real reason for companies to consider compensation for workplace death is the increasing amount of information spread through the internet, rather than the law because, in China, the law is not as effective as in the West. The fast spread of information about industrial accidents via the internet made it difficult for companies, or even local authorities, to hide the news. Even the active involvement of CCTV in reporting mining accidents is a response to public criticism of the inability of the central government to ensure a safe working environment at the local level. This is at the root of the increasing costs of casualties during exploration, whereas in North Korea the mining conditions are much better and only surface mining is needed.

To sum up, the economic activities are mainly driven by the actors below the state. Their motivations do not represent the will of the central government, while in many conditions their responses represent the shortage of preferences from the policymaking of the central government.

Drivers and Consequences of China's Economic Activities in North Korean Rare Earths

State Level: Sustain China's Control of the International Market for Rare Earth Minerals

Firstly, to Beijing, assisting the Liaoning Company to invest in North Korea helps to broaden the origins of rare earth minerals and sustain the long-term strategic domination of the international rare earth market. China has 30 per cent of global rare earth deposits, but supplies over 90 per cent of rare earth to the world market at a very cheap price (Z. Wu, 2011). Since 1998 Beijing has implemented a rare earth quota system to limit its export. This quota system was so restrictive that it led to frequent diplomatic protests from the European Union, and other countries, who considered the quota system to be a type of resource war (World Online, 2010: 28–29) (see Appendix B, point 3). However, the quota system has not been effective in the avoidance of a net loss of Chinese rare earth reserves due to rare earth smuggling of up to 20,000 tons per year (Information Office of the State Council, 2012; and see Appendix B, point 4). Thus, even China will become a net rare earth import country by the end of the twenty-first century making investment in North Korean rare earth mines a significant activity. According to one report, the deposit of rare earth minerals in North Korea is evaluated at 20 million tons (Wang and Cheng, 2011). If the global demand for rare earth minerals stabilises at its 2011 level (i.e. 70,000 tons), the North Korean rare earth deposits, which could in fact fulfil the requirements of the global rare earth market for almost 300 years, would assist markedly in China's control of the rare earth market (LIMAC Corp., 2008; Wang and Cheng, 2011). Liaoning Company's investment in North Korean rare earth mines saw its exports of rare earth minerals begin at the end of 2013. In 2014, still at the early stage of mining development, China imported about 500 tons of rare earth from North Korea. Although this amount is still small in contrast to the 20,000 tons of smuggled rare earth, with the increase of mining scale and output, as well as strengthened official curbs on rare earth smuggling, the import of rare earth should be effective to balance its loss of rare earth through smuggling.

Actors Below the State: Environmental Concerns

Differing from the long-term target of Beijing, the consideration of both regional governments and companies is to reduce the pollution associated with the extraction of rare earth minerals in China. However, separating rare earths from the original chemical mixtures may create huge pollution. Producing 1 ton of rare earth products normally creates 10 tons of waste pollution. The rare earth companies are required to deal with the waste they produce and to avoid polluting the environment (Xie and Liang, 2011). They need to pay extra tax because of the potential risks to local water resources. Unlike in China, North Korean mines are concentrated in its northwest mountainous area where they are isolated from the sources of rivers and from major cities such as Pyongyang and Gaesong. Therefore, the original blind eye turned by the DPRK regulator to Chinese investments became more lax. Thus, by investing in rare earth mines in North Korea, the heavy cost of reducing environmental pollution and dealing with the waste created during the production in China may be reduced significantly. In this way, economic activities in North Korea in the rare earth sector meet short-term requirements of local authorities in the prevention of environmental pollution and the reduction in economic costs, rather than the national interest of sustaining control of the global rare earth market.

Drivers of China's Economic Activities in North Korean Iron Mining and Central-Local Divergence

Iron ore is another key mineral for China in heavy industries and construction. With the economic reforms since the 1980s, and the accompanying rapid urbanisation, China faces the problem of low domestic supply of iron ore. Domestically, China produced around 30 per cent of its iron ore consumption at the beginning of the 2000s, and this increased to 40 per cent almost a decade later. At the state level, urbanisation in China requires an enormous supply of steel products. In the 2000s, China moved over 100 million rural residents from villages to towns and has now reached an urbanisation rate of 50 per cent (Zhao and Ni, 2012: 10–13). In the short term, there is a problem of excess production capacity in China. However, experts foresee that the speed of urbanisation in China will continue to increase in the next two decades, reaching an urbanisation rate of 65 to 70 per cent in the 2030s (Wang, Feng and Zheng, 2012: 1–3). This implies a new wave of urbanisation with a corresponding development of urban infrastructure. Thus, it is essential for China to ensure a safe supply of iron ore to be prepared should this prediction prove accurate.

Although investments in North Korean iron mines fit the resource control strategy of Beijing, such investments should be recognised as a local development-oriented economic activity. There are two reasons for this. Firstly, investment in North Korea provided approximately one-third of China Faw Group's consumption. This is a small amount of the regional resource requirement of Jilin province. In contrast to China's import of iron from Australia, which is China's largest supplier providing over half of its total import of iron ore, the amount is very limited, under 1 per cent of the imports from Australia (see Appendix B, point 5). Thus, the economic activities in North Korea in the iron ore field are actually locally oriented, rather than strategically driven.

Secondly, Chinese investment in North Korean iron ore mines comes from the regional SOEs of Jilin province, in particular the Tonghua Iron Corp, which is controlled by the province. This is related to Jilin province's local development plan which is closely linked to the steel industry and dependent on the regular supply of iron ore. On the one hand, Jilin province aims to construct a Changchun city-based centre of vehicle production. Changchun, the capital of Jilin province, is called 'China's Detroit' due to the industrial cluster around China Faw Group Corporation. Changchun is now in the process of an industrial upgrade in preparation for the production of a million cars, transmissions, and engines per annum (Cai, 2012: 30–31; Wang, 2012: 12–18). Meanwhile, the local development strategy of Jilin indeed ran against the core domestic grand development strategy of Beijing which recognised that traditional energy, steel, and vehicle industries in Northeast China were actually the industries with surplus production capacity which should be reduced and transformed. Even though China has occupied the status of the largest vehicle producer in the world since 2009, its vehicle manufacturing industry met a long-term serious problem of surplus production capacity (Sohu, 2012; see Appendix B, point 6). As early as September 2010, at the Tianjin International Vehicle Expo, Chen Bin, the Department Chief of the Industrial Co-ordination Department of the China National Development and Reform Committee, warned of the deepened risk to China's vehicle industry under its rapid expansion in the different regions occurring under the support of local governments (Ifeng, 2010). In PricewaterhouseCoopers' (PwC) China vehicle industry analysis report (2015: 5–7), from 2011 to 2018, China's vehicle industry will have an average of 20 per cent surplus production capacity with the highest point of 28.5 per cent in 2012, and the expected lowest point of 15 per cent in 2018.

On the other hand, apart from the support to the development of the automobile industry, North Korea's supply of iron ore is also significant to the construction of the physical infrastructure in Jilin province, including railways, a new airport, and new towns in its 11th and 12th five-year Plans from 2006 to 2015 (Anonymous Interviewee 4, 11 August 2014). In the sector of railway construction, during the 11th five-year plan, from 2006 to 2010, Jilin province paid most attention to the construction of its first high-speed railway between Changchun and Jilin City (Document of Jilin City National Development and Reform Committee, 2014). This high-speed railway was also the first high-speed railway in Northeast China. During the 12th five-year plan from 2011 to 2015, Jilin province made remarkable progress on its railway development. It invested 190 billion RMB in twenty-five railway programmes (see Appendix B, point 7), constructed 4180 kilometres of railway, and increased the total length of the line in Jilin to 6330 kilometres, which is almost three times its length in 2010 (Jilin.gov, 2016). Meanwhile, the density of the railway network in Jilin province is 338 kilometres per 100,000 square metres (万平方公里). This is 2.7 times the national average railway density in China, and 4.5 times the provincial railway density in 2005. Jilin province has thus connected all its towns by rail and built high-speed railways between all its major cities (Jilin.gov, 2016).

Apart from such railway expansion, the steel industry also supported the construction of other physical infrastructure in Jilin province prior to 2015. During these years, for one thing, in the sector of airport construction, Jilin province enlarged the civil-use areas of Baicheng airport and Tonghua airport, and took the further step of opening flights between these two airports to major cities in China, such as Shanghai, Beijing, and Guangzhou. Meanwhile, the civil-use airport in Songyuan and the second enlargement project of Changchun airport were also started in 2015. The construction of these airports formed the airport transport network of Jilin province. This network of 'one major & several secondary' projects centred on the airport in Changchun (Jilin's provincial capital) and connected the neighbouring airports in smaller cities, such as Baichang and Yanji (Jilin.gov, 2016). For another, by entering the era of high-speed railways, Jilin province started to construct four new cities (towns) along the Harbin-Dalian high-speed railway: De-hui West Station West New City, Changchun West Station West New City, Gongzhuling South Station West Mountain New City, and Siping East Station Southeast Natural New City. Apart from the final new city in Siping, which mainly focused on the development of leisure and agriculture, the other three, which concentrated on the area of multifunctional business, required large amounts of steel during their construction (Jilin.gov, 2016). Therefore, in the economic participation of iron ore in North Korea, the target of jurisdiction is also at the level below the state with the specific target of advancing local development, rather than the general target of resource control.

CONCLUSION

In conclusion, there are several major channels at multiple levels on the China side in Sino-DPRK economic interaction in the sector of mineral resources. First, at the state level, Beijing no longer maintains its previously dominant role of the Cold War era in decisions concerning both big and small economic affairs in Sino-DPRK relations. Apart from sustaining oil and coke supplies to North Korea for many years, it rarely became directly involved in these activities, especially after the end of the Cold War. However, it still provides institutional support in terms of legalising Chinese economic activities in North Korea by signing general agreements to promote and protect Chinese investments. It also offers necessary diplomatic aid for the achievement of economic cooperation programmes relevant to central state-owned companies and strategic resources, such as rare earth.

Secondly, at the level below the state, local government, local state-owned companies, and private SMEs formed multiple channels with North Korea. The non-state actors, such as private enterprises, played an increasingly significant role in Sino-DPRK relations, in particular in economic participation with actors outside Northeast China, who are historically considered the major source of Chinese economic actors in North Korea. At the same time, due to the rapid increase of engagement from multiple economic actors, economic cooperation in mineral resources became of primary importance in Sino-DPRK relations. The income and the relevant technological support to North Korea deepened its dependence on China, and offered opportunities for Beijing to turn the heat on Pyongyang, thereby showing its dissatisfaction with North Korea. Beijing supported a UN resolution in April 2016 and imposed the strongest sanction on North Korea by forbidding the import and export of major mineral resources in Sino-DPRK trade. On 5 April 2016, China's Ministry of Commerce (2016) announced that, except in the case of a humanitarian emergency, China would forbid the import of coal, iron ore, gold, and rare earth products from North Korea. This still allowed room for China to play a flexible role in the trade of these mineral resources with North Korea in order to meet the requirements of actors below the state.

From the way of actors' drivers, the national strategy of developing coal liquefaction is indeed the driver of the central state, and its owned companies, to participate in North Korea. However, this direct engagement from the state level is only a part of the economic activities occurring in the field of coal mining. The other actors, especially SMEs, are driven by the other specific targets of reducing economic costs and sustaining their own survival, which are not necessarily concerns of the actors at the state level. Meanwhile, in the economic participation on rare earth and iron ore, their drivers are also irrelevant to the national strategy. Although investment in North Korean rare earth mines could help to extend China's control of the international rare earth market, this long-term target could be better achieved by the strong control of the smuggling of rare earth minerals. This administrative issue at the national level is not considered by companies at the local level who are more concerned about the potential economic cost of dealing with environmental pollution. Furthermore, the economic activities in iron ore for the development of the vehicle industry and the railway network in Jilin province also ran against the national strategy of transferring and reducing the industries with surplus production capacity. The amount of iron ore imported from North Korea to Jilin province is also extremely limited at the national level. Therefore, China's economic activities in North Korea in the sector of mineral resources are mainly driven by the actors below the state with economic and environmental concerns.

References

Primary Resource

Interviews

Anonymous Interviewee 1: Interview with local official, Jinan, Shandong province, 3–5 July 2011.

Anonymous Interviewee 2: Interview with local businessmen, Jinan, Shandong province, 3–5 July 2011.

Anonymous Interviewee 3: Interview with local scholar, Dalian, Liaoning province, 12 Sep 2012.

Anonymous Interviewee 4: Interview with local official, Changchun, Jilin province, Aug 11 2014.

CHINA'S ECONOMIC ACTIVITIES IN THE NORTH KOREAN MINERAL... 43

GOVERNMENT AND CORPORATION WEBSITE

Central Government of PRC (2012) 'The amount of coal mine death falls below 2000 for the first time in 2011', 27 Mar 2012. [online] http://www.gov.cn/zxft/ft222/content_2100749.htm. Retrieved on Dec 10th 2012.

ChangBai Ethnic Korean Autonomous Town Environment Protection Bureau (2007) 'ChangBai Ethnic Korean Autonomous Town Environment Protection Bureau's Annual Review of 2007 and Working Plan of 2008'. [online] http://bs.jl.gov.cn/BsWebCms/site/cbcms/news/n3928303277.html. Retrieved on Nov 24th 2012.

Cheminfo (2011) 'North Korea Used 20 million ton rare-earth mine to exchange 300 thousand ton fertilizer and 500 thousand ton corn'. [online] http://www.cheminfo.gov.cn/ZXZX/page_info.aspx?id=350039&Tname=hgyw&c=10. Retrieved on Nov 24th 2012.

China Minmental Corp. (2005a) 'Boss Zhou went to visit North Korea with Vice Prime Minister Wu Yi and signed coal mine joint-fund agreement with North Korean side.' 14 Dec 2005. [online] http://www.minmetals.com.cn/search_detail.jsp?article_millseconds=200512140218&column_no=01. Retrieved on Nov 19th 2012.

China Minmental Corp. (2005b) 'Boss Zhou met Head of North Korean Joint-fund and Investment Committee Lee Jeu-jong'. [online] http://www.min-metals.com.cn/wkxw/200510/t20051018_25818.html. Retrieved on May 22nd 2014.

China's Ministry of Commerce (2008) 'The reply from the Ministry of Commerce about the permission of setting Liaofeng Colorful Mental Joint Corp'. [online] http://policy.mofcom.gov.cn/blank/claw!fetch.action?id=g000059546. Retrieved on Nov 24th 2012.

China's Ministry of Commerce (2014) 'Coal Import reached new record in 2013'. [online] http://acs.mofcom.gov.cn/sites/aqzn/nyaqnr.jsp?contentId=2783962029605. Retrieved on Nov 28th 2014.

Document of Jilin City National Development and Reform Committee (2014) 'The No. 11 Five Years' Plan for the National Economic and Social Development of Jilin City'. [online] http://www.jlsdrc.gov.cn/Item/Show.asp?m=1&d=2528. Retrieved on May 22nd 2014.

Information Office of the State Council (2012) 'The White Paper of China's Rare-earth Condition and Policy'. [online] http://www.miit.gov.cn/n11293472/n11293832/n13095885/14674599.html. Retrieved on Oct 31st 2012.

LIMAC Corp. (2008) 'Official Business Group of North Korean Lianfeng Community came to have a business meeting'. [online] http://www.limac.cn/limac_news_show.asp?id=131&s=1. Retrieved on Nov 12th 2012.

SASAC (2008) 'Name List of Central State-Owned Companies'. [online] http://www.sasac.gov.cn/n1180/n1226/n2425/index.html. Retrieved on Nov 24th 2012.

Shen Hua Group (2012) 'The Research and Innovation of New Coal Chemical Industry under the direction of Coal Liquefaction—Coal Liquefaction Oil Chemical Company'. [online] http://www.shenhuagroup.com.cn/cs/sh/PAGE1382682123647/ED.html. Retrieved on Nov 24th 2012.

Xinhuanet (2008) 'Huangyi: the death rate of coal mine accidents drops rapidly; a fundamental resolution needs a long-term measure'. [online] http://news.xinhuanet.com/video/2008-01/18/content_7444509.htm. Retrieved on Dec 10th 2012.

YIMA Corp. (2008) 'Corporation has signed intensive investing agreement with North Korean an-Zhou Coal Institution'. [online] http://www.ymgfgs.cn/userlist/admin/newshow-8584.html. Retrieved on Dec 10th 2012.

SECONDARY RESOURCE

BOOKS AND ARTICLES

Cai, Wanru and Xu, Hai. The effect and implementation of media's involvement to crisis resolution—Take Wang Jialing coal mine accident rescue report as an example. *TV Research*, Vol. 12 (2010), pp. 47–50.

Chen, Wei. The analysis of ethic weakness to China's mining accidents. *Journal of Taiyuan Normal University (Social Science Edition) (太原师范大学学报社科版 Taiyuan shifan daxue xuebao, shehuikexue ban)*, Vol. 5, No. 3 (2006), pp. 61–62.

Chen, Xumin. General discussion to the reasons and administration of China's mining accidents. *Journal of Shanxi Coal-Mining Administrators College (山西煤矿行政学院学报 Shanxi Meikuang Xingzheng Xueyuan Xuebao)*, Vol. 2 (2009), pp. 10–11.

Ding, Ling. The sensitive problem in the Shandong Coal Companies' Transformation. *China's Economy and Informationisation (EI survey) (中国经济和信息化 zhongguo Jingji he Xinxihua)*, Vol. 22–23 (2011), pp. 30–36.

Fan, Zhengjia. The General Research of Fundamental Infrastructure Construction and Regional Development. *Economic Forum (经济论坛 Jingji Luntan)*, Vol. 6 (2012), pp. 26–28.

Hao, Shengyun. The reasons for the frequent happen of mining accidents in China and strategy'. *Frontline (前线 Qianxian)*, Vol. 4 (2007), pp. 155–158.

Lan, Qing-xin. Study on Resources Enterprises' Overseas Mergers and Acquisitions of China in Recent Years. *International Trade Problems (国际贸易问题 Guoji Maoyi Wenti)*, Vol. 8 (2011), pp. 152–163.

Li, Yungang, Cheng, Wenhao and Wang, Guoliang. China's oil security problem and response research. *Sci-Tech Information Development and Economy (科技信息发展和经济 Keji Xinxi fazhan he Jingji)*, Vol. 7, No. 17 (2007), pp. 91–92.

Montinola Gabriella, Qian Yingyi and Weingast Barry R. Federalism, Chinese Style: The Political Basis for Economic Success. *World Politics*, Vol. 48, No. 1 (1996), pp. 50–81.

Ren, Min. The exploration of Musan Iron mine in North Korea and the Construction of China's Northeast Eastern Border Railway. *Railway Transport and Economy. (铁路交通和经济 Tielu Jiaotong he Jingji)*, Vol. 1 (2006), pp. 11–12.

Shu, Yuan. China's oil security: Challenge and Response. *The Journal of Yunnan Provincial Committee School of the CPC (云南省委党校学报 Yunnan Shengwei Dangxiao Xuebao)*, Vol. 9, No. 5 (2008), pp. 106–109.

Wang, Yonglun. Discuss the diversification of our country's oil energy security strategy. *Sichuan Reform (四川改革 Sichuan Gaige)*, Vol. 4 (2007), pp. 44–49.

Wang, Haiyan (2012) *New Geo-Economics: China and Central Asia*. Beijing: World Knowledge Publish, pp. 212–213.

Wang Ya-nan, Feng Kui and Zheng, Ming-mei. The Development Trend of China Urbanization - China International Forum on Urbanization in 2012. *Urban Studies (都市研究 Dushi Yanjiu)*, Vol. 06 (2012), pp. 1–3.

World Online. The West competitively store China's Rare-Earth and increase pressure to China together. *Focus News*, Vol. 9 (2010), pp. 28–29.

Wu, Hongwei (ed.) (2011) *Regional Development and International Cooperation Mechanism in Central Asia*. Beijing: Social Science Academic Press, pp. 330–331.

Wu, Zhengxiao. A simple discussion of China's rare-earth export quota system. *Energy Technology and Management (能源技术和管理 Nengyuan jishu he Guanli)*, Vol. 3 (2011), pp. 121–122.

Xie, Qingyu and Liang, Guangyuan. Reduction of Rare-earth pollution forced the industrial upgrade. *Southern Daily*, Mar 1st, 2011, p. 16.

Yin, Jian-ping and Ding, Qi. Developing Coal Liquefaction Industry must insist the principle of stable expansion. *Journal of China University of Petroleum (Edition of Social Sciences) (中国石油大学学报社科版 Zhongguo shiyou daxue xuebao)*, Vol. 22, No. 5 (2006), pp. 1–5.

Zhang, Feng. Win-Win in the cooperation and complementation: Analyze the exploring condition of China-North Korean mineral resource. *Korean Studies*, Vol. 3 (2006), pp. 188–192.

Zhao, Zheng and Ni, Pengfei. The characteristics, problems and policy-advise of current China's urbanization. *China National Conditions and Strength*, Vol. 2 (2012), pp. 10–13.

ONLINE RESOURCES

Cai, Peng (2012) 'The Study on Competitiveness Evaluation and Promotion Measures of Changchun Automobile Industrial Cluster', Master Paper in China's National Knowledge Infrastructure, pp. 20–31. [online] http://www.cnki.net/KCMS/download.aspx?filename=2VDU6J0aNp3Np1EeURDWYRne0IVUaNmTpF0QOlVQ1cnaWl2arYmUK9iR3dzVmNnY4tEN24UdzRlTDhTYxdVc3BFUxNFR==QcsFETIpkR6h3YURTYBVWQlVkNJZVR1kjM0YGSnRnT59GWqdzdLZWe31EWi9UR39kRQdkUulVZpZjNOVkYCp0Kq9Ub&dflag=readonline&tablename=CMFDLAST2012. Retrieved on Dec 10th 2013.

ChinaIRN.com. (2013) '枣庄市煤炭企业数量"缩水"严重 Zaozhuan Coal Mining Enterprises' Amount Reduced Heavily'. http://www.chinairn.com/news/20131220/102616425.html. Retrieved on Jan 31st 2019.

China's Ministry of Commerce (2016) '2016-No.11 Announcement of Ministry of Commerce and General Administration of Customs about the outline of abandoned North Korea mineral products' (商务部、海关总署公告2016年第11号 关于对朝鲜禁运部分矿产品清单公告). http://www.mofcom.gov.cn/article/b/e/201604/20160401289770.shtml. Retrieved on December 17th 2018.

Ifeng (2010) 'Chen Bin: Insisting resisting the over-production of vehicle industry' (陈斌:坚决抑制汽车工业产能过剩). http://auto.ifeng.com/news/special/qichechanye10/20100904/414582.shtml. Retrieved on Nov 26th 2013.

Lin Jinshu, Sino-DPRK trade's status quo and countermeasure. *Yanbian Daxue Xuebao, Social Science Edition* (延边大学学报:社会科学版), Vol. 42, No. 1 (2009), pp. 37–43.

SINA (2005) 'TongGang Group used 7 billion RMB to get the Musan Iron mine in North Korea'. [online] http://finance.sina.com.cn/chanjing/b/20051101/16322085037.shtml. Retrieved on Nov 24th 2012.

Sohu (2012) 'China has 233 million vehicles and 247 million vehicle-drivers'. [online] http://news.sohu.com/20120717/n348375776.shtml. Retrieved on Nov 24th 2012.

Wang, Hongtao (2012) 'Changchun Automobile Industry Cluster Development Study', Master Paper in China's National Knowledge Infrastructure'. [online] http://www.cnki.net/KCMS/download.aspx?filename=XhmTBxGZEd3LOBDRyATZtdzbaFHayZGeq1kQ2ZmZ0cWSMNkZW12UHx2dq9iSLtiU1JndWtSVGBlTqd2LCZGV4NUQSl0Q==QOjdWOyN1bZRjTYlnd3kVYzgDZkpHdEhXYLZHS1AjazVmWk9ENHpXQLR1aXdUaJl2UyJWNPl1M2JzT4lWMvEjeyRXY&dflag=readonline&tablename=CMFDLAST2012. Retrieved on Dec 10th 2013.

Wang, Gang and Cheng, Gang (2011) 'South Korean Media claims that North Korean rare-earth mine opens to China'. [online] http://news.cntv.cn/20110817/107530.shtml. Retrieved on Nov 12th 2012.

CHAPTER 3

China's Economic Activities in the North Korean Fishing Industry

INTRODUCTION

The previous chapter discussed China's economic activities in DPRK's mineral sector. It found that Chinese economic activities in North Korea in the sector of mineral resources were mainly implemented by actors below the state, such as provincial and city-level governments, local state-owned companies, and private enterprises. These activities were driven by non-traditional security (NTS) concerns, such as resource scarcity and environmental considerations, as well as other reasons such as reduction of economic cost, improvement of social welfare, and local industrial transition. This chapter continues the preceding analysis by focusing on Chinese investment in North Korea's fishing industry.

Access to clean and affordable food is an important priority for the Chinese government that has to feed the world's largest population especially when total amount of seafood consumption in China increased from 1.76 million ton to 2.98 million ton in the first decade of 21st Century (The Central Government of People's Republic of China, 2000, 2010). Just as

---

This chapter has been previously published and includes the complete source citation as follows: Bo, Gao. 'China's economic activities in North Korea on the Fishery Industry', *Journal of Asian Politics and History* (ISSN 2227-9105), Fall 2016, No. 9, 77–99.

© The Author(s) 2019

B. Gao, *China's Economic Engagement in North Korea*, Palgrave Series in Asia and Pacific Studies, https://doi.org/10.1007/978-981-13-0887-1_3

48 B. GAO

access to strategic mineral resources, like coal and iron ore, is vital for the country's continued development, so too has securing access to large quantities of seafood been a major objective for the Chinese government at all levels. In recent years China's fishing industry has come under attack from the Sino-ROK inter-state agreement to reduce China's fishing area. This situation, along with the need for protection from environmental hazards and overfishing, has driven Chinese economic activities in the fishing sector to expand rapidly overseas. This chapter argues that China's economic activities are motivated by NTS issues, especially the food safety problems caused by environmental concerns. It analyses how these activities in North Korea can reduce such threats. In doing so, it distinguishes between the objectives of the central government in Beijing and those of actors below the state, mainly regional governments and private fishing companies. The chapter also argues that the actors driving these policies are mainly those below the state level, such as local government, private and state-owned companies, and non-government organisations. Except as the broker of fishing opportunities in North Korea and the provider of diplomatic support to contingencies, the central government rarely plays an essential or active role in these activities. During the Cold War era, it relinquished its unchallenged role of organising negotiations over fishery cooperation by signing all the agreements (as a part of general treaty) with North Korea.

The following paragraphs outline the specifics of China's economic activities in North Korea's seafood sector in the post-2003 era. This information includes the purchase of fishing licences, technology transfer, civil cooperative programmes, joint enterprises, and direct investment. After that, the NTS issues, including the reduction of traditional fishery areas, environmental pollution, and the short-term impact of the Fukushima nuclear accident, which influenced the seafood security and pushed the actors to implement seafood activities in North Korea, are discussed with the positive influences of these economic activities in North Korea on China's seafood supply identified.

CHINA'S ECONOMIC ACTIVITIES IN NORTH KOREA IN THE FISHING INDUSTRY

Before 2003, the fishery cooperation between China and North Korea was directly controlled by the central governments of the two countries. The first agreement to include fishery is the Sino-DPRK Economic and Cultural Cooperation Agreement signed in 1953 in support of Liaoning province and North Korea's construction of a reservoir, with China's assistance in fishery management in the reservoir area. The first single ocean fishery agreement between China and North Korea official fishery representative groups was signed on 10 August 1959, after one week's dialogue which briefly discussed the fishing areas of the two countries in the Yellow Sea. After that, Beijing signed the same agreement with North Korea regularly in 1969 and 1981. These agreements hold more symbolic than practical meaning because, before the 2000s, neither China nor North Korea had a strong requirement or the ability to send large fishing fleets to fish in the ocean territories of others, especially in the exclusive economic zones. The normalisation of Sino-ROK diplomatic relations in 1992 became a turning point in Sino-DPRK relations because in the next decade top official interaction and visits completely stopped and China and North Korea did not sign any further fishery agreements. However, in the late 1990s, during the great famine of North Korea, in order to reduce material shortages, Beijing asked North Korea, through its embassy in Pyongyang, to allow Chinese fishermen to develop a barter trade with the North Korean navy in the coastal areas in order to gain permission to fish in North Korea's ocean territory; permission was indeed granted.

Since 2003, China's economic activity in the sector of fishery has become a significant part of the activities among all the sectors in North Korea. In 2003 and 2004, seafood products achieved over 52 per cent of North Korea's total export to China. Although seafood products lost the status as the product with the top import output, due to the rapid increase of mineral resource imports from North Korea after 2005, they remained among the top five products imported from North Korea (Lin, 2009: 39–40). Chinese involvement in the North Korean fishing industry can be categorised into six different kinds of activities (for specific information see Table 3.1). Firstly, buying fishing licences to fish in North Korea is the major choice. From 2003 to 2011, the Ministry of Agriculture in Beijing played the role of general agent for collecting information from sub-level governments and buying fishing licences from North Korea. From 2012, this duty was transferred to the China Distant Fishing Association (CDFA), whose members are made up of public fishery institutions, fishery companies, and other relevant individuals in China. The corresponding partner in North Korea is the North Korean Fishery Association. However, due to the sensitivity of the special relationship between China and North Korea, although CDFA succeeded in dealing with fishery disputes between China and other countries, it still only took responsibility for communicating with North Korea for

Table 3.1 Chinese economic activities in North Korea on fishery industry

Actor	Activities	Time	Output value	Sources
Liaoning Baohua Group; Liaoning Changping Industry and Commerce Company (North Korea; Success Commercial Firm)	Sino-DPRK civil fishery cooperation programme; joint venture (Great West Sea Programme by the North Korean side)	28 May 2010–2012 (350 fishing boats in 2010, 500 in each of 2011 and 2012)	2 billion RMB in 2010 2.2 billion RMB in 2011 2.3 billion RMB in 2012 (whole industrial chain)	Liaoning Ocean and Fishery Bureau (2010b); Anonymous Interviewee 8, 14 September 2012
Joint venture Sino-DPRK Investment, Cooperation and Trade Commercial Firm (Liaoning Baohua DPRK Long-Xing Economic Community)	Sea Cucumber Cultivation Base (13 sq. km.) in Haeju, North Korea	Started from 2011	Baohua Group funded 30 million USD, annual output 150 million RMB	LnBaohua.com (2011); Ifeng (2012a)
Changhai town (under Dalian city)	Fishing activities and officially offered training sessions	April–September 2010 (96 fishing boats)	240 million RMB (seafood only) 5 million RMB per pair of ships	Liaoning Ocean and Fishery Bureau (2010a) Weihai News (2012)
Weihai city	Fishing in the east marine territory of North Korea	June–August 2012 362 fishing boats		
Rongcheng Ocean Fishery Company (local state-owned company) (North Korea: Yu-liu Commercial Firm)	Fishing in the east marine territory of DPRK	2004 10 fishing boats	500 tons squid per pair of ships	Weihai News (2011); Yonhapnews (2004)
Rongcheng Ocean and Fishery Bureau; Rongcheng Ocean Fishery Company	Developing the new fishing area in the North Korea East Sea	June–October 2005 92 fishing boats	600 tons squid per pair of ships	Weihai Fishmarket News (2005)

Penglai Xingdong Fishing Seedling Cultivation Company (Private enterprise)	Trade of technology transfer from China to DPRK on fish seedlings; investment of research and development on the cultivation of fish seedlings	2004 and 2005 (trade); 2006 and 2007 (investment)	200,000 RMB (trade); 30 million RMB (investment) Import of 70 tons of shrimp (5 million RMB) in 2010 Import of 150 tons of shrimp (11 million RMB) in 2011	SC-fishery.com (2008); Yantai Daily (14 March 2010, p1); Anonymous Interviewee 4: 10 August 2012; Shui Mu Website (2010) (China Water Transportation, 2005; Siyang Mofcom, 2005); Anonymous Interviewees 1, 2, and 3: 9 September 2011, Zhoushan CDFA (2012)
Zhoushan Zhengyang Deep-Sea Fishing Corporation Putuo Deep-Sea Fishery Company (local state-owned companies)	Cooperative programme with Dandong companies; buying fishing licence; technology support	2005; 2010	Slight financial loss in 2005	
CDFA (North Korea: mutual fishing association)	Signing fishing agreement with DPRK on developing the eastern marine territory fishery resource	2011; 2012	The general framework and rule that should be followed by all the Chinese fishing boats working in North Korea eastern marine territory	

buying fishing licences. China's Ministry of Foreign Affairs still has to deal with any disputes and conflicts with North Korea in the fishery industry. As the real consumer of fishing licences in North Korea, there are many local governments buying fishing licences. For example, as early as 2004, the Rongcheng government from Shandong province bought fishing licences for ten local boats. Then in 2005, the rapid increase of boats from ten to ninety-two, which required fishing licences for the North Korea east marine territory, enlarged the fishing area in North Korea. As another city in Shandong province Weihai's local government bought fishing licences and sent 362 local boats to North Korea in 2012.

The second type of activity is investing in new facilities located in the coastal area of DPRK, such as the fish seedling project of Penglai Xingdong Fishing in North Korea. Penglai Xingdong Company, which developed a project named 'Domestic Seedlings for External Cultivation 内育外养', constructed its fishery facilities in North Korea by funding 40 million RMB in 2006 and 2007. It cooperated with Penglai local research institutions to develop advanced fishery seeds and used North Korea's clean environment for production. Thirdly, training in the fishing regulations provided by the sub-level governments (e.g. Changhai local government) to both Chinese fishermen and North Korean officials in order to clarify important issues, such as specific formalities, significance of equipping regular GPS facilities, allowed and prohibited fishing areas (not only the exclusive economic zones of North Korea but also the disputed areas between North Korea and South Korea), and avoidance of illegal cross-border fishing activities. What is more, Chinese companies also joined the North Korean fishery development programme by setting up joint ventures with North Korean commercial partners. From 2010 to 2012, two companies from Liaoning province, Baohua Group and Changping Corp, joined the Great West Sea Programme with the cooperation of the North Korean Success Firm. From 2011, the Baohua Group also funded 30 million dollars to found a joint venture with the North Korean LongXing Firm and to construct a Sea Cucumber Cultivation Base (13 square kilometres) in Haeju. Another type of economic activity is that of fishing technology transfer and support. For example, fishing boats from Zhoushan Putuo Distant Fishery Company offer explanations and assistance on the technology of double-ship trawling (see Appendix C, point 1) to North Korean partners who only use underdeveloped single-ship trawling (see Appendix C, point 2). Usually they give advice about the suitable types of double-ship trawling facilities for North Korean partners according to the real conditions of North Korean boats. They also invite North Korean fishermen to observe the practical control required for cooperation of two fishing ships in the double-ship trawling progress, especially how to keep two boats in step at the same time (radio interaction between the captains and chief mates of two boats), as well as the cooperation of sailors in the close-net stage. Finally, in addition to these official, legal activities, there are also media reports about underground interaction between Chinese individuals and North Korean troops about the sale of illegal fishing licences and monopolisation of fishery resources by attacking Chinese fishing boats in the name of illegal cross-border fishing in the Sino-DPRK ocean border near Yalu River (see Appendix C, point 3).

According to the information above, it is clear that over the last ten years there have been multiple channels of interaction at both official and non-official levels between China and North Korea. The inter-state interaction still continued, but it weakened from the dominant control of Sino-DPRK fishery affairs in the Cold War era to a single diplomatic channel for emergencies. At the level below the state, cases concerned cooperation between sub-level governments on training officials and sessions for Chinese fishermen about fishing regulations in North Korea. At the same time, social fishery associations of the two countries followed the decentralised power for dialogue and the trade of fishing licences. There was also illegal cooperation between companies of the two countries concerning investment in marine facilities, technology transfer within the fishery industry, construction of joint ventures, and mutual development of fishery programmes, as well as the underground, illicit sale of fishing licences.

Chinese economic actors in the North Korean fishing sector are driven by particular concerns. These include the reduction of traditional fishery areas and access to fresh fishing stocks, as well as fears of environmental pollution, including nuclear contamination from Fukushima. The next section will discuss what prompts Chinese companies to involve themselves in DPRK, paying particular attention to the impacts of the fishery agreement between China and South Korea, signed in 2000, on reducing the scale of China's traditional fishing area.

Driver 1: Response to the Reduction of China's Fishing Area Caused by the Signing of the China-ROK Fishery Agreement

After outlining China's specific activities in the sector of seafood in North Korea in the previous section, three motivations for these activities, their background, and their implications are discussed. This section mainly focuses on the first motivation: the response to the reduction of China's

54   B. GAO

fishing area caused by the signing of the China-ROK fishery agreement, which has been effective since 30 June 2001. It has resulted in a large reduction in the number of Chinese fishing boats in historical fishing areas such as Tsushima and Chejudo (Li, 2004: 16).

Difference Between Old and New Agreements
In the past, agreements between China and neighbouring countries were signed under the principle that international waters are open to commercial fishing. In other words, all the fishing boats that choose to fish in the international waters outside the 12 sea-mile exclusive economic zone can benefit from unrestrained fishing without any supervision by authorities. The old principle caused damage to natural fishery resources near small countries due to the unsustainable fishing carried out by fishing fleets from large countries. For example, large numbers of Chinese fishing boats can fish wherever they can reach, except in the exclusive economic zones (Li, 2004: 13–15).

The new agreements between China and neighbouring countries, especially South Korea and Japan, were signed under the Ocean Law Treaty of the UN in the early 2000s. Despite the 12 sea-miles special economic zone, the authority of the central government has expanded to cover 200 sea-miles and the final achievement of the continental shelf. Under this treaty, China now has a 300 square sea-mile fishing area, 20 per cent less than previously. Furthermore, the 300 square sea-miles includes the overlapping ocean between China and neighbouring countries, which is 70 per cent of the total scale and has to be supervised by both authorities under the institutions of Tentative Measures waters (Li, 2004: 16).

Sino-ROK Fishery Agreement: Impacts
Before the Sino-ROK fishery agreement in 2001, there were over 20,000 fishing boats in these areas; however, from 2001 to 2005, the number has been reduced to below 5500, and after 2005 a further reduction has been made in order to ensure the number of fishing boats from China stays under 2000 (Sino-ROK fishery agreement). In other words, almost 90 per cent of fishing boats have been removed from traditional external fishing areas and forced to compete inside the domestic offshore fishing areas for very limited fishing resources (Li, 2004: 16).

The new fishery agreement was recognised as a major problem in three ways at that time, and led to the rapid rise of discontent among fishermen (Xu, 2002: 5). The permanent loss of traditional fishing areas caused a

CHINA'S ECONOMIC ACTIVITIES IN THE NORTH KOREAN FISHING... 55

huge reduction in the number of fishermen. The original offshore natural environment had already been very weak and now this condition must be worsened with huge numbers of fishing boats forced to return from traditional fishing areas. The fishermen normally followed a traditional family path in entering the fishery business. According to the record of Lin and Liu (2006: 71–74), in Liaoning province alone, from 2000 to 2004, the fishery agreement between China and South Korea caused the loss of 40 per cent of the traditional external fishing area and 30 per cent of fishing boats in the mutual fishing area. In 2005, in the Yellow Sea and the East Sea, the number of fishing boats reduced to one-third of the number in 2000. Meanwhile, the final fishery quota in 2005 was less than 10 per cent of that in 2000. Over 4000 fishermen and 700 fishing boats have been forced to retire or seek new jobs. Liaoning is the tip of the iceberg.

Implications: Solution and Competition

The loss of traditional fishery areas due to the Sino-ROK agreement is one of the main drivers behind China's engagement with DPRK in the area of fishing. It pushed the coastal areas near Bohai and the Yellow Sea to implement solutions, such as changes to fishing areas and upgrading the industry to maintain the livelihood of fishermen affected by the agreement. North Korea is one of the most significant alternative places to replace the lost traditional fishing areas. Take Shandong province as an example—depending on the different financial conditions, several cities in Shandong province chose to buy fishing licences and go fishing in North Korea in different periods after 2001. The local authorities and fishery companies of Rongcheng, a less developed town in Shandong, responded to the reduction of traditional fishing areas quickly by starting to apply for fishing licences in North Korea from 2003. In contrast, the fishermen from Weihai, a relatively developed city in Shandong, chose Chile as their first alternative fishing area in the early 2000s, and did not buy licences for fishing in North Korea until 2012 (Weihai Year Book, 2013). According to the China Fishery Year Book (2007, 2012), during the first decade after 2001, the yearly number of Shandong boats that went fishing in North Korea increased from 30 to more than 700. With the enlargement of permitted fishing areas, around 4000–5000 people in Shandong province who had originally lost jobs due to the signing of the China-ROK fishery agreement continued their original business as boatmen or in fishery product transport and food processing.

Apart from being an alternative to the traditional fishing areas, North Korea's ocean territory also became the front line of competition between Chinese and South Korean fishing boats. Although the inter-Korea fishery cooperation started as early as the 1970s (see Appendix C, point 4), the number of Chinese fishing boats still had an overwhelming advantage over the South Korean side. Needless to say about the amount of boats from other cities. One example is the 300 fishing boats under the control of Dandong companies which remain unchallenged by South Korea's boats. The 300 fishing boats under the name of Dandong companies have already been unchallenged to South Korean boats (Ifeng, 2012a). Especially for the fishing fleets from Shandong province, which are the major victims of the Sino-ROK fishery agreement, the competition with South Korean fishing boats can be seen as a type of revenge by China on South Korea, particularly by the use of their advantages in terms of the number of fishing boats they have. In 2005, one year after the signing of a contract between the North Korean Shangming Trade Corporation and the Beijing Huatong Trade Company on opening the marine territory of DPRK near Wonsan to Chinese fishing boats, South Korean media expressed strong concern over the potential negative impacts, especially the decline of fishery migration to South Korea, because this area partly covers the inter-Korea mutual fishing area (Yonhap News Agency, 2004). In 2010, the serious decline of squid migration from the Yellow Sea to Russia via the South Korea coastal line was confirmed by Mr. Choi, the leader of the Goseong fishery association, because the permanent numbers of Chinese fishing boats in the North Korea sea area increased threefold, from twenty to sixty (Yonhap News Agency, 2010). However, although the South Korean fishermen called for a response from Seoul, Seoul could do nothing because the allowance of Chinese fishing boats to fish in North Korea is a domestic affair for Pyongyang.

Therefore, Chinese economic activities in North Korea in the fishery sector successfully provide an empirical grounding for the coexistence of jurisdiction concepts in the two different modes of multi-level governance. It was a target jurisdiction which represented the will of the victims of Sino-ROK agreements in the coastal areas, and specifically aimed to use North Korea's underdeveloped fishery resources as an alternative to the resolution of fish scarcity, in turn due to the reduction in the traditional fishing area in the Yellow Sea caused by the Sino-ROK new fishery agreement. The diversified economic activities, such as the investment of coastal marine facilities and buying fishing licences, are evidence of flexible jurisdiction. There are also very clear, limited numbers of jurisdiction levels with no overlapping fields between Beijing and the actors below. On the one hand, the central government in Beijing provided an institutional framework for Chinese economic activities in North Korea during the early period of operating the Sino-ROK fishery agreement. In China's economic cooperation with North Korea, it paid most attention to the transmission of information from North Korea about commercial fishery opportunities. In other words, Beijing played a mediating agency role by mainly collecting the specific requirements from the actors below the state, and providing information about the opportunities from North Korea. It neither pushed all the affected fishermen to choose North Korea as an alternative fishing area through top-down administrative commands nor influenced the quota of fishing licences on the North Korean side because, under the market-oriented principle, the quota is determined by the requirement from China. On the other hand, the regional governments, local state-owned companies, and private enterprises took responsibility for developing relations with North Korea under the inter-state framework to develop the underdeveloped North Korean fishery resources as an alternative seafood source, and thereby make up for the loss of traditional fishing fields. The responses of actors below the state to the Sino-ROK fishing agreement, especially Beijing's compromise on reducing the scale of China's fishing area, can be seen as evidence of their core status and subjectivity in the jurisdiction of this issue. Although the Sino-ROK fishery agreement came into effect in all the relevant provinces and cities at the same time, the impact on actors below the state in the coastal area was not equal in terms of their purchase of fishing licences and sending fishing boats to North Korea. For example, in Shandong province, as early as 2003, Rongcheng became the first city to apply for fishing licences in North Korea. In contrast, other cities such as Weihai and Penglai did not implement the resolutions until several years later. It can be seen that, in resolving problems of seafood security (i.e. scarcity), Beijing played a relatively limited role in contrast to its superior, unchallenged status in Sino-DPRK relations during the Cold War era. The actors below the state became the real drivers of China's economic policy towards North Korea. This section has shown how the Sino-ROK fishery agreement caused the long-term, in fact, an almost permanent, reduction to China's traditional fishing fields. This incident pushed North Korea to be selected by many Chinese fishery companies and local governments in the coastal area as their alternative fishing field. The section below analyses how Chinese actors below the state are motivated by environmental pollution, another mid-term (though probably long-term) factor with a negative impact on fishery resources, to develop North Korea marine resources.

58   B. GAO

Driver 2: Seeking a Clean Alternative Fishing Area Due to the Heavy Environmental Pollution in the Offshore Area of China

In addition to the driver of fishery resource scarcity due to the loss of traditional fishing fields seen in the section above, environmental pollution is another major driver of Chinese economic activities in the North Korean fishery industry. This section first outlines the background to China's environmental pollution in the coastal areas, and the negative impact on the coastal fishery industry. After that, it explains specifically how China's fishery industry has benefited from North Korea's clean ocean environment.

Environmental Pollution: Background and Impacts

Environmental pollution, especially water pollution, is a serious new NTS threat to China and includes groundwater pollution and underground water pollution. Ocean pollution is considered as the worst of the groundwater pollution problems due to its large scale and difficulties of recovery. In 2011, Wu Xiao-qing, the Vice Minister of the Ministry of Environment Protection of the People's Republic of China, made a speech about the protection of the sea in the Seventh Chinese Ecology and Health Forum. As she pointed out,

> Although all levels of Chinese governments have made a great contribution to protect the sea in the Eleventh Five Years Plan Period, the condition of protecting Chinese immediate offshore area is still very difficult. The major expressions are: the problems of pollution and ecological damage in the immediate offshore area are still serious; the conflict between coastal business development and bearing capacity of resources-environment is increasingly sharpen; the abilities of environmental monitoring and supervision are still needed to improve. (Li, 2011: 69–71)

For example, in the period 2000 to 2008, in Liaoning province, the nearest coastal province to North Korea, the Bohai Sea near Liaoning was the most polluted area in China (Lin, Lu and Luo, 2008: 1–5). Between 2000 and 2003 there were thirty-two red tides (see Appendix C, point 5) with over 100,000 square kilometres of the Bohai Sea affected. From 2004 to 2008, the number of red tides increased to forty-eight and the affected area doubled (Lin et al., 2008: 1–5).

The environmental pollution had three negative impacts on the local fishery industry. First of all, the pollution directly reduced the amount of production and decreased the patterns of the seafood catch. The red tides in the Bohai Sea resulted in the reduction of marine production fishery output by 5 to 10 per cent every year (Zhang and Ke, 2005: 95–101). The annual economic loss of seafood production caused by red tides in the Bohai Sea reached 500 million RMB on average (Yin and Li, 2005: 15–18). For Liaoning province, the productive area of Liaodong Bay in the northeast part of Bohai had a 3 per cent yearly drop. It produced 650,000 tons of seafood in the Ninth Five Year Plan Period of PRC's National Economy and Social Development (1995–2000) (九五时期), 550,000 tons in Tenth Five Year Plan Period of PRC's National Economy and Social Development (2000–2005) (十五时期), and 480,000 tons in the Eleventh Five Year Plan Period of PRC's National Economy and Social Development (2005–2010) (十一五时期) (Liao, 2006: 24). Secondly, the ocean species diversity decreased. Since the 2000s, only five of the eleven traditional major fishery products in the Bohai Sea remain. In contrast, output of the other six types dropped by 80 per cent (Wang, 2008: 117–119) (see Appendix C, point 6). Thirdly, environmental pollution also indirectly led to overfishing. As the continuative structure of fishery products in the Bohai Sea has been damaged, in order to maintain the quantity of production under the condition of fish scarcity, fishermen have started to catch small fish. The specific case can be found in the first table in Appendix.

Effectiveness of Fishing Activities in North Korea
As mentioned in the section above, environmental pollution, which causes fishery resource scarcity directly and overfishing indirectly, is the main threat to Chinese seafood security. The ocean condition of North Korea, where fishing is relatively underdeveloped and the water is clean has benefited the fishery industry in China's coastal areas in two major ways (Ifeng, 2012b; Ministry of Commerce of People's Republic of China, 2009; see Appendix C, point 7).

Firstly, developing the fishery industry in the North Korean ocean territory has promoted the quality and quantity of fishery products by avoiding the negative impacts of environmental pollution on fishery seedlings. Take the example of the Penglai Xingdong Company, which developed a project named 'Domestic Seedlings for External Cultivation *内育外养*', in short of '*国内育苗国外养殖*' and constructed its fishery facilities in North Korea. Its first batch of 179.78 tons of mussel products grown in North Korea were of a better quality, even under the shortened cultivation period (two years in North Korea, three years in China) than the same domestic products (SC-Fishery.com, 2008; Shm.com.cn, 2010; Shuichanyangzhi, 2010: 27). During its four years of investment in North Korea, the

Xingdong Company succeeded in achieving mussel output of 50 per cent more than its normal domestic output (Anonymous Interviewee 4, 10 August 2012).

What is more, the successful cases of Chinese economic activities in the North Korean fishery industry also reduced the pressure on domestic fishing and offered opportunities for local authorities to implement programmes of fishery resource recovery. For example, from 2005, the Ocean and Fishery Department of Shandong province started a regional fishery resource recovery programme after getting positive feedback from Rongcheng's first-year fishing activities in North Korea in 2004 (HSSD. gov.cn—Shandong Ocean and Fishery Department Official website, 2005). In the following years, local authorities in Shandong also set up special policy priorities to encourage local enterprises to develop fishery programmes in North Korea. Thus, with the reduction of local fishing activities, the fishery resource recovery programme increased the number of cities and partners involved from 4 regions and 28 partners in 2007 to 15 regions and 114 partners in 2012 (Guo, Ma and Wang, 2007: 71–72; Wang and Sun, 2013: 21–26). Indeed, not all regions and partners were involved in the economic activities in North Korea, although cities such as Weihai and Rongcheng, and their relevant companies, remained on the list.

In general, besides the fishery scarcity caused by the Sino-ROK fishery agreement, Chinese economic activities in North Korea in the sector of fishery are also motivated by environmental requirements, in particular the avoidance of pollution in the ocean. In the case of this second motivation, the jurisdiction concepts in the different modes of multi-level governance still coexist in a similar way to the first motivation of fishery scarcity. There remain flexible ways of jurisdiction, limited levels of jurisdiction that provide institutional support at the state level and deal practically with specific problems below the state level, without overlapping responsibilities. As a target jurisdiction, the actors below the state, particularly the fishery companies, were anxious to leave the original heavily polluted fishing areas. This target is still irrelevant to, and different from, Beijing's general purpose of keeping regional peace and stability. It cannot be denied that environmental protection was recognised by Beijing as a national strategy since economic reform, in order to prevent contamination from happening in the first place. However, Beijing's overwhelming attention to economic profits and development made it difficult to implement this strategy at the regional level and lacked effective restraint on the unsustainable development of regional administration. In this section and the one above, Chinese economic activities are seen to be motivated by the long-term impacts brought about by both environmental pollution and the inter-government fishery agreements. In contrast to these two causes with their long-term impacts, the next section discusses how Chinese fishery companies were pushed by the short-term temporary impact of the Japanese nuclear accident in 2011.

Driver 3: Influence of the Nuclear Accident in Japan

Background and Impact
The Japanese nuclear accident at the Fukushima nuclear plant in March 2011 is also an important driver for Chinese fishing boats to choose North Korea's marine territory as an alternative fishing area to the North Western Pacific near Japan. The accident was caused by the breakdown of the electrical supply to two nuclear plants and eventually led to fire and the explosion of nuclear facilities. Indeed, the radioactive particles from Fukushima did not directly enter the air to spread with the same speed as occurred in the Chernobyl accident in 1986. However, because the Fukushima nuclear plant is located in the eastern coastal area of Japan very close to the Northeast Pacific Ocean, the Japanese government pumped 10,000 tons of polluted waste water into the nearby ocean under severe international criticism (SINA, 2011a). The Hong Kong media pointed out two major directions for this nuclear pollution: one towards the southeast, the major ocean currents would come close to the nearby sea area of the first island chain rather than to the coastal area of China; and one towards the northeast, taking the radioactive particles into the deep Pacific Ocean and away from the continent. However, the latter direction results in the pollution of ocean-living beings in the Northeast Pacific. As the French Research Center of radioactive prevention and nuclear security claimed at its New Release Conference on 27 October 2011, 27.1 quadrillion Becquerels of the radioactive element Cs-137 spread into the ocean during the first week after the accident (SOHU, 2011; Xinhua Net, 2011). The Japanese nuclear accident in Fukushima has become the largest issue in history concerning human-made radioactive particles entering the ocean. Although the ocean currents could thin the concentration of these radioactive elements to a safe level after several years, the deep water fish, the fish at the top of the food chain, and molluscs are the easiest living creatures to be polluted due to their living conditions, or through the effect of food chain enrichment, which leads to an accumulation of toxins in the bodies of the beings at the top of the food chain.

62   B. GAO

Response: Fishing to North Korea
As mentioned in the section on economic activities, the fishing fleets of the companies from Zhoushan have changed their fishing areas for large squid from the Northwest Pacific to North Korea's marine territory. Two responses from Chinese society motivated companies to fish in North Korea. One response is the Chinese public's awareness of the influence of the Japanese nuclear accident on ocean products. It caused a short-term reduction in the sale of ocean fish products. The other response is the official implementation of radioactive examinations. This becomes a long-term increase to the cost of the seafood production.

Firstly, public awareness in China of the security threats of nuclear contamination on ocean production created a short-term reduction in the sale of ocean fish products. During the first two weeks after the accident, seafood sales in the coastal area and in Northeast China decreased rapidly. Although several local governments made an official denial of possible nuclear contamination to seafood, and promised to implement radioactive examination of seafood products, these activities only strengthened the confidence of local dealers rather than that of consumers (SINA, 2011b; Qingdao News, 2011). For example, the sale of seafood at both the terminal market and the supermarket in Dezhou decreased by over 70 per cent compared to the previous sale one week before the rumours (Dezhou Daily, 2011). Changchun fell into a worse situation where its seafood shops were forced to close down (Xinwenhua, 2011). To the social anxiousness about nuclear pollution, one top manager of a fishery admitted the negative impacts but also denied it to be a big problem:

> *Our sale is indeed influenced by the news of possible pollution. Many small companies tried to use this chance to lower the price in order to promote their marketshare. A small number of business partners in Southwest China stopped buying seafood products from us. However, it is not a big problem. Our company does not fear. I am very confident about our products. They are completely safe. We have rented a temporary place to store our products. The price is not cheap, but still affordable. Next year our company will build a new food-store with the enlargement of the company's scale. This is only an automatic emergency response to the disaster, just like the knee-jerk reaction, which you have learnt about in the biological classes of Junior Middle School. It is involuntary. We can sell them a few weeks later after the end of social panic. It is only a very small reason for us to change our fishing area.* (Anonymous Interviewee 2, 9 September 2011)

Compared to the short-term reduction of seafood sales due to social panic, the official implementation of radioactive examination has more influence on the companies. In order to prevent any possible risk of selling the seafood products in China which are contaminated by radioactive particles from Japan, the relevant local governments ordered the establishment of special inspection and supervision departments to implement examinations. The fishing boats which had worked in the Northwest Pacific, with either freshly frozen or processed dry seafood products, had to go to a specified port to undergo an official inspection for nuclear pollution, and even to destroy products on the spot if necessary. For example, the fishing fleets which belong to companies from Zhoushan are required to berth in Shanghai, before returning to their home port, for radioactive examination. Due to the temporary nature of this process, huge numbers of fishing boats created long queues in the port and the examination took two or three days. According to another interviewee (Anonymous Interviewee 1, 9 September 2011), the decision to set up temporary radioactive examinations created huge inconvenience in terms of sales. Secondly, because of the higher transport costs of reaching an inspection port, the cost of retaining the freshness of the food, fuel, and electrical costs also increase. Thirdly, although the payment for the radioactive examination of seafood in one fishing boat is relatively low (200 RMB per type per boat), for a fishing fleet which has about 20 per cent of China's squid-fishing boats, the cost is no small amount. After all extra costs are taken into account, the estimation for every boat is over 1000 RMB if it carries only five fishermen. Moreover, if the companies decide to continue their fishing plans in the Northwest Pacific, they have to buy and build special facilities on their boats to check for nuclear pollution in the seafood.

Thus, fishing in the North Korea marine territory is becoming an economic choice for the seafood companies that have fishing programmes in the Northwest Pacific. Just like the responses in the previous sections towards the loss of traditional fishing areas due to the Sino-ROK fishery agreement and the decline of seafood products under the worsened ocean environment, this was another target jurisdiction that aimed to save time and avoid extra cost around the radioactive examinations. In contrast to the two motivations above, the impact of the nuclear accident in Japan is temporary, meaning it may be more effective to show the subjectivity of the actors below the state. In Zhejiang province there are many fishing boats. However, only a few companies from Zhoushan, rather than all of the fishing companies in Zhejiang province, chose to go fishing for squid in North Korea. Many other companies sent boats to fish in the South China Sea and West Africa as different companies had different coping strategies according to their own financial condition and scale of operation. Again, different levels of jurisdiction concerning the potential risk of the nuclear accident did not overlap because the local governments mainly declared the real condition and implemented radioactive checks in order to satisfy an anxious public, while the fishery companies paid most attention to the selection of substitute fishing areas. Similar ocean conditions, with the same fishing target (squid), is also a reason for the companies to make the decision to fish in the North Korea area in order to replace the previous working area in the Northeast Pacific near Japan. The fishing facilities can continue to be used. The companies need not upgrade the facilities or worry about the waste of their boats, with their advanced equipment, because of the extra cost of many idle functions. After discussing how the negative impacts of three factors influenced Chinese actors motivated to develop economic relations with North Korea in the fishery sector, the next section further examines the independence of actors below the state level, especially local state-owned companies and private enterprises, through the negative impacts of their economic cooperation with North Korea, from Beijing's general foreign and domestic strategy.

Divergence Between Central Government and Local Actors

The sections above discussed three major drivers of Chinese economic activities in the North Korean fishery industry. In these sections the central government in Beijing played the role of broker by introducing potential opportunities in North Korea. Meanwhile, the actors below the state are the main actors of different economic activities in North Korea. Although two activities of Beijing, the signing of the Sino-ROK fishery agreement and the administrative decision to implement radioactive checks of fishery products, have created a negative background which pushed actors below the state to fish in North Korea, generally, securing access to fishery resources is still the mutual target of Beijing and actors below the state. However, there remains divergence between the central government and local actors on the distribution of North Korean fishery resources. The central government tries to regulate fishing activities and provide equal, regular opportunities for fishing in North Korea to all the fishing boats from different provinces, whilst the local actors aim to maximise their own economic profits by monopolising the fishery resources and selling illicit licences.

Background of Fishery Incident

From the specific details of Chinese economic activities in North Korea in the section above, it is found that there is a clear distribution of North Korean fishing areas. Only boats belonging to companies from Dandong, and their partners (such as companies from Zhoushan), could fish in the west marine territory of North Korea. In contrast, the fishing boats from other cities in Liaoning, and other provinces, such as Shandong, could only fish in the east marine territory of North Korea. Although both of these marine territories are relatively underdeveloped and clean, the west side near the Yellow Sea has the advantage of better conditions, with warmer water and a larger amount of natural fish feed spread around the mouth of the Yalu River as it meets the sea. This area was indeed monopolised by North Korean military strength in the coastal area and its Chinese agent in Dandong based on a historical relationship.

The 5.8 fishery incident was the first well-known North Korean kidnapping of a Chinese fishing boat in China. According to Chinanews (2012), on 8 May 2012, three Chinese boats (from Dalian) with twenty-nine Chinese fishermen on board were fishing in the China side and were attacked by unidentified North Korean armed men, kidnapped, and taken to North Korea. The Chinese fishermen were asked to call their relatives in China for a 1.2 million RMB ransom (increased to 2.7 million RMB on 18 May). The relatives called the police and contacted the Liaoning province government for help as the news was released through the Internet. China's Ministry of Foreign Affairs became involved in this affair from 16 May. After one week's diplomatic communication and interaction, the three Chinese boats with all the fishermen returned to China safely.

Although the Chinese fishermen and the boats were returned safely after the emergency diplomatic dialogue between China's Embassy in Pyongyang and North Korean top officials, the Chinese media unearthed the history of North Korea's frequent attacks on Chinese boats in order to get a ransom. Several scholars discussed this incident during the interviews. Lv Chao, from Liaoning Academy of Social Science, admitted that their internal research had already found the existence of underground sales of North Korean fishing licences through local Chinese agents in Dandong (Ifeng, 2012a). Even Zhang Liangui, the top scholar in North

66   B. GAO

Korean studies in China, confirmed the involvement of North Korean military units, rather than the mafia, in these incidents, and in an interview with the media criticised North Korea saying it should not have allowed the incident to happen (Ifeng, 2012a).

Beijing's Punishment: Worsened Short-Term Sino-DPRK Relationship

Monopolising the fishery resources of the North Korean west marine territory, especially allowing North Korean local partners—in fact they are military units—to rob other Chinese boats who fish with legal licence in North Korea, and even attack those who fish in the Chinese marine territory, in the name of illegal cross-border fishing, has worsened Sino-DPRK relations from the original disagreement on the nuclearisation of North Korea. China insisted on denuclearising North Korea from the first round of the Six Party Talks in 2003 and recognised it as the core national interest in the region while at the same time North Korea continued to speed up its nuclear development (Roy, 2015: 97–99). Yet the North Korea kidnapping incident discussed above became a turning point in China's domestic view of North Korea. Beijing met huge domestic pressure on the direction of developing a relationship with North Korea. Chinese people are increasingly dissatisfied that this neighbour is turning from being a blood ally to being a troublemaker. As a medium of the CCP, a Global Times' editorial (2012) pointed out that Pyongyang should understand the Chinese public's anger over this incident and realise what influence and support from Beijing could be provided to Pyongyang in the future. Another Global Times' editorial (2015) also claimed that after the latest nuclear test in North Korea, Chinese public opinion of North Korea has changed since the incident of kidnapping Chinese boats. Now over 60 per cent of Chinese citizens recognise North Korea as a burden, or even as a bad neighbour to China. Although in the end, due to the sensitivity of Sino-DPRK relations, there was no further news about the real identity of North Korean military units and their Chinese agents in Liaoning who were involved in the underground sale of fishing licences and activities of quashing dissenters from other provinces, Beijing's response shows its changed position to some extent. One month after the incident, in June 2012, Beijing temporarily stopped the import of North Korean fishery products and then withdrew this prohibition after dialogue and communication with North Korea. Then on 28 June 2013 and 8 July, Beijing issued an emergency announcement to forbid all Chinese boats to fish in the

North Korea east marine territory from July (Ministry of Agriculture, 2013). These two responses, especially the latter, cut off North Korea's major income of selling fishing licences to China, except for the income from their agents, and were recognised as punishment from Beijing to North Korea for its connivance of local units to develop underground connections with their agents in Liaoning province.

Although Beijing has tolerated previous similar violations by North Korea in order to sustain their traditional friendship, under strong domestic pressure it still took the first step of punishing North Korea for issues irrelevant to its nuclear development. The traditional friendship between Beijing and Pyongyang was weakened by the traditional underground relationship between Dandong companies and North Korean coastal units. Beijing played the role of a passive responder in the face of divergence between its general strategy and the interests of actors below the state.

Conclusion

There are several major channels at multiple levels in Sino-DPRK economic interactions in the sector of seafood. First, at the state level, Beijing no longer retains its previously dominant role of making decisions on both big and small economic affairs in Sino-DPRK relations, as it did in the Cold War era. It rarely became directly involved in these activities, especially after transferring its power to issue fishing licences in the territory of North Korea to the fishing bureau of Liaoning province. Even the recent signing of the fishing cooperative programme was achieved between North Korea and the national fishing association. However, Beijing still provided institutional support by legalising Chinese economic activities in North Korea through the signing of the inter-state treaty in the beginning. Besides, it also offered necessary diplomatic channels for emergency inquiries, such as the kidnapping of Chinese fishermen by North Korean military units.

Secondly, at the level below the state, local government, non-government organisations, local state-owned companies, private enterprises, and even social groups formed multiple channels with North Korea. Especially the non-state actors, such as private enterprises and social groups, played an increasingly significant role in Sino-DPRK relations. On the one hand, the non-government national association replaced the official department to sign treaties with North Korea. On the other hand, through underground trade with North Korean militants, a few private enterprises even created negative impacts on the Sino-DPRK relationship by weakening the Chinese public's positive emotions towards North

Korea. At the same time, as a part of Sino-DPRK economic interaction, with the increase of the fishery actors from the coastal areas, fishery cooperation became progressively important again after being exceeded by the mineral cooperation and third-industry cooperation. The income and relevant technology support to North Korea deepened its dependence on China and offered opportunities for Beijing to turn the heat on Pyongyang to show its dissatisfaction. By using North Korea's fishery resources as a substitute for historical fishing areas, and for clean seafood products from unpolluted waters, the actors below the state were motivated to resolve NTS problems in both the short and the long term. This target was irrelevant to Beijing's general purpose of maintaining regional peace and stability at the strategic level. Thus, these activities practically promoted the relevant independence of North Korea's peripheral areas from the control of Pyongyang, increased the uncertainty of Sino-DPRK relations, and led to a rise in domestic dissatisfaction in China towards North Korea.

Although Beijing provided an institutional framework and diplomatic channels for emergency inquiries, the local government and the departments below it mainly operated administrative activities. Despite providing training for the restraint of illegal cross-border fishing activities, the local government of different provinces, particularly the local bureau of ocean affairs, normally played a double role, either as decision-makers, which directly recognised the North Korea marine territory as the alternative fishing area, or as the agents who collected the information about what local fishermen required, and offered fishing licences after buying them from the Liaoning marine bureau. In some cases, the role of local governments also extended to assistance on food quality inspections. The local state-owned companies and private companies were the practical actors of fishing activities in North Korea's marine territory whose decision-making was independent from Beijing, as it did not push them to fish in the North Korea marine territory from several choices. The specific activities, such as buying fishing licences, technology support, and setting up branches in North Korea, were diversified to govern these NTS problems. It can be seen that China's economic activities in the sector of seafood are motivated by the NTS concerns over environmental factors and fishery safety. The actors below the state are the major policy drivers. In contrast, the central government plays a less important role as a broker providing potential economic opportunities in North Korea, and as a diplomatic supporter in the event of emergencies between the two countries, in contrast to its historical dominant role of controlling all Sino-DPRK affairs.

REFERENCES

PRIMARY RESOURCE

INTERVIEWS

Anonymous Interviewee 1: Interview with local businessmen, 9 Sep 2011. Zhoushan, Zhejiang province.

Anonymous Interviewee 2: Interview with local businessmen, 9 Sep 2011. Zhoushan, Zhejiang province.

Anonymous Interviewee 3: Interview with local businessmen, 9 Sep 2011. Zhoushan, Zhejiang province.

Anonymous Interviewee 4: Telephone Interview with local businessmen, 10 Aug 2012. Penglai, Shandong province.

Anonymous Interviewee 5: Interview with local businessmen, 12 Sep 2012. Changhai, Liaoning province.

Anonymous Interviewee 6: Interview with local businessmen, 13 Sep 2012. Changhai, Liaoning province.

Anonymous Interviewee 7: Interview with local scholars, 14 Sep 2012. Dandong, Liaoning province.

GOVERNMENT AND CORPORATION WEBSITE

China Distant Fishing Association (2012) 'CDFA signed the agreement of cooperative program on the sector of fishery resource in North Korea Eastern Marine Territory with North Korea'. [online] http://www.cndwf.com/. Retrieved on Feb 24th 2013.

China's Ministry of Agriculture (2007) *China Fishery Year Book*. Beijing: China Agriculture Publisher.

China's Ministry of Agriculture (2012) *China Fishery Year Book*. Beijing: China Agriculture Publisher.

De Zhou Daily (2011) 'Seafood can be eaten without nuclear pollution'. [online] http://www.dezhoudaily.com/news/dezhou/folder135/2011/03/2011-03-23224441.html. Retrieved on Feb 24th 2013.

HSSD.gov.cn (2005) 'Rongcheng reached a breakthrough on Coastal and Distant Fishing 荣成市远近洋捕捞实现新突破'. http://www.hssd.gov.cn/xwzx/sxdt/200501/t20050110_509931.html. Retrieved on May 26th 2017.

Liaoning Baohua (2011) 'Baohua Corp invests North Korea seafood industry'. www.lnBaohua.com. Retrieved on Feb 24th 2013.

Liaoning Ocean and Fishery Bureau (2010a) 'The condition of Dandong-DPRK Civil Fishery cooperative program's stage operation is fine'. [online] http://www.lnhyw.gov.cn/kjhz/dwhzjl/201007/t20100719_553049.html. Retrieved on Feb 24th 2013.

Liaoning Ocean and Fishery Bureau (2010b) 'The fishing boats of Changhai town came back fully loaded after fishing in the marine territory of DPRK'. [online] http://www.lnhyw.gov.cn/yyfz/hypl/201010/t20101009_578744.html. Retrieved on Feb 24th 2013.

Ministry of Agriculture (2013) 'Emergent Announcement of Suspending Distant Fishery Project in North Korea East Sea Ocean Territory'. http://jiuban.moa.gov.cn/zwllm/tzgg/tfw/201308/t20130828_3589469.htm. Retrieved on May 12th 2016.

Ministry of Commerce of People's Republic of China (2009) 'The nearby fishery resource of Korea Peninsula and the status-quo of economic cooperation'. [online] http://ccn.mofcom.gov.cn/spbg/show.php?id=8638. Retrieved on Feb 24th 2013.

Qingdao News (2011) 'Seafood can be eaten without nuclear pollution'. [online] http://epaper.qingdaonews.com/html/qdzb/20110324/qdzb228232.html. Retrieved on Feb 24th 2013.

Shui Mu Website (portal site of Yantai city) (2010) 'From a female worker to boss, Penglai Xingdong Fishery Manager: Sun Piqing'. [online] http://www.shm.com.cn/special/2010-03/24/content_2876974.htm. Retrieved on Feb 24th 2013.

Siyang Mofcom (2005) 'Zhoushan Fishing program in North Korea started comprehensively'. [online] http://siyang.mofcom.gov.cn/aarticle/zhongyaozt/200512/20051201154064.html. Retrieved on Feb 24th 2013.

The Central Government of People's Republic of China (2000) 'PRC's statistical bulletin of national economic and social development 1999'. [online] http://www.gov.cn/gongbao/content/2000/content_60106.htm. Retrieved on Feb 24th 2013.

The Central Government of People's Republic of China (2010) 'PRC's statistical bulletin of national economic and social development 2009'. [online] http://www.gov.cn/gzdt/2010-02/25/content_1541240.htm. Retrieved on Feb 24th 2013.

Weihai Fishmarket.com (2005) 'The fishing boats won the first battle of fishing in North Korea, 1500 tons of squid have been sent to Shi island'. [online] http://www.wh-fishmarket.com/NewsInfo.aspx?ID=70638. Retrieved on Feb 24th 2013.

Weihai News (2011) 'Rongcheng Ocean Fishery Company: collaboration for sailing in the international fishing area'. [online] http://www.whnews.cn/2011-08/19/content_1698592.htm. Retrieved on Feb 24th 2013.

Weihai News (2012) '362 Weihai fishing boats gained the license of fishing in the east marine territory of DPRK'. [online] http://www.whnews.cn/news/node/2012-07/13/content_5375205.htm. Retrieved on Feb 24th 2013.

Weihai Year Book (2013) www.hswh.gov.cn. Retrieved on Jun 13th 2015.

Xinhua Net (2011) 'Japanese nuclear accident may become the largest ocean nuclear polluted incident'. [online] http://news.xinhuanet.com/world/2011-10/29/c_122211566.htm. Retrieved on Feb 24th 2013.

SECONDARY RESOURCE

BOOKS AND ARTICLES

Guo Min, Ma Xuexin and Wang Yunzhong. Repair Biological Resource and Construct a harmonious hometown for fishery—Theory, Practice and Innovation of Shandong's Fishery resource recovery program. *China Aquatic Product (中国水产 zhongguo shuichan)*, No. 6 (2007), pp. 71–72.

Li Linghua. Simple discussion to the new PRC-Japanese and PRC-ROK Fishery Agreement and the delimitation of ocean border. *Modern Fisheries Information (现代渔业信息 Dangdai Yuye Xinxi)*, Vol. 19, No. 5 (2004), pp. 15–16.

Li Ming. Ocean Pollution's Origins and Countermeasure. *Science, Economy, Market (科技、经济、市场 Keji、Jingji、Shichang)*, No. 8 (2011), pp. 69–71.

Liao Hai. Seafood Industry is becoming a major industry of Liaoning province. *Modern Fishery Information (现代渔业信息 Xiandai Yuye Xinxi)*, No. 12 (2006), pp. 34–34.

Lin Feng-ao, Lu Xingwangn and Luo Hao et al. The History, Status quo and features of Red-tides in Bohai Sea[J]. *Ocean Environmental Science (海洋环境科学)*, Vol. 27, No. S2 (2008), pp. 1–5.

Lin Jinshu. The Status-quo of Sino-North Korean trade and countermeasure. *Journal of Yanbian University (Social Science) (延边大学学报社科版 Yanbian daxue xuebao)*, Vol. 42, No. 1 (Feb 2009), pp. 37–43.

Lin Yuejiao and Liu Haiying. The influence of the implementation of PRC-ROK fishery agreement to Liaoning's fishery industry and strategy. *Chinese Fisheries Economics (中国渔业经济 Zhongguo Yuye JIngji)*, No. 04 (2006), pp. 71–74.

N. A. North Korea-produced Chinese Mussel is landing Penglai. *Shuichuanyangzhi 水产养殖*, No. 4 (2010), p. 27.

Wang Run-bo. The Existed Problems and Advices of China-North Korea Trade Settlement. *Jilin Finance Research. (吉林金融研究 Jilin Jinrong Yanjiu)*, Vol. 6 (2008), pp. 48–50.

Wang Xiyuan, Sun Gang. Shandong Peninsular Coastal Fishery Resource Recovery and Sustainable Development Strategy[J]. *China Fishery Industry Economy (中国渔业经济)*, Vol. 31, No. 6 (2013), 21–26.

Xu Bolong. Respond calmly to PRC-ROK Fishery Agreement. *Ocean Development and Management (海洋发展与管理 Haiyang Fazhan yu Guanli)*, No. 02 (2002), pp. 50–51.

Yantai Daily, 'Seed Cultivation in China and Grow up abroad for one year's reduction of growth period: North Korean produced shrimp landed Penglai'. March, 14th, 2010. Page 1.

Yin Zengqiang and Li Jiuqi. Early Research about Liaoning province's coastal fishery resource. *Hebei Fishery Industry (河北渔业 Hebei Yuye)*, No. 5 (2005), pp. 15–18.

Zhang Yinghui and Ke Na. Liaoning Province Ocean Industry's problem and countermeasure. *Ocean Developement and Management (海洋开发与管理, Haiyang Kaifa Yu Guanli)*, Vol. 22, No. 1 (2005), pp. 95–101.

OTHER WEBSITES

Chinanews. (2012). '中国被朝鲜扣押28名渔民返回大连 船员详述经过' 28 Chinese fishermen returned Dalian from North Korea and told the experience specifically. http://www.chinanews.com/gn/2012/05-21/3904758.shtml. Retrieved on Jan 31st 2019.

China Water Transportation (2005) 'Zhoushan Fishing boats went to North Korea for Fishing'. [online] http://www.zgsyb.com/GB/Article/ShowArticle.asp?ArticleID=37494. Retrieved on Feb 24th 2013.

Ifeng (2012a) 'The previous top officials of the United States: the rocket-launching of North Korea reflects the domestic struggle between Kim Jong-en and militants'. [online] http://news.ifeng.com/world/special/chaoxianfasheweixing/content-4/detail_2012_04/10/13755567_0.shtml. Retrieved on Feb 24th 2013.

Ifeng (2012b) North Korea attracts attention by talking up foreign investment' http://finance.ifeng.com/news/hqcj/20121107/7264376.shtml. Retrieved on Feb 24th 2013.

Roy, Denny (2015) The North Korea Crisis in Sino-US Relations. In Simon Shen (ed.) *North Korea and Northeast Asian regional security*. London: Routledge, pp. 101–105.

SC-fishery.com (2008) 'Going abroad to invest North Korea, Sun Piqing: looking for the gold from ocean seedling'. http://www.scfishery.com/hyxxview.asp?newsid=5666. Retrieved on Jan 11th 2013.

SINA (2011a) '11 thousand tons of nuclear polluted water was pumped into ocean'. [online] http://finance.sina.com.cn/roll/20110405/03159639351.shtml. Retrieved on Feb 24th 2013.

SINA (2011b) 'Five official departments of Shanghai claimed that the seafood in Shanghai are safe'. [online] http://news.sina.com.cn/c/2011-03-19/094522144268.shtml. Retrieved on Feb 24th 2013.

SOHU (2011) ' French institution announced that the Japanese nuclear accident as the largest ocean nuclear polluted incident'. [online] http://news.sohu.com/20111029/n323809455.shtml. Retrieved on Feb 24th 2013.

Xin Wen Hua (2011) 'Changchun's seafood production dropped rapidly'. [online] http://news.xwh.cn/news/system/2011/04/14/010175874.shtml. Retrieved on Feb 24th 2013.

Yonhap News Agency (2004) 'North Korea opened the front sea of Wonsan to Chinese fishing boats'. [online] http://app.yonhapnews.co.kr/yna/basic/articlechina/new_search/YIBW_showSearchArticle.aspx?contents_id=ACK20040907003500999. Retrieved on Feb 24th 2013.

Yonhap News Agency (2010) 'Chinese fishing fleets fished in North Korea and influenced our fishery gains'. [online] http://chinese.yonhapnews.co.kr/allheadlines/2010/07/15/0200000000ACK20100715003500881.HTML. Retrieved on Feb 24th 2013.

CHAPTER 4

Chinese Cross-Border Economic Activities in North Korea

INTRODUCTION

The previous chapter discussed China's economic activities in DPRK's fishing industry. It found that Chinese economic activities in North Korea in this sector were mainly implemented by actors below the state, such as provincial and city-level governments, local state-owned companies, and private enterprises. These activities were driven by non-traditional security (NTS) concerns such as resource scarcity and environmental consider-ations, as well as for the reduction of economic costs and the impact of the Japanese nuclear accident. This chapter continues the preceding analysis by focusing on Chinese cross-border activities in North Korea's sectors of light industry, physical infrastructure, agriculture, and the tourism indus-try. These economic activities are summarised as cross-border activities because they involve the flow of people and equipment between the bor-der areas of China and North Korea and connect the border areas of the two countries. They are different from the activities discussed in the two previous chapters where only Chinese economic actors participated in North Korea.

Maintaining the social stability and safety of the border area is an impor-tant priority for the Chinese government as China borders numerous countries and encompasses over fifty ethnic minority groups. In contrast to the European Union, which has a higher level of domestic integration, China could not open its border for free population flow because it may

© The Author(s) 2019
B. Gao, *China's Economic Engagement in North Korea,*
Palgrave Series in Asia and Pacific Studies,
https://doi.org/10.1007/978-981-13-0887-1_4

immediately meet the drug trafficking from Vietnam, Laos, and Cambodia, terrorists from Central Asia, and refugees from North Korea. Just as access to fishery resources is vital for the country's daily public consumption, so too has securing the border areas been a major objective of the Chinese government at all levels. The border between Northeast China and North Korea is 1400 kilometres long. Unlike the threats of separatism, terrorism, and religious extremism, and the drug trafficking problem in Southwest China, the NTS problems in Northeast China have received less attention. The target of reducing population outflow and labour shortages, which in recent years have occurred as Northeast China has become less attractive to youth, as well as preventing illegal immigrants from North Korea, has driven Chinese cross-border economic activities in North Korea to expand rapidly. This chapter argues that China's economic activities are motivated by NTS issues, especially the cultural decline and border control problems caused by geographical isolation and the difficult economic situation in North Korea. It analyses how these activities in North Korea can reduce these threats. In doing so, it distinguishes between the objectives of the central government in Beijing and those of actors below the state, mainly regional governments and private companies. The chapter also argues that the main actors behind these activities are those below the state, such as the local government, private and state-owned companies, and non-government organisations. Except as the signatories of a few inter-state agreements, the central government rarely plays an active role in these activities. This is what multi-level governance argues for—that the central government acts at a distance and they regulate rather than govern directly.

The chapter begins with a discussion of the drivers of Chinese cross-border economic activities in North Korea's border areas in two parts: economic security and border security. Economic security refers mainly to the socio-economic problems associated with labour shortages in Northeast China. Border security refers to illegal cross-border activities, particularly escapees from North Korea (illegal immigration in the official announcement of Beijing). The background to, and the negative impacts of, these security threats is discussed. After that China's economic activities in the border area of North Korea near China are outlined for several different fields: construction of physical infrastructure (roads and railways), light industry cooperation, border policing, agriculture, and tourism. Thirdly, the effectiveness of these economic activities in resolving, or at least mitigating, the security threats above is discussed.

China's Drivers for Implementing Economic Activities in North Korea's Border Areas

Economic Security

The labour shortage problems in Northeast China are presented in two major ways: purely labour outflow in the major area of Northeast China and a combination of labour shortage and a reduction in the ethnic Korean population in Yanbian Ethnic Korean Autonomous Prefecture (延边朝鲜族自治州), which is located in the eastern part of Jilin province, borders North Korea, and has the largest number of ethnic Korean citizens in China. This is called Ethnic Shrinking in Chinese. These problems not only influence normal industrial operations, but also threaten cultural continuation.

Following the opening-up policy in the 1980s, changes were made to the national developing strategy shifting from heavy to light industry. Apart from the energy industry, for example, oil, there has also been a transition in the focus of development which has shifted from Northeast China to the eastern coastal area. As a result, Northeast China lost its previous priority and became less attractive to its own citizens. Recently the central government implemented a national strategy called the Northeast Rejuvenation Plan, and in some young cities in Liaoning province, such as Dalian, the human capital inflow exceeded the outflow by a factor of two. However, most cities in Northeast China still lack the attractiveness to keep their younger citizens in their hometowns. This has caused a serious shortage of labour in Northeast China; since the late 1980s the yearly human capital inflow to Jilin province has averaged 57 per cent of outflow. A worse condition exists in Heilongjiang with an outflow as great as three times that of the inflow. Youth, especially highly educated students, account for the majority of the outflow (Liu, 2012; Meng, 2013: 39–42).

In Yanbian Ethnic Korean Autonomous Prefecture, the establishment of formal relationships between China and South Korea in 1992 worsened the labour problem. Due to its geographical isolation, Jilin province, in particular the Yanbian Ethnic Korean Autonomous Prefecture, cannot attract enough external investment to employ local cheap labour. This caused a large population outflow towards South Korea from Yanbian Ethnic Korean Autonomous Prefecture for nearly twenty years up to 2011. As they have dual identity in terms of both culture and ethnicity, ethnic Korean minorities from China can easily find jobs in both South Korea and the inner lands of China, which have attracted large amounts of investments from South Korea. In 2008 over 1 million Chinese Korean civilians left for other places: 380,000 to South Korea; 100,000 to Japan, the US, and Australia; and a further 500,000 to other areas of China (Jin, 2011; Guan, 2010). These 1 million Chinese Korean civilians represent half of the Chinese Korean population.

The population outflow caused a crisis in the shrinking ethnic Koreans' settlement in Yanbian. Firstly, the outflow of population from Yanbian is bad for local enterprises, which cannot employ enough workers because they cannot pay the high salaries that companies in South Korea pay to their workers. In 1993, the salary of construction workers in China was 80 US dollars per month, while in South Korea it was 850 US dollars. Currently, the official designed lowest salary in Jilin has increased to 300 US dollars per month. However, this amount is still lower than it was in South Korea even a decade ago. Secondly, the outflow of population deepened the problem of an ageing population. In 2008, the population in the 60+ age group represented more than 15 per cent of the total population; this is considerably higher than the international average of 10 per cent (Jin, 2011). This ageing population structure, especially the rapid increase of aged people living alone, forced the local government to redesign and reduce its administrative region so that between 1993 and 2008 this reduced by 17 per cent. This part of the administrative territory under Yanbian was redistributed to the neighbouring cities. Finally, within the population outflow, 42 per cent of those leaving are women, which is quite significant. Several thousand of these women are of reproductive age and marry South Koreans, which lowers the birth rate and adds to the reduction in the population of Chinese Koreans in Yanbian Ethnic Korean Prefecture (within Chinese borders). In the previous twenty years, over eighteen ethnic Korean schools have shut down due to a lack of students (Jin, 2011). Yanbian Ethnic Korean Prefecture also experienced a continuation of negative population growth rate for a decade until 2011. Thus, it is clear that local economic security problems, especially labour shortage and population outflow, are major NTS threats to Northeast China. This problem belongs to low politics, rather than to the military threat of high politics, with the latter being especially relevant to the nuclear issues of North Korea.

Border Security: Illegal Immigrants

North Korean escapees are the illegal immigrants from North Korea who have entered China and other neighbouring countries since the late 1990s. The estimated number of escapees is between 500,000 and 2 million according to different academic scholars and research centres. Over 95 per cent of escapees first enter China and then over half of them successfully enter South Korea (Piao and Li, 2011). Apart from a few famous people, such as the previous chairman of DPRK Workers' Party Hwang Jiang-yep, who escaped from North Korea for political reasons, most North Korean escapees are ordinary civilians. They and their relatives live near the Sino-DPRK border areas and are motivated to leave for economic reasons. In contrast to the North Koreans who live inland (excluding Pyongyang) and have no idea about external conditions, these escapees usually have a good understanding of the changes in China and of the real conditions in South Korea. In the late 1990s, many hungry North Koreans entered China due to the famine in their own country. In contrast, from the late 2000s onwards, the North Korean escapees want to live in China, enter South Korean institutions through China, or use China as a hub to enter a third country for further repatriation to South Korea. North Korean escapees are becoming a part of illicit smuggling from North Korea (human, narcotics and counterfeit currency) which harms the border area of northeast China (Chestnut, 2007; Clarke, 2008: 73–93; Zhao, 2009).

Indeed, apart from the escapees captured by Chinese policemen and sent back to North Korea, most of the North's escapees who successfully enter China and South Korea have improved their own living conditions. However, their existence creates social problems, in particular adding to local unemployment and criminal activity in the border areas of China with North Korea, especially in the Yanbian area.

Illegal Immigrants Increased Local Unemployment
As noted above, with the change in the national development strategy, Northeast China's traditional heavy industrial bases lost their previous developing priority. Since the beginning of economic reforms in the 1980s, most previous industrial companies, not only a large number of small companies under privatisation, but also large local state-owned industrial companies in key areas such as steel and coal, began to implement Western-style structural reforms and lay off their employees. In the original plan of regional governments, unemployed civilians and people who lost their jobs (Chinese word 'Xia Gang', 'stepping down from one's position') could be recruited by the new businesses, especially in the tertiary industry or the service sector, such as tourism or food.

North Korean escapees influenced the original official plan because they provided extremely cheap labour. They did not create the unemployment but just worsened the situation. A part of victims of local state-owned

78   B. GAO

companies' reform, Northeast Chinese locals who were laid off, gave up the idea of keeping face. They turned to other jobs such as doing private businesses. Yet the rest chose to refuse the official training for working in the South Korean light industry. In contrast to these people, the illegal immigrants took the advantage of age, salary, and education level. Furthermore, their extremely strong will of survival drove them to work hard in order to exchange the food and accommodation (Xuan, 2009: 66–68). Thus, the local employers of North Korea's escapees saved costs and also used some of them to corrupt local policemen and administrative officials in order to avoid routine inspections. In Dandong, Hunchun, and other border cities near North Korea, the business of illegal agents/people traffickers for the introduction of illegal labourers from North Korea has been an open secret. Indeed, the employers of these escapees, agents, and local inspectorates all benefited from this chain while local unemployment increased with the occupation of at least several thousand positions by the escapees (Piao and Li, 2011: 7).

Illegal Immigrant and Their Later Generations' Problems on Influencing the Public Security

Despite the seizure of job positions, North Korean escapees, and their second generation, also contribute to the increase in public security problems. Since the early 2000s the majority of Chinese Koreans in the Sino-DPRK border areas did not welcome the North Korean escapees because two generations of escapees account for a lot of public security problems in the Sino-DPRK border areas.

On the one hand, for the escapees themselves, their journey to China remains risky even after successfully leaving North Korea. Since the mid-2000s, border-crossing for escapees have been organised by human traffickers. Under an increasingly strengthened level of border supervision and inspection, if the illegal agents could not succeed in corrupting, or avoiding, border inspectors, the escapees must continue their journey alone with no further help from the traffickers. In the China/North Korea border region of other Chinese provinces with fewer ethnic Koreans, such as Dandong, escapees are easily captured by the local police as they use a different language to the local dialect. Therefore, the escapees always use illegal ways to get food and money in order to survive and wait for the agents. This is the first type of social problem created.

On the other hand, the second generation of North Korean escapees in China met worse conditions in China than their parents did. Because the female escapees did not have Chinese Citizen ID and Hukou, these children are all 'black children' without Hukou, education, social welfare, or even basic skills. According to the words of one ethnic Korean interviewee in Northeast China, the second generation of North Korean escapees became a new social problem in the border area. The number of social problems among escapees' children has steadily increased every year, although the total number of this group is only several thousand: 'They bring nothing but only dissatisfaction to the environment and even to their families. Maybe they can find temporary work but will soon lose it because they have to move up and—hide. They have nothing to lose so they can do whatever they want to do. The worst result, either being killed in the violent conflicts, or being sent back to North Korea, is actually same to them' (Xuan, 2009: 66–68; Autonomous Interview, September 2012, Dalian).

Many interviewees used the word violation of law and crime to describe the public security problems, such as stealth and robbing, brought by the North escapees and their second generation. However, according to the No. 13 regulations of China's Criminal Law, the case which has slight circumstance without huge negative social impact is not recognised as the commit a crime. It should be seen as the violation of the Law of PRC on punishments in public order and security administration and given the administrative punishment only, without criminal punishment (2013, Chap. 1). Most of North escapees' activities, which caused social problems, could be found in the third chapter: 'The activities which violate the public order and security administration; Punishment' of Law of PRC on punishments in public order and security administration (2013, Chap. 3):

'No. 19 The case that has one of the activities below which interrupt the public order but not enough for criminal punishment, should be given to custody under fifteen days, fine under 200 RMB or warning:

(1) Interrupting the order of government departments, groups, enterprises and public institutions and preventing the normal daily work, producing, management, medical treatment, education and scientific research but haven't created huge loss.'

'No. 22 The case that has one of activities of violating public or private wealth below but not enough for criminal punishment, could be given to custody under fifteen days or fine under 200 RMB.

(1) Beating other people and creating slight injure;
(2) Illegally restraining other people's individual freedom or illegally entering other people's house.'

'No. 23 The case that has one of activities of violating public or private wealth below but not enough for criminal punishment, could be given to custody under fifteen days, warning or fine under 200 RMB.

(1) Stealing, cheating and robbing small amount of public or private wealth.'

(All the information above about public security and criminal law has been translated by the author; see the original names in Mandarin and pinyin in Appendix D, point 11)

Therefore, driven by the requirement of food and money for survival in China or seeking asylum in foreign institutions (mainly South Korea), the North escapees might have violated the Law of PRC on punishments in public order and security administration frequently and caused a large number of small social problems. However, their activities are not criminal. This should be differentiated from the relatively rare case of North Korea soldiers' cross-border killing of China's villagers in the border areas. The ideas of interviewees about the type of escapees' activities, in particular about the large percentage of illegal immigrants' activities in the local crime cases, should be misunderstanding. Two major reasons might have caused this misunderstanding. On the one hand, common citizens are lacking knowledge about laws such as the Criminal Law and the Law of PRC on punishments in public order and security administration, which are relatively distant from their daily life. Their moral judgement and standard in Chinese society deepen the confusion surrounding these activities. For example, stealth could be measured as crime or administrative violation of law according to the level and impact to the society whereas the public opinion might recognise stealth as a type of crime simply because the thieves might be criticised morally beyond the law. On the other hand, the public view in China regarding North Korea has turned negative due to the frequent reports of North Korea's nuclear problems and domestic dictatorship. The North escapees, who are rarely known to the public, could be easily recognised in a negative way due to their nationality.

Thus, local border security problems, especially illegal immigration from North Korea, are a major NTS threat to Northeast China, particularly in Yanbian, Jilin province. Not only does this problem belong to low-politics concerns all things about social or human security, rather than to a military threat within high politics which concerns the state's survival and strict national security, and especially the nuclear problems of North Korea, this threat to human security, which originates in North Korea but impacts heavily on China, also blurs the differences between external and internal affairs.

To sum up, labour shortages, population outflow, and illegal immigration from North Korea causes different types of social problems and negative influences in the border area of China near North Korea. Because the origin of escapees is North Korea and not China, this pushes Chinese local authorities to resolve these problems by implementing economic activities in North Korea. Although it seems that the number of North Korean escapees who have entered Northeast China may compensate for the population outflow, there are two reasons why this is not the case. First of all, the quality of outflowing population is higher than that of the illegal immigrants. Secondly, North Korean escapees mainly enter South Korea through China rather staying in Yanbian.

Economic Activities

Having outlined the local NTS problems above, this section details specific information about China's cross-border economic activities in North Korea with regard to the mutual management of the Rason Special Economic Zone and cooperation on infrastructure use and construction, light industry, agriculture, and tourism, implemented by actors on different levels and within relevant agreements. These specifics are preceded by a short introduction about the targets of these initiatives.

The Mutual Management of the Rason Special Economic and Trade Zone

On 2 September 2010, Li Longxi, the mayor of the Yanbian Korean Autonomous Region, and Kim Su-wol, the chairman of the North Korea Rason Special City People's committee, signed an agreement on a framework for building a cooperative arrangement between their respective institutions (Hunchun.gov.cn, 2010a; Xinhuanet, 2010) (see Appendix D, point 1).

Two years later, on 14 August 2012, China and North Korea reached a mutual development agreement for Rason economic trade area, Golden Floor, and Granville Island. Chen Deming, the minister of China's department of Commerce, and Jang Sung-taek, the central administrative minister of the North Korea Workers' Party, inaugurated the two economic zones' committees of mutual management (Sohu, 2012). The information released by China's department of Commerce claims that the agreement includes the foundation of an operations management committee, economic technological cooperation, agricultural cooperation, and electrical supply from

China to Rason. The signing of this agreement marked the operation of these two economic zones coming into practice. Jilin's local government agreed to send at least hundred officials to enter and manage the Rason economic zone (Sohu, 2012).

On 26 October 2012, after the opening ceremony of Yuanting to the Rason highway, representatives from China and North Korea joined the management committee of the Rason Special Economic and Trade Zone to hold a ceremony marking the formation of the Sino-North Korean Management Committee for the area (Hunchun.gov.cn, 2012b) (see Appendix D, point 2). This mutual management of the North Korean special economic zones (SEZs) means that Chinese officials take a direct role in the border management of North Korea, especially border control and construction, in order to reduce the number of escapees by improving living standards and administration of North Korean border areas.

Physical Infrastructure Cooperation and the Chang-Ji-Tu Project

Since 2002, there have been three major cooperative projects regarding physical infrastructure in the Sino-DPRK border area. They are the repair project of the cross-border Tumen River Bridge, the project known as 'Domestic trade with external transportation: Jilin-Rason Transport Experiment Cooperation', and the Sino-DPRK Road-Harbor-District Integration Project (Hunchun. gov.cn, 2010b; Mofcom.gov.cn, 2006b; see Appendix D, point 3). These projects aim to change the historical, geographical block of China's access to the sea. At the same time, the improved physical infrastructure, with advanced inspection facilities, is also helpful for border control. These projects are under the Jilin province-led national strategy called the 'Chang-Ji-Tu Developing Strategy 长吉图开发战略', which aims to seek access to the Japanese Sea by connecting Jilin province and North Korea Rason Harbor in order to promote the local economic development.

On 29 December 2009, an agreement was signed by Jiang Hu-quan, the city mayor of Yanji, and Kim Su-wol, the chairman of the Rason SEZ People's Committee, regarding the repair project of the cross-border Tumen River Bridge, which connects Quanhe port of Hunchun in Jilin with Yuantingli in North Korea (Hunchun.gov.cn, 2009). The local top officials also reached an agreement on repairing the road from Yuantingli to Rason and building a new bridge from Quanhe port of Hunchun to Yuanting. The repair project started on 15 March 2010 and was expected to be finished by the end of June; however, it was in fact completed one month earlier than the original plan at the end of May 2010 (Yonhapnews Agency, 2010).

Hunchun and Rason reached an agreement on cooperation in an experiment by China with regard to domestic trade and cross-border transport. The experiment was supported by China's Custom Hall in its official announcement on 4 August 2010. On 7 December 2010, eleven heavy trucks with 380 tons of coal, produced by Hunchun Mineral Corporation, left Hunchun's Quanhe border port for Shanghai and Ningbo and onwards to North Korea's Rason Harbor (Hunchun.gov.cn, 2010b). This was the first group of products (coal products from Hunchun Mineral Company) used to test China's domestic trade via cross-border transport. In Rason the work took place in a special port rented by China's company (Hunchun.gov.cn, 2010b; Shanghai.gov.cn, 2011).

On 10 July 2005, two Chinese investors, Jilin Hunchun Dongling Economic Trade Corporation and Bonded Company of the Hunchun Border Economic Co-operation Zone, and their North Korean partner, Rason People's Commission's economic coordination firm, signed a cooperation agreement and formed the North Korea Rason International Linguist Co-management Company in order to push the development of the 'Road-Harbor-District Integration Project' (Small-Mid Enterprises of Jilin.gov.cn, 2007). On 23 August 2005, this company received its company registration licence from Rason city and, up to the end of 2006, the company has since gained licence from North Korea for ocean transport and oil management with the aim of opening up the customs and product transport businesses from Rajin to Southeast China, Japan, and South Korea. It signed a cooperation contract with South Korea's Daya High Speed Ocean Transport firm and reached cooperative intentions with several big logistics companies in Shanghai, Zhejiang, and Shandong. In September 2005, the agreement on the Hunchun-Rason Road-Harbor-District integration project was formally signed. In order to gain access to the sea from Jilin, and even Northeast China, Donglin Economic & Trade Company provided support to road construction around Rajin port in Rason, effectively ending fifty years of single operation rights at the port. Meanwhile, Hunchun also gained the use of 5 to 10 square kilometres in Rason to construct an industrial region. The Jilin local government permitted changes to the rules of combined land-sea transport from Hunchun to Southeast China through North Korea. They also reached an agreement with the Rason side with regard to the tax preference policy for the China-oriented North Korea-processed products. These products were not subject to the same custom inspection process as those goods imported from other countries.

In July 2007, Hunchun Dongling Economic and Trade Company and US Madeli Corporation signed the cooperation project for Sino-DPRK

84   B. GAO

Road-Port-District Integration. The total amount of the investment is 8 billion RMB; Chinese companies will invest 6.53 billion RMB through equipment and funds; North Korea's Rason side will invest 1.47 billion RMB through the licensing of land use and harbour operations (see Appendix D, point 4).

In September 2012, the reconstruction of the North Korean Yuantingli-Rason road was finished. This road connects Quanhe port in Hunchun in the north of the SEZ with Rason port in the south. The whole length is over 500 kilometres. The reconstruction project comes under the mutual development and management of China and North Korea but is constructed by Hunchun city (Xinhuanet, 2012b).

The project, which aims to strengthen road transport in the area, began in June 2011, lasted for more than three months, and cost 226.8 million RMB (Mofcom.gov.cn, 2006a; China News, 2007; Jilin.gov.cn, 2008).

Indeed, the majority of this book aims to examine the key role of China's actors below the state in the implementation stage of China's foreign economic policy in North Korea. However, in the policymaking and designing stage, from the extremely limited number of open-accessed materials, 'Chang-Ji-Tu National Strategy' is a special case which could show the dominant and subjective status of local government at the province level in policymaking by changing the idea of central government. The Chang-Ji-Tu Initiative mainly targeted to connect Jilin province to Rason in North Korea through physical infrastructure. It covered the original geographical scale of the UNDP cooperative programme in the Tumen River Region. Therefore, on 25 March 2008, in the discussion about designing the regional development strategy, Du Ying, vice director of National Development and Reform Committee and the leader of the Tumen River Developing Coordination Group, suggested that Jilin province should still keep the name of the Tumen River developing programme, keep Changchun and Jilin (current and previous capital of Jilin province) away from the centre but focus on the Tumen River Region and set it as the core of total programme. An interviewee introduced the general ideas of officials from Beijing about Chang-Ji-Tu National Strategy (Interviewee 12, 2014):

> 'The officials from Beijing asked us whether this developing strategy will focus Chang-Ji-Tu Cooperative Zone or Tumen River Opening and Developing Cooperative Zone. In other words, whether it locate at Tumen

River, or Tumen River plus Jilin and ChangChun with all of these three regions as the policy-priority zone? In their view, we should pay all the attention to develop Tumen River zone now and then properly expand it to Changchun and Jilin as the support of Tumen River border areas. At the same time, the name of developing strategy/initiative is still Tumen River in order to keep coherence with the UNDP and understanding of international society but expanding to Chang-Ji-Tu is the issue in the future. However, we had different ideas with them and still insisted our main strategic scale of Tumen River zone, Changchun and Jilin and submitted the proposal. Finally our plan was still approved.'

From the interview above, it can be seen that Jilin province diverges from Beijing on the scale of the regional developing plan. Jilin province attempts to cover its important area as much as it could in the plan but the central government tries to restrain the scale only in Tumen River. However, from the paragraphs below, the reply of China's National Developing and Reform Committee to Jilin province's proposal about China's Cooperation and Development Strategy of Tumen River Region, it could be found that apart from keeping the characters of Tumen River in the title of the developing strategy, the central government's suggestion was almost rejected by Jilin province. Changchun and Jilin are still recognised as the core of the Tumen River Zone. They share the same status with Yanbian Prefecture (the historical Tumen River Zone in UNDP Tumen River developing programme) as the policy-priority regions. However, the central government still made a compromise to approve this regional development strategy: 'Agreeing on "China Tumenjiang Region's Cooperation and Development Plan Proposal—Setting Chang-Ji-Tu as the Developing and Opening Pioneer zone" (Proposal in short) in principle. Please carefully organise and implement it Jilin province's Changchun City, Jilin City and Yanbian Prefecture (Chang-Ji-Tu in short) is the core region of Tumen River Zone' (The Central Government of PRC, 2009, translated by the author; see original Mandarin text and pinyin in Appendix D, point 12).

Therefore, it could be examined that in contrast to the central government, Jilin province has played a dominant role in designing the Chang-Ji-Tu Developing Strategy which actually guided the cross-border economic cooperation between Jilin province and the North Korea Rason region in the sector of physical infrastructure cooperation and further cooperative programmes in tourism and agriculture.

Labour/Light Industry Cooperation

There are two cooperative arrangements between Jilin province and North Korea on the labour use in the light industry. The first is known as the 'Going abroad processing' experiment. This experiment was approved by Jilin province with coordination and cooperation from North Korea. On 11 December 2012, Changchun Custom Hall's request to implement 'going abroad for processing and returning business' was agreed to by China's Custom Hall. Four local clothes processing companies (Hunchun Yunda Clothes Corporation, Jilin Telai Clothes Company, Hunchun Hongfeng Clothes Company, and Small-Island Clothes Corporation) make up the first experimental group to use the perfect labour resource of North Korea. Those four companies are allowed to start 'going abroad business' from January 2013 for two years (Hunchun.gov.cn, 2012a).

Apart from the cooperation discussed above, Jilin and Liaoning provinces also reached labour cooperation agreements with North Korea. In January 2012, Jilin province and North Korea completed negotiations on the use of North Korean labour in Jilin. As a result, in the next decade, over 20,000 North Korean labourers will work in the Tumen Sino-DPRK Labour Co-operation Zone and in other cities in Jilin province (Globaltimes, 2012). In April 2012, Liaoning province and the North Korea Co-operation Committee reached an agreement on using North Korean labour in Liaoning province. Around 40,000 North Korean technicians will enter Liaoning province to work in the following years (Globaltimes, 2012). After two years almost 6000 North Korean labourers are working in China under this scheme: 3000 in the Tumen cooperative zone, 1000 in Hunchun, 1500 in Dandong, and 500 in other towns in Northeast China. These initiatives aim to counter the population outflow from Jilin and Liaoning.

Tourism Cooperation

Since 2007, several cooperative projects on tourism have been achieved between China's border cities and North Korea. They provide numerous jobs for ethnic Koreans, in particular as tourist guides and drivers. In 2007, the Dandong Tourism Bureau and its North Korean partner reached an agreement for two tourist trips to North Korea: Dandong-Sinujiu one-to two-day trip, and a longer Dandong-Sinujiu-Pyongyang trip. The latter includes a seven days' plan to tour Pyongyang, Kaesong, and Sinuiju with a visa-free policy for all mainland Chinese citizens. It changes the previous non-landing tourist trip available to Chinese citizens whereby Chinese tourists can only stay on boats in the Yalu River to view North Korea but cannot land in the country. Before 2007, the one-day border tourist trip in Sinujiu was in an experimental period and only open to 210 Dandong local citizens each year (Sina, 2007; China News, 2012b; Anonymous Interviewee 3, 14 August 2014).

From 2008 to 2011, the Tumen tourist bureau developed two tourist projects and one tourist rail-line in North Korea. The two projects are the Onsong one-day trip and the Namyang two-day walking trip (Yanbian News, 2008; Yanbian News, 2011). The rail-line is the Tumen-Namyang-Qibao Mountain Line which first ran on 8 October 2011. Tumen River International Tourism repaired the trains and improved the accommodation standards for tourists by adding soft sleeper compartments (CNTA/China's National Tourist Administration, 2014).

From May 2011 a sea tour began, which was developed by Dafeng International Corporation under the opening of the Kumgang Mountain Special Tourist Zone (STZ) initiated by Rason. Yanbian Tianyu International Tourism Group is the deputised partner of Dafeng International in China. The first tour was organised from 29 August to 2 September 2011 (Yanbian News, 2011).

On 26 April 2011, after a two-week field research trip from the end of March to early April of 2011, the Hunchun local government signed an agreement with the Rason local authorities on cross-border tourism cooperation. It started the first self-driving tourist line to North Korea and allowed Sino-Russia-DPRK round-trip cross-border tourism (Hunchun. gov.cn, 2011). One month later, on 1 June 2011, Hunchun started the first tourist group of Sino-DPRK self-driving. Both Hunchun and Rason local governments have achieved an agreement on the length, range, security checks and guarantees, cross-border tourist licences, and normalisation of this tourism project (Hunchun.gov.cn, 2011; CNTA/China's National Tourist Administration, 2011).

On 12 July 2012, Yanji Tianyu International Tourist Company signed an agreement for direct tourist flights from Yanji to Pyongyang with North Korea's airline. There are two tourist flights to Pyongyang every Thursday and Sunday (China News, 2012a). The passenger transport line between Yanji and Rajin has been opened since 17 August 2012. From then up to 6 November 2012, the traffic line was in an experimental operation period. After 7 November 2012, with the completion of the road from Yuanting to Rason, the international bus transport line formally came into existence. The cost of this traffic line, 3 million RMB, is invested by two local companies: Jilin Northeast Passenger Transport Corporation and Jilin Yubieer Transport

Corporation. Both Chinese and North Koreans can take this transport line to enter the two countries with specific cross-border documents (Xinhuanet, 2012a; Mofcom.gov.cn, 2012; Yanbian, 2012). On 4 August 2014, based on the experience of the foundation of the previous transport line in 2012, Yanji opened a direct line for tourists to Rason (one per day) for the two-day trip in Rason (People.cn, 2014). On 2 May 2014, Tumen developed a bicycle trip for tourists to Namyang (Yanbian News, 2014).

On 3 December 2013, the government of Ji-an (town), under Tonghua city, signed an agreement with North Korea Tourist Administration to begin a one-day tourist trip to Mampoo. The first three tourist groups from Ji-an to Mampoo left Ji-an on 25 December and returned by 28 December (China News, 2014). These initiatives aim to provide jobs to attract the large outflow of females to return to Jilin, especially to Yanbian because of market requirements and considerable salary, which will be explained specifically in the sections later.

Agricultural Cooperation

Hunchun-Rason Agriculture Cooperation Projects
The Hunchun-Rason agricultural cooperation project started from April 2011. In 2011, the Hunchun Agricultural Bureau finished the design of the construction plan of mushroom and rice planting demonstration zones in Rason. Then three agricultural cooperative projects between China and North Korea were launched in Rason area. They included greenhouse construction (see Appendix D, point 5), chicken farm construction and stock-raising experience sharing (see Appendix D, point 6), pig farm construction and stock-raising experience sharing. The greenhouse and chicken farm projects successfully passed the test period and continued, while the pig farm failed and was stopped (see Appendix D, point 7) (Hunchun.gov.cn, 2013b; Anonymous Interviewee 1, 12 August 2014).

Yatai Agricultural High-Efficiency Test Zone
The BeiDahuang agricultural branch of Yatai Corporation, a local state-owned company of Changchun, signed an agreement with the Rason People's Committee in August 2012. The aim of BeiDahuang is to build a high-efficiency agricultural demonstration zone with 500 hectares of rice in Rason (People.com.cn, 2012a). In 2014, following a successful test, the size of this zone increased to between 2000 and 3000 mu, the Chinese unit of field measurement, which is as much as 1300 to 2000 hectares (Anonymous Interviewee 1, 12 August 2014).

CHINESE CROSS-BORDER ECONOMIC ACTIVITIES IN NORTH KOREA 89

To sum up, in the specific cross-border economic activities discussed above, on China's side, the central government at the state level, and the actors below the state level at the regional and local level, formed multiple channels between China and North Korea. The central government in Beijing, as well as its departments such as China Custom Hall, mainly provided institutional support, such as signing general agreements with North Korea and approving a domestic regional development plan. The actors below the state, such as local governments and local state-owned companies, mainly implemented the specific cross-border economic activities in North Korea. Thus, the jurisdictions of governance are only limited at three levels: state level, regional level, and local level below the state. The intersecting memberships are also very limited because the approval from the state level to the level below the state happened only during the limited time of the experimental exercises. Furthermore, under the general framework agreement signed between Pyongyang and Beijing, the governments at the city and provincial levels also signed agreements with North Korea. Although agreements signed at the central state level are more general and of larger scale than the ones signed at the regional and local level below the state, they still represent a system-wide architecture.

THE EFFECTIVENESS OF CHINESE ECONOMIC ACTIVITIES IN NORTH KOREA ON RESOLVING AND MITIGATING THE NTS ISSUES IN CHINA'S BORDER AREAS NEAR NORTH KOREA

Labour Shortage and Population Outflow

Labour shortage and population outflow have been mitigated by labour cooperation in the light industry, the successful construction of the Road-Harbour Integration project, and cooperation on tourism.

Labour Cooperation
Labour cooperation in the light industry directly relieved the labour shortage in the textile industry of Northeast China's border areas. According to interviewees from Jilin (Anonymous Interviewees 4 and 6, 15 August 2014), in the past two years, there existed 5000 North Korean labourers in Jilin province who worked as hard as 6000–7000 Chinese workers. Most of the companies who employ North Korean labourers, and who have labour cooperation with North Korean communes, improved their production

load from less than 40 per cent to 90 per cent. Some companies even offered extra prizes for workers (mainly the team leaders) to persuade the North Korea labour team leader to extend working hours. By paying only half the wages paid to Chinese workers, these companies achieved a rapid increase in net profit from 16 per cent to 84 per cent. 'One North Korean labourer could save 1500 RMB at least per month and produce over 30 % productivity with simple training. You could count how much the companies can earn from them,' the interviewee said. Introduced by another local official (Anonymous Interviewee 8, 10 August 2014), due to concerns regarding management conditions, currently cooperation occurs only in the light industry. The Chinese enterprises that hire North Korean labour have to keep their percentage below 20 per cent of the total amount of its workers. The interviewee said, 'The use of North Korea labor has attracted the attention of companies from other parts of China and even of international companies. We are doing research into the current advantages of using North Korean labour in China and applying to ease the restrictions in labour cooperation' (Anonymous Interviewee 8, 10 August 2014). Thus, the labour cooperation between North Korea and cities in Liaoning and Jilin provinces is the first task-specific jurisdiction at the level below the state which aims to resolve local labour shortages. Indeed, currently China also faces the problem of rapid national ageing, although this problem has not shown a clear negative influence on China's economic development yet. Meanwhile, the population problem in the Yanbian area is much more serious than at the national level.

Road-Harbour Integration

The successful construction of Road-Harbour integration has changed the isolated geography of the Yanbian Ethnic Korean Autonomous Prefecture. As noted above, the failure of regional integration of Yanbian, Russia's Far East, and North Korea kept Yanbian in an isolated geographical position and hampered it from attracting its local citizens to remain or from gaining external investments. Thus, the connection between Yanbian and North Korea's harbour resolved the problem of population outflow and ethnic shrinking in two ways: by attracting foreign investments with the massive creation of jobs and by improving the salary level of Chinese workers.

On the one hand, Yanbian has attracted a large number of foreign companies who hold positive views on the prospects for regional economic development, but could not previously open branches in North Korea. Take Hunchun as an example, from 1993 to 2010, almost 150 foreign companies

(80 from South Korea, 20 from Japan, 12 from the US, and a few from other countries such as Russia and Ireland) have invested in Hunchun, but only 25 of them, less than 20 per cent, entered Hunchun before 2005 (Hunchun.gov.cn, 2009). These companies have created 70,000 jobs for local ethnic Koreans. In April 2011, Posco, a South Korean company in the world top 500, started a two-year cooperation programme for the construction of a logistic district in Hunchun. This logistic district can prospectively create over 10,000 jobs (SEAC, 2012). With the rapid increase in the requirement of local workers to develop business with Japan, Korea, and Russia, salaries increased quickly. In 2013, the salary of a normal waiter in Hunchun was around 2000 RMB. Foreign trade agents can earn a basic salary of 4000–5000 RMB, which is commensurate with a white-collar salary in the secondary cities of China.

On the other hand, with the increase of foreign companies in Hunchun and improvement of income for local workers, the outflow of population still continues, but it has decreased significantly. Compared to the huge annual population outflow in the 1990s, and with illegal immigration to South Korea, since 2006 the structure of the outflowing population has changed (Li, 2007). Mid-level technicians, who go overseas to receive short-term professional training, and the businessmen who leave to develop businesses in Southeast China now represent the majority of that outflow. To the former group of ethnic Korean citizens in Yanbian they normally returned Hunchun to take up a higher position, such as that of technician manager in a foreign company. The jobs created in Yanbian will make local workers stay rather than emigrate to South Korea. Even though they earn less than what they would in South Korea, they do not want to afford the high cost of living in South Korea and compete with South Korean workers who have better education and skills. Liu (2012) and Gao (2011) claim that due to the increased attraction of Chinese Korean workers and intellectuals to move overseas, and under the internationalisation of Yanbian, in 2009, there has been a balance between human capital outflow and inflow, while since 2010 the inflow has been slightly more than the outflow (1 per cent). While the internationalisation of Yanbian has stopped the long history of serious human capital outflow, it can be expected that with increasing regional integration there will be a large turnover of human capital flow in Yanbian, and even in the whole of Northeast China. Thus, the cooperation of using North Korea's Harbour in Rason is another task-specific jurisdiction at the level below the state (regional and city level). As with labour cooperation, this aims to reduce local population outflow by providing access from the landlocked Yanbian region to the Sea of Japan, thereby improving the attractiveness of the area to external investment and increasing the number of better-quality jobs.

Tourism Cooperation

Booming tourism has benefited Yanbian by reducing the outflow of females. Since the beginning of border tourism with North Korea, the need for tourist guides, especially female guides, has increased enormously with the growth of tourist cooperation with other domestic tourist enterprises, and the growth in the number of tourists every year. According to a border tourist businesswoman in Hunchun, who also has working experience in Dandong, during 2007, the first year in which North Korea offered its visa-free tourist policy to Chinese citizens, less than 40,000 tourists (25,000 from Dandong and 10,000 from Jilin) went to North Korea (Anonymous Interviewee 3, 12 August 2014). Half of them chose to go to Sinujiu for one day. However, in 2012, 40,000 was only the number of tourists who went to North Korea from Hunchun for one peak month in the summer and autumn. The annual average of tourist numbers to North Korea after 2012 is over 200,000 from Hunchun and 250,000 from Yanbian Prefecture (including Yanji, Hunchun, Tumen, and Ji-an). In other words, the number of tourists from Yanbian to North Korea increased twenty-five times in five years. Thus, the number of ethnic Korean tourist guides increased correspondingly.

Two factors attracted local young females to stay and work as tourist guides: market requirement and considerable salary. Firstly, under the positive background seen above, the gender concern of tourist enterprises was a decisive factor in offering jobs to local females. Meanwhile, most of the tourist guides in North Korea for Chinese tourist groups are female, so that for convenience Chinese tourist companies also employ female tourist guides for tourist trips to North Korea. Currently, there are dozens of tourist enterprises in Yanbian with several thousand positions for professional tour guides, part-time tour guides, and other relevant workers. One official (Anonymous Interviewee 1, 10 August 2014) says, 'Now Yanbian only has developed two large cities in North Korea (Pyongyang and Rason) as tourist targets. These two cities' tourism has created several thousand positions here. Last year there were a few other new SEZs in North Korea with tourist co-operation programmes. I believe that a large number of young local girls will choose to work in the tourism field.'

Secondly, the salary level is another essential factor of consideration. Indeed, tourist enterprises could hire female tourist guides by offering a salary lower than that for male tourist guides, but this does not mean a low income for female guides. This is because, apart from the mid-level basic salary they receive, they gain considerable bonuses from the large consumption by Chinese tourists of adequate non-polluted natural products, especially medical materials in North Korea. Male tourist guides mainly take responsibility for tourist groups to Far East Russia because of potential risks. A professional tourist guide could have a very comfortable life in Yanbian. Although local daily costs are not low, the price of flats is around 5000 RMB, which is relatively low compared to the national average (Anonymous Interviewee 3, 11 August 2014). Therefore, in Yanbian Prefecture, work as a tourist guide, and in other positions related to the industry, is considered a respectable job for local young females. This has had a clear impact on the decreased female outflow from Yanbian as local females are increasingly attracted to stay in their hometown rather than to emigrate. This can be examined from the annual growth rate of ethnic Korean population in Yanbian. Before 2011, ethnic Koreans in Yanbian had a decade of negative annual growth rate (−1 per cent per year), whereas in 2011, for the first time this index turned into a positive growth rate at 1 per cent. The gender comparison of Yanbian also dropped from 104.5 to 102 (Li, 2014: 30). Thus, the numerous cooperative projects on tourism between Chinese and North Korean cities on the Sino-DPRK border are the third and final task-specific jurisdiction at the regional and local level below the state. The aim had been to stop the local population outflow, especially that of young females of fertility age, by offering attractive working opportunities with competitive salaries, and change the local negative annual growth rate to a positive one.

North Escapees

According to Reuters (2013) the number of North escapees who arrived in South Korea reduced significantly from 2706 in 2011 to 1509 in 2012. UN officials recognised the reduction as the result of strengthening border control under the command of Kim Jong-un (Yonhapnews Agency, 2012b). At the same, Kim Jong-un also softened its punishment to the captured escapees in order to gain the support from the people (Yonhapnews Agency, 2012a).

However, since the 2000s, North Korea has had a strict policy of border control. For more than a decade, Chinese villagers in the Jingxin village on the Sino-DPRK border became used to hearing the noises of shooting and finding the floating corpses of North Korean escapees in the Tumen River. They did recognise the reduction of escapees but denied the possibilities of strengthened control because the deaths in the river in 2014 were relatively less than in the past (Anonymous Interviewee 3, 11 August 2014; Yanji). Thus, the explanation for strengthening border control is not persuasive.

During the interviews and discussions with local officials and scholars, the operation of Sino-DPRK mutual management of Rason SEZ, especially the use of China's own experience, was considered as the most important reason for the strengthening of border controls. One scholar (Anonymous Interviewee 2, 14 August 2014), in Changchun, argues, 'Why did Hunchun try to develop itself as the second Shenzhen? What experience of Shenzhen has been learnt by Hunchun? Hunchun should develop itself as a second Hong Kong because now China is much more developed than North Korea and Rason is learning Shenzhen under Chinese management.'

This section shows how China's previous experience of avoiding escapees has been used in Rason with adjustment to North Korean local conditions. It outlines the reproduction of Shenzhen's experience in Rason first and then discusses extra targeted activities, with North Korean characteristics, to local conditions. In contrast to the sections above about resolving the problem of labour shortage and population outflow through domestic means at the local and regional level, this section shows the connection between local problems of North Korean illegal immigrants in Jilin and the effects of Chinese cross-border economic activities in North Korea on preventing these illegal immigrants escaping from North Korea.

Applying Shenzhen's Experience to Rason

China has a longer history of refugee output than North Korea. From the mid-1950s to the end of the 1970s (with the continuation of a small number of escapees following the return of Hong Kong to the PRC in 1997), almost 1 million illegal immigrants walked or swam across the border between Shenzhen and Hong Kong. This incident is called the Big Flee to Hong Kong and is recognised as the largest group escapee incident of the Cold War era due to the numbers involved and the length of time over which this occurred. The reasons for the creation of these escapees from China are

CHINESE CROSS-BORDER ECONOMIC ACTIVITIES IN NORTH KOREA   95

almost the same as the historical motivations of the North escapees: famine, political torture, and the expectation of better living standards in the neighbouring areas. However, with the implementation of two policies and activities in Shenzhen, the historical escapee wave was almost stopped.

The first policy was called 'second border'. This policy did not aim to strengthen the border control between Shenzhen and Hong Kong; rather, its purpose was to build an additional border between Shenzhen and the other parts of China with extremely strict entry inspection. In June 1982, the State Council No. 92 document approved the set-up of the management line (the second line) of Shenzhen SEZ. The border inspections, which maintained the management standard of the border supervision between Shenzhen and Hong Kong, began during the first half of the new border construction. Four years later, with ten supervision stations, the construction of this 84.6 kilometre 'iron net' between Shenzhen and other parts of mainland China was completed and became fully operational. Before 2003, visitors to Shenzhen could not get across this management line without a special border pass which had to be issued by both the Shenzhen SEZ government and their original local government. Thus, the second line of Shenzhen played the role of filtering out suspicious persons. From 1986 to 2003, the supervision stations on this second border stopped 6 million people entering Shenzhen illegally.

One interviewee says that when the Rason SEZ was first founded in 1984, there was a similar plan of special pass inspections; however, North Korea had no idea about how to develop an SEZ. As a result Rason was left for almost twenty years without any strong border inspection in practice (Anonymous Interviewees 6 and 9, 13 September 2012. Dalian). Rason is geographically very similar to Shenzhen, as can be seen in Table 4.1:

Table 4.1   Comparison of geographical condition of Shenzhen and Rason

	Shenzhen	*Rason*
Escapees' target	Hong Kong	Hunchun
Ethnic relationship	Yes (Cantonese)	Yes (ethnic Korean)
Geographic blockade	River and sea	River and sea
Only origin of escapee	Yes	No (but very important)
Size	395 square kilometres	470 square kilometres

Source: Jilin Province Map, 2012; Anonymous Interviewee 5, 15 August 2014. Changchun; Anonymous Interviewee 6, 13 September 2012. Dalian

96   B. GAO

After the foundation of a mutual agreement committee, Chinese officials started to implement a similar policy in Rason as had been done in Shenzhen. However, in Rason they met difficulties, especially the limitations of the mutual management scale. The mutual management area does not cover the whole of Rason city but only 470 of the 830 square kilometres. The 'iron net' only separated the mutual management zone from the rest of North Korea. As an important exit route for North escapees, the rest of Rason remained connected to the rest of North Korea. When one official was asked about the number of escapees who were blocked by the 'second border', he said, 'It reaches up to a thousand. The second border is still too short, otherwise the reduction of North escapees will be more than the current amount' (Anonymous Interviewee 3, 11 August 2014).

To the escapees from places outside Shenzhen, the local authority of Shenzhen constructed the second border. Meanwhile, in order to increase the confidence of local people by improving local living conditions, a policy of trade relaxation was implemented in the villages of Shenzhen in early 1980s. Except for special forbidden products, such as poppies, in certain markets villagers were allowed to sell their own agricultural and fishery products to Hong Kong citizens in order to earn extra income to improve living standards. This policy is now copied in Rason. According to one scholar (Anonymous Interviewee 7, 23 November 2014), who visited Rason in August of 2014, a similar special market was also established in the mutual management zone of Rason in order to provide opportunities for local citizens to gain through trade with Chinese tourists. Most importantly, in Rason, RMB and the DPRK won are both used freely. Thus, local citizens always ask Chinese tourists to pay in RMB because, to these people whose annual income is as low as 300 to 400 RMB, every RMB is extremely valuable.

Effects of Physical Infrastructure Cooperative Construction

Although Chinese officials could not apply the experience of Shenzhen to the whole of Rason due to the limited area of mutual management, Chinese experience was still applied in another cooperative project in order to strengthen the border control directly. The reconstructed road and railway from Rajin to Yuanting port requires a special pass to enter. These new traffic systems are closely inspected by camera facilities, a new experience popularised from China. Currently there are tens of thousands of cameras set up in each large or middle city of China (People.com.cn, 2012b). Besides being used as tools for recording traffic violations, the cameras are also very useful for tracking criminals. The camera inspection system is connected to both China and North Korea. This activity aims to push the two countries towards the promotion of good border control and, at the same time, to negate the responsibility of allowing escapees to get across the border. In the past, both China and North Korea believed that the other side should take the major responsibility of allowing escapees to get across the border; North Korea criticised Chinese shortage of border inspection troops, while Chinese newspapers pointed out bribery issues in the exchange of money and freedom between North Korean soldiers and escapees.

Effects of Other Activities

Apart from the administrative methods discussed above, Chinese economic activities in Rason were also effective in reducing the existence of economic-oriented illegal immigrants in North Korea, especially in Rason. As seen in the administrative methods used, these activities were also non-military ways of reducing North Korean illegal immigrants.

Agricultural Programme Ensures the Supply of Food

As the largest agricultural country in the world before economic reform, apart from the serious famine from 1958 to 1960, Beijing did not need to worry about a shortage of food in the country. Like other places in China, Shenzhen also has its agricultural foundation; therefore, the construction of the Shenzhen SEZ did not require the attraction of external agricultural projects.

In contrast, after the end of the Korean War, because the northern part of the Korean Peninsula is mountainous and not suitable for agriculture, North Korea never achieved self-sufficiency in agricultural products, especially the major grains. During the Cold War it imported grains from the Soviet Union and China. After the end of the Cold War, it mainly received aid in the form of grains and fertilisers from China (Hwang, 2008). In Rason, the shortage of food is also a problem. In addition to food distributed from Pyongyang, the agricultural cooperation programme offered a basic grain supply for Rason. If the relaxation of trade is an extra gift to the citizens in Rason, the consolidation of grain supply and the increase of plant varieties are the foundation for stabilising the Rason local condition. As noted above, a considerable number of Rason citizens are from families related to politicians and the army. Pyongyang cannot ignore the requirement of these people because their families are more important to the

98   B. GAO

regime than ordinary civilians. Meanwhile, it cannot be denied that some-times the natural desire for food under extreme hunger can still motivate people to give up their original loyalty, especially the new generation of interest groups sent to the Sino-North Korea border who do not have memories of the most difficult period in North Korea's history. Thus, ensuring the food supply to Rason SEZ is significant in order to consoli-date the loyalty of local North Korean elites to their regime and avoid their escape because of hunger.

Tourism Cooperation

North Korea has a different political background from China's back-ground. The most important one is the totalitarian domination of the country. It blocks external news in order to prevent the overthrow of the regime. Under external sanctions, North Korea is short of foreign cur-rency, resulting in a compromise by North Korea to allow the participa-tion of China in the construction and mutual management of an SEZ in its border area. This is different from China's subjectivity and strong will of establishing an SEZ in Shenzhen. Therefore, the blockade function of North Korea SEZ is clear, but despite its original role of screening and stemming external information, the effects of preventing North escapees during the construction of its tourist zone, and its further transformation to SEZ, should not be ignored.

Tourism cooperation can be considered as a warm-up preparation period for Pyongyang to relocate a large number of young elites to the border cities and to train another part of youth to be skilled labourers in the SEZ. These people are recognised in North Korea to have the highest loyalty to the regime. Meanwhile, North Korea has also relocated a few original citizens in the region to the other side. From the song '*The Story of Spring*' (*ChunTian de Gushi* in Chinese), the setting of Shenzhen SEZ is described as 'An old man drew a circle on the coast of South China Sea'; the 'tourist zone—special economic zone' mode in the border area of North Korea can be seen as a mode of 'small circle, big circle & point, line and area'. When North Korea agreed to open one border town as a tourist zone, it drew a circle on its border and cleaned the fields inside the circle. Chinese is moving forward and close to them so Pyongyang does not want its citizens to escape again. Then with the foundation of an SEZ based in, or near, the tourist zone, another circle will be cleaned. With the increase and enlargement of cleaned circles in the border areas, the original lines formed by a few points become cleaned areas in the Sino-DPRK border and form a comprehensive blockade to the escapees from inland of North Korea. Chinese interviewees said, 'North Korea set up 14 SEZs in its border area at the end of 2013. Kim Jong-un hurried to popularise the successful experience of Rason in attracting funds and stopping escapees. He did not learn from the failure of his father and grandfather in developing Rason. It is another Great Leap Forward. Without Chinese involvement in infrastructure construction, it can be expected that these SEZs will be abandoned again. They will still become paper windows made in North Korea but not steel fences made in China' (Anonymous Interviewee 1, 14 August 2014; Anonymous Interviewee 5, 19 August 2014).

To sum up, no matter copying China's general experience of Shenzhen to Rason, or developing the agricultural industry and tourism with North Korean specific characteristics, Chinese economic activities in North Korea use economic, and administrative, ways of resolving the problem of North Korean illegal immigrants in their homeland rather than in China. These ways are different from the North Korean traditional military way of resolving the problem by asking soldiers to kill the illegal cross-border citizens. They blur the difference between the domestic requirement of reducing local unemployment and social instability caused by North Korean illegal immigrants, and external issues of developing tourism and the agricultural industry in North Korean border areas through resolving the problem of North Korean illegal immigrants.

REASONS FOR BEIJING'S DISTANT GOVERNANCE IN SINO-DPRK CROSS-BORDER COOPERATION

From the specific information of Chinese economic activities in the second paragraph, it can be found that Beijing was almost absent from these cooperation and mutual management activities. This section explains the reason these NTS issues are important to local authorities, such as ethnic shrinking, but are not influential at the national level. In other words, reducing NTS problems, such as North escapees, labour shortages, and population outflow, is the task-specific jurisdiction at the regional (Jilin and Liaoning provinces) and local levels (Yanji Korean Autonomous Prefecture), rather than a general jurisdiction directly dealt with by Beijing.

Illegal Immigration

The central government in Beijing rarely becomes involved in the problem of North escapees for two major reasons. The first is that human rights are no longer an effective tool of external criticism of Beijing. China's human rights have always been criticised by the West, particularly after the incident in Tian'anmen in 1989. The assistance of Beijing to Pyongyang on returning illegal escapees has been criticised as a violation of human rights. The human rights issue was a very strong tool used by other countries to increase diplomatic pressure on China in the 1990s and early 2000s, especially the negotiation of China's WTO membership (Nathan, 1994; Dittmer, 2001). However, with the increase in China's economic strength, Beijing is more confident to face these criticisms and even use its soft power, particularly its economic power, to ease external criticism on human rights issues. The economic interests from economic interdependence between China and other countries, especially the requirements of the huge market in China, and huge funds from China, have weakened the voice of criticism and made a few countries (see Appendix D, point 8) stop talking about human rights issues with China as an extra requirement of joining WTO, and China even began to build its own reputation for human rights in the world (see Appendix D, point 9) (Potter, 2007; McFarland and Mathews, 2005).

The second reason is that the direct political negative impact of North escapees on Beijing is not very big. This is a result of the unwillingness of Seoul to criticise Beijing on human rights issues due to the deepened economic interdependence between China and South Korea. Meanwhile, two further factors help reduce the criticism about North escapees to China. On the one hand, in contrast to other human right issues, such as the Tibet problem under the frequent activities of the Dalai Lama, and apart from the incident of four North escapees rushing into Japanese Consulate in Shenyang on 8 May 2002 (see Appendix D, point 10), during this time information about China's treatment of North escapees was rarely released. Most information is about China's capture and return of these people to North Korea. Although China's official choice to return these people to North Korea is always questioned because it always leads to the torture of these people in North Korea, the number of returned North escapees, usually several hundred, actually is only a very small proportion of the thousands of North escapees. As reported by South Weekly (2013), there have been tens of thousands of North escapees travelling across the whole of China, from Northeast China to Southeast China, to enter Southeast

Asia. In other words, Beijing actually has a very relaxed policy towards North escapees. On the other hand, the condition of North escapees who have successfully entered South Korea is good in general, especially who were in high positions in North Korea, received awards, priority treatment, and protection in South Korea. However, most escapees who were normal citizens in North Korea still struggle in South Korea because of isolation from society, social discrimination, and weak official support from the South Korean government (Nan Kang, 2009: 50; Anonymous Interviewee 7, 23 November 2014). Recently, with improved economic conditions in North Korea and a softened policy towards North escapees, a few of those escapees have actually chosen to return to North Korea. They are seen as heroes in North Korea by describing the difficult days in South Korea and criticising the corrupted life of capitalism. They also encouraged other North escapees in South Korea to return home. Thus, to Beijing, the North escapee problem itself is actually a very small diplomatic issue. In other words, it only needs to be resolved from a task-specific jurisdiction at the regional and local levels rather than from a top-down general jurisdiction at the national level. The stand-by role of Beijing to the decision-making and policy implementation of local government also presents a non-intervening independent jurisdiction condition.

Cultural Decline and Labour Shortage

The cultural decline of Chinese Koreans is actually not a problem to the central government at all for two reasons, the official policy of nation building and the special status of ethnic Koreans in China and the world. Firstly, the central government does not care about cultural decline under its policy of nation building; Beijing always aims to popularise recognition of China as a civil nation beyond the identity recognition of ethnic minority groups through modernisation. Beijing actually pushes ethnic assimilation by offering priorities on policies concerning ethnic minority groups to motivate them to move from rural areas to urban areas and speed up their integration into the developed Han-dominant society (Kipnis, 2012). Under the effects of urbanisation and modernisation, apart from special ethnic and religious characteristics very different from the Han culture, most normal ethnic characteristics disappeared, or at least rarely appeared, in daily life except in special situations, such as the traditional holidays of those ethnic groups. In terms of cultural protection, the central government pays more attention to the historical research of ethnic minority groups.

102   B. GAO

Secondly, the cultural decline is also caused by the special status of ethnic Koreans in China and the world. Compared to other ethnic minority groups, such as the Uygur and the Tibetans, ethnic Koreans in China are not a large group, though they do have clear ethnic differences from Han in terms of race and religion; and their special ethnic characteristics are language and costume. However, in contrast to Uygurs and Tibetans, who only exist within China, or whose majority ethnic population lives in China, ethnic Koreans around the world have their own countries and the same language and culture as Chinese Koreans. This means that the ethnic assimilation of Chinese Koreans will not influence the existence of ethnic Koreans at the international level. Deepening globalisation also promotes communication and interaction between Chinese Koreans and Koreans in the two Koreas to sustain the survival of cultural characteristics (Cui, 2004; Xu, 2013). Meanwhile, according to some South Korean scholars, the existence of Chinese Koreans is a potential risk to China. In the future, once the two countries in the Korean Peninsula achieve unification, the ethnic Koreans in China could become the new Kosovars in the Far East (Anonymous Interviewee 7, 23 November 2014). Thus, the central government in Beijing does not need to worry about the ethnic shrinking of the Chinese Korean autonomous region. In contrast to the issue of North escapees, which still attracts diplomatic attention to some extent, the ethnic shrinking of ethnic Koreans in Yanbian is a problem which exists, and impacts, only at the regional and local levels, but not at the central government level. Resolving this problem also requires only a task-specific jurisdiction at the regional and local levels.

CONCLUSION

In conclusion, there are two major types of NTS problems in the low-politics field in the Jilin and Liaoning provinces in Northeast China: socioeconomic security and border security. The former problems include the ethnic shrinking of ethnic Koreans in Yanbian Korean Autonomous Prefecture and labour shortage. The latter problem concerns illegal immigration from North Korea (North escapee). Firstly, the problem of ethnic shrinking is caused by the reduced attraction to local labour and qualified personnel of underdeveloped local economic conditions in the Yanbian Korea Autonomous District, as well as in the whole of Northeast China. This contrasts strongly with the developed areas of China in big cities and the eastern coastal area. It made a potential crisis of the existence of the

Yanbian Korea Autonomous District due to the net outflow of population, which also resulted in a rapid ageing population. Secondly, North escapees also created big social problems in Northeast China, particularly those who lost contact with their illegal immigration agents in China. They always cause big problems: in the past, they tried to enter every type of foreign diplomatic institution in China for asylum which always led to diplomatic clashes; and recently, because the illegal immigration agents in China chose a new route from Northeast to Southwest China, the escapees, who cannot deal with this type of complicated issue, created increased crimes in the border area.

The local governments and enterprises in Northeast China have implemented many economic activities, such as economic investments in social infrastructure, economic cooperation in the field of agriculture, the establishment of SEZs, and the implementation of tourist programmes in North Korea. These activities could help to resolve the socio-economic and border security problems in Northeast China to some extent. In contrast to the previous military ways of the North Korean side, these non-military means are more effective. To the problem of labour shortage and ethnic shrinking, a few local private enterprises have developed OEM relationships with North Korea business communities; the economic investments in the social infrastructure of Rason port, as well as the fifty-year lease of Rason port, is a big step in the promotion of regional integration. It has attracted a few foreign companies to enter Yanbian and seize local markets to prepare for future developments. These companies have created many attractive job opportunities and slowed down the tendency of population outflow. To the problem of North escapees in Northeast China, the economic activities cannot fundamentally resolve the problem because the root cause, that is, the underdeveloped conditions in North Korea, cannot be resolved easily in the short term. These economic activities can only provide some help. The tourist programmes in North Korea are also helpful to reduce the illegal escapees by pushing population relocation in the border area; members of interest groups come to replace the original citizens. The agricultural cooperative programme can be helpful to consolidate the food consumption of the local population in the North Korean border area in order to lower the possibilities of illegal immigration due to the shortage of material. The setting up of cameras in the border areas, and especially the construction of roads, is also useful to monitor the activities of illegal immigration. Thus, the origins and resolutions of these problems, which directly and indirectly exist in North Korea, blur the differences between domestic and external issues. The economic activities are also more effective than the traditional military ways of border policing in North Korea.

These activities are rarely done by the central government because the negative influences of security threats are mostly limited in the region of Northeast China rather than on the national level. The human rights issues can no longer pressure Beijing. Meanwhile South Korea cannot treat North escapees well. Under this condition, the previous problem of North escapees is not a problem anymore. Now the existence of escapees provides opportunities for Beijing to show its kindness to Seoul because some captured escapees are returned to South Korea. The special status of ethnic Koreans in China, and in the world, also determines that the central government pays little attention to any resolution to the outflow of population and the subsequent reduction in the local population of Yanbian. Thus, dynamic provincial and city governments, as well as non-state actors, have diversified the multiple channels of interaction between China and North Korea on the China side.

References

Primary Resource

Interviews

Anonymous Interviewee 1: Interview with local official, 10 Aug 2014. Hunchun, Jilin province.

Anonymous Interviewee 2: Interview with local businessmen, 12 Aug 2014. Hunchun, Jilin province.

Anonymous Interviewee 3: Interview with local businessmen, 11 Aug 2014. Yanji, Jilin province.

Anonymous Interviewee 4: Interview with local official, 15 Aug 2014. Changchun, Jilin province.

Anonymous Interviewee 5: Interview with local scholar, 15 Aug 2014. Changchun, Jilin province.

Anonymous Interviewee 6: Interview with local scholar, 13 Sep 2012. Dalian, Liaoning province.

Anonymous Interviewee 7: Interview with local scholar, 23 Nov 2014, Seoul, South Korea.

Anonymous Interviewee 8: Interview with local official, 10 Aug 2014. Tumen, Jilin province.

Anonymous Interviewee 9: Interview with local scholar, 13 Sep 2012. Dalian, Liaoning province.

CHINESE CROSS-BORDER ECONOMIC ACTIVITIES IN NORTH KOREA   105

GOVERNMENT AND CORPORATION WEBSITE

China National Tourism Administration (2011) 'Sino-DPRK self-driving tourism formally operates'. [online] http://www.cnta.gov.cn/html/2011-6/2011-6-14-15-26-97981.html. Retrieved on Nov 12th 2013.

China National Tourism Administration (2014) 'The Tourist train from Tumen to Qibao Mountain ran again'. [online] http://www.cnta.gov.cn/html/2014-4/2014-4-21-10-23-22271.html. Retrieved on Aug 30th 2014.

China News (2007) 'Overseas Chinese Businessmen signed agreement and invested 3 billion RMB to start the "Road Harbor District" Project'. [online] http://www.chinanews.com/cj/cyzh/news/2007/09-05/1018625.shtml. Retrieved on Nov 12th 2013.

China News (2012a) 'Jilin's Yanji started to launch the direct tourist flight to Pyongyang'. [online] http://www.chinanews.com/df/2012/07-06/4014989.shtml. Retrieved on Nov 12th 2013.

China News (2012b) 'Several North Korea tourist companies held exhibition for customers in Dandong'. [online] http://finance.chinanews.com/cj/2012/10-13/4245453.shtml. Retrieved on Nov 12th 2013.

China News (2014) 'Ji-an of Jilin province successfully sent tourist groups to North Korea'. [online] http://www.jl.chinanews.com/news1-90379.html. Retrieved on Aug 30th 2014.

Hunchun.gov.cn (2009) 'Hunchun and Rason increase practical cooperation'. [online] http://www.hunchun.gov.cn/user/index.xhtml?menu_id=182&mode=view_content&page=1&news_content_id=989. Retrieved on Nov 12th 2013.

Hunchun.gov.cn (2010a) 'Lee Longxi and Jin Xiuyue signed cooperation framework agreement'. [online] http://www.hunchun.gov.cn/user/index.xhtml?menu_id=442&num=280&gallery_mode=content. Retrieved on Nov 12th 2013.

Hunchun.gov.cn (2010b) 'The first batch of goods in the experiment point of domestic-trade with cross-border transport in Jilin province applies to get across the border'. [online] http://www.hunchun.gov.cn/user/index.xhtml?menu_id=442&num=307&gallery_mode=content. Retrieved on Nov 12th 2013.

Hunchun.gov.cn (2011) 'Hunchun actively plans the Sino-DPRK self-driving tourism'. [online] http://www.hunchun.gov.cn/user/index.xhtml?menu_id=532&mode=view_content&page=1&news_content_id=3824. Retrieved on Nov 12th 2013.

Hunchun.gov.cn (2012a) 'The first patch of Chinese going abroad processing gets permitted'. [online] http://www.hunchun.gov.cn/user/index.xhtml?menu_id=182&mode=view_content&news_content_id=8805. Retrieved on Nov 12th 2013.

Hunchun.gov.cn (2012b) 'Rason Mutual Committee formally operates'. [online] http://www.hunchun.gov.cn/user/index.xhtml?menu_id=179&num=514&gallery_mode=content. Retrieved on Nov 12th 2013.

Hunchun.gov.cn (2013a) 'Hunchun is constructing the cross-border tourism base which faces to northeast Asia'. [online] http://www.hunchun.gov.cn/user/index.xhtml?menu_id=182&mode=view_content&page=1&news_content_id=9125. Retrieved on Nov 12th 2013.

Hunchun.gov.cn (2013b) 'Hunchun developed Agricultural Cooperation Project to North Korea'. [online] http://www.hunchun.gov.cn/user/index.xhtml?menu_id=272&mode=view_content&page=1&news_content_id=9045. Retrieved on Nov 12th 2013.

Jilin.gov.cn (2008) 'The Proposal of pushing the operation of "Road Harbor District" Project'. [online] http://www.jl.gov.cn/zt/lhzt2008/wyta/200801/t20080102_350477.html. Retrieved on Nov 12th 2013.

Mofcom.gov.cn (2006a) 'The Pre-project of Sino-DPRK Road-Harbor Integration has finished'. [online] http://www.mofcom.gov.cn/aarticle/difang/jilin/200603/20060301712354.html. Retrieved on Nov 12th 2013.

Mofcom.gov.cn (2006b) 'China and North Korea provided a green channel for the "Road Harbor District" Project'. [online] http://www.mofcom.gov.cn/aarticle/difang/jilin/200603/20060301773313.html. Retrieved on Nov 12th 2013.

Mofcom.gov.cn (2012) 'Hunchun-Rason International Passenger Traffic line formally operates'. [online] http://www.mofcom.gov.cn/aarticle/difang/jilin/201211/20121108426853.html. Retrieved on Nov 12th 2013.

People.com.cn (2012a) 'BeiDahuang of Yatai Branch will enter Rason'. [online] http://finance.people.com.cn/stock/n/2012/0910/c67815-18962437.htmlReference. Retrieved on Nov 12th 2013.

People.com.cn (2012b) 'Ningbo has made a video-invigilation web for security control'. [online] http://nb.people.com.cn/n/2012/1021/c200892-17609817.html. Retrieved on Nov 12th 2013.

Shanghai.gov.cn (2011) 'Shanghai Custom Hall tries it best to ensure the successful experiment point of domestic-trade with cross-border transport in Jilin province'. [online] http://www.shanghai.gov.cn/shanghai/node2314/node2315/node18454/u21ai479346.html. Retrieved on Nov 12th 2013.

Small-Mid Enterprises of Jilin (SMEJL).gov.cn (2007) 'Hunchun Donglin Economic and Trade Company and American Corporation signed the agreement of operating Sino-DPRK Road-Harbor Integration Project'. [online] http://www.smejl.gov.cn/assembly/action/browsePage.do?channelID=1127270051672&contentID=1188952587098. Retrieved on Nov 12th 2013.

State Ethnic Affairs Committee (SEAC) (2012) 'Hunchun-POSOC Linguistic Region constructs well'. [online] http://www.seac.gov.cn/art/2012/9/11/art_36_165674.html. Retrieved on Nov 12th 2013.

UNHRC (2013) 'China Main Page'. [online] http://www.ohchr.org/EN/countries/AsiaRegion/Pages/CNIndex.aspx. Retrieved on Nov 12th 2013.

CHINESE CROSS-BORDER ECONOMIC ACTIVITIES IN NORTH KOREA 107

Xinhuanet (2010) 'Yanbian and Rason signed bilateral cooperation framework agreement'. [online] http://www.jl.xinhuanet.com/newscenter/2010-09/07/content_20836105.htm. Retrieved on Nov 12th 2013.

Xinhuanet (2012a) 'Yanji firstly launched the international tourist direct coach to North Korea Rason'. [online] http://www.jl.xinhuanet.com/2012jlpd/2014-08/04/c_1111914954.htm. Retrieved on Nov 12th 2013.

Xinhuanet (2012b) 'The re-construction of road from Rajin Harbor to Yuantingli was finished'. [online] http://news.xinhuanet.com/world/2012-09/04/c_112956185.htm. Retrieved on Nov 12th 2013.

Yanbian News (2008) 'The agreement of Walking Tourism from Tumen to Namyang was signed'. [online] http://www.ybnews.cn/news/ybnews-bdnews/200805/49833.html. Retrieved on Nov 12th 2013.

Yanbian News (2011) 'Yanbian opened a new tourist line. Let's get across the sea and watch Kumgang Mountain'. [online] http://www.ybnews.cn/news/local/201109/126602_2.html. Retrieved on Nov 12th 2013.

Yanbian News (2014) 'Tourists can go to North Korea by bicycle from May 2nd'. [online] http://www.ybnews.cn/news/local/201404/212220.html. Retrieved on Aug 30th 2014.

Yanbian Dong-Bei-ya (2012) 'Yanji-Rason transport line opens'. [online] http://www.ybdongbeiya.com/2NewsyInfo.asp?id=380&intID=2&ClassID=10. Retrieved on Nov 12th 2013.

Secondary Resource

Books and Articles

Chestnut, S. Illicit Activity and Proliferation: North Korean Smuggling Networks. *International Security*, Vol. 32, No. 1 (Summer, 2007), pp. 80–111.

Clarke, R. Narcotics Trafficking in China: Size, Scale, Dynamic and Future Consequences. *Pacific Affairs*, Vol. 81, No. 1 (Spring, 2008), pp. 73–93.

Cui Qingzhi (2004) China's national policy, the history, current condition and future of Chinese Korean under the background of Globalization. *Collective Papers of Ph.D student in Chinese national knowledge infrastructure.*

Dittmer, L. Chinese Human Rights and American Foreign Policy: A Realist Approach. *The Review of Politics*, Vol. 63, No. 3 (Summer, 2001), pp. 421–459.

Gao Jijun (2011) *Research on Agricultural Labor Transfer of Yanbian Autonomous Prefecture of Jilin province.* Collective Papers of Ph.D student in Chinese national knowledge infrastructure.

Guan Yanjiang (2010) *A research on the labor export of Yanbian area to South Korea.* Collective Papers of Ph.D student in Chinese national knowledge infrastructure.

Hwang Jang-Yap (2008) *Hwang Jang-Yap Memoirs.* Shanghai: Hua Xia Publisher.

Jin Qiangyi. The Crisis of Chinese Korean Social Shirking and its choice of developing pathway. *Journal of Yanbian University (Social Science)* (延边大学学报社科版 *Yanbian Daxue Xuebao)*, Vol. 44, No. 6 (December 2011), pp. 25–30.

Kipnis, B. Constructing Commonality: Standardization and Modernization in Chinese Nation-Building. *The Journal of Asian Studies*, Vol. 71, No. 3 (August 2012), pp. 731–755.

Li Meishan (2007) *Northeast Asia regional cooperation and Chinese ethnic Korean social economic development.* Collective Papers of Master student in Chinese national knowledge infrastructure.

Liu Xinrong. Analysis of the human capital loss in Northeast China. *New Long March* (新长征 *Xin Chang Zheng)*, No. 2 (2012), pp. 46–47.

McFarland, S. and Mathews, M. Who Cares about Human Rights? *Political Psychology*, Vol. 26, No. 3 (June 2005), pp. 365–385.

Meng Lijun. Research of the factors which influences border security of Jilin and strategy. *The Border Economy and Culture* (边疆经济和文化 *Bian jiang jing ji yu wen hua)*, No. 7 (2013), pp. 39–42.

Nan Kang. South Korea has a serious problem of North Escapee. *Prosecutorial View*, No. 20 (2009), p. 50.

Nathan, A. Human Rights in Chinese Foreign Policy. *The China Quarterly*, No. 139 (September 1994), pp. 622–643.

Piao Jianyi and Li Zhifei. The Internationalization and Influences of North Escapees. *Modern International Relations* (现代国际关系 *Xiandai Guoji Guanxi)*, No. 7 (2011), pp. 3–9.

Potter, Pitman B. China and the International Legal System: Challenges of Participation. *The China Quarterly, No. 191, China's Legal System: New Developments, New Challenges* (September 2007), pp. 699–715.

Xu Qingxing (2013) *The influence of South Korea Culture to Chinese Korean.* Collective Papers of Master student in Chinese national knowledge infrastructure.

Xuan Songhe. The origins and strategy of cross-border crimes in Yanbian. *Journal of Yanbian Party School* (延边党校学报 *Yanbian Dangxiao xuebao)*, Vol. 24, No. 6 (2009), pp. 66–68.

Zhao Wei (2009) *The Research about the status-quo of drug crime in China's border and strategy.* Collective Papers of Master student in Chinese national knowledge infrastructure.

Other Websites

EEO (E-Economy Observation). 'Using Harbor of North Korea, Jilin found the channel to the Sea of Japan'. [online] http://www.eeo.com.cn/eeo/jjgcb/2006/07/15/40480.shtml. Retrieved on Nov 12th 2013.

Globaltimes (2012) 'North Korea sent 40 thousand labor into China'. [online] http://world.huanqiu.com/roll/2012-07/2876201.html. Retrieved on Nov 12th 2013.

Li ed. (2014) *Yanbian Yearbook 2014*. Yanji: Yanbian People Publishing.

People.cn (2014) '延吉至朝鲜罗先国际旅游直通车将于8月2日开通' 'The International Tourist Directline from Yanji to Rason in North Korea will open at August 2'. http://leaders.people.com.cn/n/2014/0730/c121615-25369172.html. Retrieved on Jan 31st 2019.

Reuters (2013) 'The number of North escapees has a significant reduction'. [online] http://cn.reuters.com/article/CNTopGenNews/idCNC-NE99T09I20131030. Retrieved on Nov 12th 2013.

SINA (2007) 'Chinese tourists can go to North Korea with visa free'. [online] http://news.sina.com.cn/c/2007-04-03/011611551396s.shtml. Retrieved on Nov 12th 2013.

Sohu (2012) 'China and North Korea started the mutual management of Rason, Golden Floor and Granville Island'. [online] http://roll.sohu.com/20120816/n350763675.shtml. Retrieved on Nov 12th 2013.

South Weekly (2013) 'The Visitors from North Korea'. [online] http://www.nbweekly.com/news/special/201312/35397.aspx. Retrieved on Dec 26th 2013.

The Central Government of PRC (2009) '国务院正式批复中国图们江区域合作开发规划纲要' State Council formally approved Chang-Ji-Tu Cooperation and Development Proposal. http://www.gov.cn/jrzg/2009-11/16/content_1465540.htm. Retrieved on Jan 31st 2019.

Yonhapnews Agency (2010) 'Cross-border bridge between Hunchun to Rajin will be used by the end of this month'. [online] http://chinese.yonhapnews.co.kr/allheadlines/2010/05/18/0200000000ACK20100518004300881.HTML. Retrieved on Nov 12th 2013.

Yonhapnews Agency (2012a) 'Kim Jong-un reduces the collective punishment in order to get the support from civilians'. [online] http://chinese.yonhapnews.co.kr/newpgm/9908000000.html?cid=ACK20130212001600881. Retrieved on Nov 12th 2013.

Yonhapnews Agency (2012b) 'The amount of North Escapees reduced rapidly after Kim Jong-un coming into power'. [online] http://chinese.yonhapnews.co.kr/newpgm/9908000000.html?cid=ACK20120701001100881. Retrieved on Nov 12th 2013.

CHAPTER 5

The Regional Impact of Chinese Economic Activity in North Korea

The earlier chapters outlined the specificities and motivations of Chinese economic activities in the mineral resource sector, fisheries, and cross-border issues, such as tourism and physical infrastructure, and examined the leading role of actors below the state in these economic engagements in contrast to a weakened role of the central government in Beijing. This chapter discusses the regional impact of these economic activities on the Korean Peninsula. It first shows a positive impact in terms of how Chinese economic activity reduced domestic barriers within North Korea and advanced the process of economic reform there. Then two kinds of negative impact are discussed. One is the prevention of the resolution of the Sino-ROK Ieodo Island dispute, accompanied by an escalation in China-South Korea struggles for fishery resources in the Yellow Sea. The other is the reduction in the bargaining leverage of aid from the US and South Korea to North Korea in the Six Party Talks, which directly led to both the withdrawal of North Korea from Six Party Talks and further uncertainty over the nuclear weapons of North Korea, a setback for Washington and Seoul as well as a negative impact in the sense that tensions remain in the Korean Peninsula.

© The Author(s) 2019
B. Gao, *China's Economic Engagement in North Korea*,
Palgrave Series in Asia and Pacific Studies,
https://doi.org/10.1007/978-981-13-0887-1_5

The Implications for North Korea Economic Reform and Opening Up

Under its totalitarian regime and planned economy, North Korea is seen as the country most isolated from external conditions in the world. For a long time North Korea also experienced failure of its economic reforms. Since the mid-2000s, with the rapid increase of Chinese economic engagement in North Korea, the country is increasingly opening up. This section aims to show that North Korean economic reform and opening up has benefited from Chinese economic activities. First, it reviews the history of failed economic reform and opening up in North Korea. Then it outlines the domestic barriers to reform. Finally, it discusses the positive impact of Chinese economic activities on the reform process in North Korea.

The History of Failed North Korean Economic Reform and Opening Up

North Korea has been ruled by the Kim family for more than half century, from the late 1940s at the end of the Second World War. In contrast to its socialist neighbours in East Asia, such as China and Vietnam, its pace of economic reform had been slow. Economic reform has been delayed over various incidents, that is, the sudden death of Kim Il-Sung, Kim Jung-il's focus on nuclear weapons, and the coming to power of young Kim Jong-un.

The Trend of Economic Reform in the Era of Kim Il-Sung

North Korean economic reform was first known to the external world when, in 2002, Kim Jong-il implemented the '7.1 Reform'. However, the earliest trend towards economic reform and opening up began under Kim Il-Sung more than one decade before. North Korea experienced economic difficulties at the end of the Cold War and the collapse of the economic system in the socialist camp. Kim Il-Sung began to consider the possibility of economic reform and opening up to avoid economic recession, and as a result he visited the Eastern European countries which had recently experienced economic reform. North Korea also signed agreements with West Germany and France to found joint companies for developing its oil reserves (Cha, 2013: 77–79). However, Kim Il-Sung died of a heart attack in 1994 before he could implement significant economic reforms.

The Failed Economic Reform of Kim Jong-il

As the second leader of North Korea, contrasted to his father, who was unable to turn the idea of economic reform into reality, Kim Jong-il successfully implemented some economic reforms, although the overall experience was a failure. In 2002, he implemented economic reform policies in several fields under the general name of '7.1 reform'. In the ideological field, Kim Jong-il developed his Juche idea and called for new thinking to abandon the old collective ideological blockade to economic development (Li, 2006: 38–41). However, Kim Jong-il only pushed his new ideas for economic reform for several months without reviewing the old collective ideas. At the end of 2012, he emphasised the significance and continuation of the planned economic system in North Korea in a public talk (Tudor, 2015: 40–43). In the agricultural field, Kim Jong-il copied the Chinese experience of releasing the subjectivity of peasants on agricultural production by encouraging the free trade of agricultural products and allowing the people to use individual idle land and water to raise chicken and fish. However, without corresponding policies, his experiment failed again and he was forced to cancel it because, in the short term, the underground economy, or the black market, quickly grew out of control and threatened state-owned firms (Tudor, 2015: 50–54). The third failure of Kim Jong-il's reform was the establishment and operation of North Korean special economic zones (SEZs). He set up four SEZs in North Korea: Kim-Kong Mountain, Kaesong Industrial Zone, Rason, and Sinuiju. Apart from the well-managed Kaesong Industrial Zone with the support of South Korea, the others were not successful. The Kim-Kong Mountain International Tourist Zone was closed due to the breakdown of cooperation with South Korea (Abt, 2014: 77–79). Due to poor infrastructure, the Sinuiju SEZ remained unattractive to external investors and failed to develop; because of its favourable geographic location near the Sea of Japan and the efforts of Jang Sung-Taek in cooperation with China, in 2011 the Rason SEZ attracted funding and mutual management and joined the Kaesong SEZ to become the only two properly run SEZs.

The only real success of Kim Jong-il's economic reform and opening up was the modernisation of North Korea's information technology (IT) sector. Under his leadership, IT rose in the government's economic agenda and developed rapidly. With the foundation of the North Korea Computer Center, the Computer Scientific Technology University, and the Kim Il-Sung Comprehensive University, North Korea successfully formed its own national scientific research system of IT skills (Bechtol, 2013: 175–177). Under the policy of concentration on the development of software, North

114   B. GAO

Korean IT teams succeeded in developing document processing software, for example, the North Korean Linux Operation System, Red Star, and Go Chess software. The rapid development of the IT sector also benefited a few other fields, such as productivity and resource efficiency in the manufacturing, mining, light industry, and agricultural industries, which improved with the popularisation of a corresponding upgrade in IT skills (Bechtol, 2013: 178). After outlining the general history of North Korea's economic reform under its previous two leaders, the following section considers the more recent specifics of North Korea's opening up under its third and current leader, Kim Jong-un.

Economic Reform Under Kim Jong-un: The Legacy of Jang Sung-Taek
After the death of Kim Jong-il at the end of 2012, Kim Jong-un started his rule of North Korea. In contrast to his conservative father, Kim Jong-un made numerous changes to his public image, such as allowing Mickey Mouse to join North Korea's official evening parties, becoming the first North Korean leader to be accompanied by the first lady and seen in the media, extending the first official invitation to a US basketball team to visit North Korea, and discarding Kim Il-Sung's and Kim Jong-il's signature in the official dressing, which has been a tradition of all the North Korean citizens for decades (French, 2014: 366). However, even though at the beginning of his governance Kim Jong-un noted the importance of economic development in his public speeches, he did not make a great economic contribution because he continued to reinforce the significance of nuclear development at the same time. Although he was responsible for the execution of Jang Sung-Taek, who was his uncle and the most important pro-China official in North Korea, currently Kim Jong-un continues to follow Jang's original opening-up strategy in terms of setting up mutual management economic zones with China, but without any further steps of economic reform.

The Domestic Barriers to North Korea's Opening Up

North Korea's three leaders have made some efforts in pushing the economic opening up in North Korea. However, due to three domestic barriers, North Korea's economic reforms mostly failed. This section discusses these major blocks to reform: concerns about political stability, limited domestic economic conditions, and the lack of public support and leadership for economic reform.

'Dare Not Reform': Concerns for Political Instability

North Korea is a highly centralised country under a traditional socialist Juche ideology and military-first doctrine. The economic reforms of other ex-socialist countries were implemented with the transformation from a planned to a market economy. Pyongyang worried about the attraction of external investment, especially from South Korea, Japan, and Western countries. Such concerns are based on the belief that the cultural invasion caused by the entrance of these external sources of funding could lead to the ideological decay of North Korean officialdom, and the citizenry at large, and result in a crisis of legitimacy for the ruling Kim family. Meanwhile, the awareness of the need for political stability also came from the imbalance of economic strength between North Korea and its neighbours. For one thing, North Korea continued to be anxious about its overdependence on China. In ancient history, the Korean Kingdom in the Peninsula always tried to escape from the domination of a central empire on the continent, although it accepted its status as a vassal state. There have been several wars between the Korean Kingdom and Chinese Emperors, such as Han and Tang, until the Japanese invasion and occupation of the Peninsula following its victory in the Japanese-Qing War in the late nineteenth century. Even after the Korean War, Kim Il-Sung required China's Volunteer Army to withdraw from North Korea as soon as possible (Cumings, 2005: 73–75). In order to avoid an overwhelming Chinese presence in the North Korean economy, Kim Jung-il even chose an Egyptian telecommunication company to develop its domestic mobile phone market, rather than accepting the experienced Chinese companies.

For another, in contrast with the historical struggle against China, Pyongyang's awareness of the threat from South Korea is stronger. In the post-Cold War era, South Korea experienced a steady increase in its economic strength. Compared to North Korea, South Korea's GDP is several times higher and the average salary in South Korea is more than forty times higher than that of North Korea. No matter the soft Sunshine policy of Kim Dae-Jong (fifteenth South Korea President from 1998 to 2002) and Roh Moo-hyun (sixteenth South Korea President from 2003 to 2007), or the 'Denuclearization, opening up, 3000' plan of the pro-American Lee Myung-Bak doctrine (seventeenth South Korea President from 2008–2012), due to the huge economic disparity between the two Koreas, Pyongyang continues to pay attention to the prospect of what may be termed as 'the second collapse of Berlin Wall' in the Korea Peninsula (Jin, 2014).

'Don't Want Reform': The Little Will of Leadership to Opening Up and Public Opinion of Pushing Economic Reform

Apart from the concerns of regime collapse, the problematic leadership and the lack of public support in North Korea also prevented economic reform in contrast to China, whose economic reform has been successful.

Firstly, in non-democratic countries, the political leaders are usually very powerful in the decision-making on national affairs. As the neighbouring country of North Korea, China had the same totalitarian system and planned economy as North Korea during the first thirty years of the Cold War. On the decision-making of economic reform and opening up, China's powerful leadership played a determining role. As the major designer of China's economic reform, Deng Xiaoping had a very clear understanding of the target, the principles, and the steps required for economic reform. He gave up the planned economy and replaced it with a limited market economy. He also used his personal influence and gave speeches during his visit to South China (Shanghai, Shenzhen, Wuhan, and Zhuhai) in 1992 to strengthen confidence in the economic reform. This trip happened when the top leader of China at the time, Jiang Ze-min, lacked the confidence to instigate economic reform. He even expressed doubt about the opening up policy in his talk reviewing Mao Zedong's Rectification Campaign in the early 1940s towards right-wing capitalist ideology in Yan'an (Vogel, 2011: 354).

By contrast, neither Kim Il-Sung nor Kim Jong-il held a strong will during their rule of North Korea. Indeed, as outlined in the section above, a few opening up activities were made, such as the establishment of joint companies with France and West Germany on oil exploration, the setting up of SEZs in the final days of Kim Il-Sung era, and the July-first economic adjustment of Kim Jong-il (Harrold, 2004; Christopher, 2005: 823–842). However, because these activities were recognised as temporary resolutions to North Korea's economic difficulties by attracting foreign funds, without a long-term plan most of them were suspended soon after they began. The only exception might be the underground marketisation for commodity trade between citizens which guaranteed their survival but the scale is still under strict control (Smith, 2015: 211–220). The two SEZs in North Korea, Rason and Sinuiju, are a case in point. As SEZs founded before 2000, there was no specific development strategy for them, especially Sinuiju. Sinuiju's development failed in the beginning with the imprisonment of the first Head of City (Yang Bin) in China due to financial crimes. However, since then, North Korea stopped its attempt to look for his successor (French, 2014: 44). As the second leader of North Korea, and although he visited China several times, Kim Jong-il mainly praised the

THE REGIONAL IMPACT OF CHINESE ECONOMIC ACTIVITY... 117

results of Chinese economic reform in exchange for limited economic aid from China. Once he returned to North Korea, he, nevertheless, stressed the significance of the Juche ideology and the planned economy in his public talks (Tudor, 2015: 106–108). More importantly, from the late 2000s and until his death in 2012, his trips to China served to secure Chinese support for his third son, Kim Jong-un, who was about to become the third generation of the Kim family of North Korean leaders (Beck, 2012: 65–71). Kim Jong-il's visits to China were an opportunity for his cousin, Jang Sung-Taek, to learn from the Chinese experience of economic reform and to launch economic cooperation with China (Gause, 2011: 82–84). However, the short-term practical control of North Korean power by Jang Sung-Taek and the Sino-DPRK top-level cooperation were actually not expected by China in Pyongyang's power-transfer era (from Kim Jong-il to Kim Jong-un), according to the one-decade freeze in bilateral interaction at the top level from 1992 to the early 2000s, and the disagreement on the North Korean nuclear problems.

Secondly, in China, strong public opinion also contributed to creating an atmosphere conducive to economic reform. Since the end of the Cultural Revolution, public opinion supported economic reform, especially when the introduction of the world's advanced technology, by intellectuals, to the public consolidated the foundation of mass citizens (Vogel, 2011: 97–103). By contrast, there is no significant public support for economic reform in North Korea. There is little dissatisfaction with the current regime in North Korea, that is, the Kim family, and any dissatisfaction voiced is quickly dealt with by the secret police. The propaganda of North Korea is under strict control and everything is praised in order to maintain the domestic status quo. Most officials and citizens have no idea about the external world (Liu, 2008: 75–81; Lankov, 2013). Thus, North Korean leaders have not been under domestic pressure to implement economic reform.

'Unable to Reform': North Korea's Domestic Limitations to Economic Reform
In addition to blockage from the leadership and public apathy, North Korea also had other problems which negatively influenced its short-term economic reform. The condition of the fundamental physical infrastructure of North Korea was not attractive to external investors. North Korea experienced severe power supply problems from the 1980s onwards. In the 2000s, even in Pyongyang, the only stable power supply at night was used to light up Juche Tower and the buildings of Kim's family (Gause, 2011: 88–90). The SEZs in Rason and Sinuiju also faced the problem of insufficient supplies of electricity and water. This was seen by external businessmen as a lack of sincerity on the

part of North Korea to attract external investment. North Korea's imperfect legal system was another negative factor. Although North Korea had enacted specific laws on foreign investment, problems remained in the implementation of those laws. In particular, the laws failed to protect external investors when they faced problems caused by the local economic actors who intentionally provided false commitments in contracts, or even scrapped contracts without justifiable reason. For example, Xiyang Corp from China was forced to withdraw from North Korea after its first year of experimental production because its contract was cancelled by the North Korean commercial firm which had benefited from the technological transfers from Xiyang. This incident resulted in a loss to Xiyang of over 200 million RMB (Wu and Wang, 2013: 58–61).

Thus, the concerns over political instability, weak leadership, and limited domestic economic foundation were the three major barriers to North Korea's economic reform and opening up. It lacked the confidence to allow external economic engagement or temporary and tactical opening up without long-term plans and provided little attraction to external funding. The following sections discuss how helpful Chinese economic activities are in pushing forward the economic reform of North Korea by resolving the domestic barriers discussed above.

The Role of Chinese Economic Activities in North Korea in Promoting North Korea's Own Economic Reform and Opening Up

After introducing the history of North Korea's failed economic reform and opening up under Kim Jong-il and the major corresponding domestic barriers, this section discusses the role of Chinese economic activities in pushing North Korea's economic reform forward, especially making North Korea accept opening up and to gain confidence in reform by supporting ideological change, and reducing the concerns of external impacts by offering benefits.

'Accept Opening Up': Driving a Top-Down Ideological Reform Through Elite Cooperation and Increased External Interaction Through Training

From the section above about North Korean domestic barriers to economic reform, it is seen that the ideological blockade by the top elites of North Korea is the most important factor to cause the regression of North Korea's economic reform with very limited progress. However, North Korean economic reform and opening up still benefited from Chinese economic activities from the mid-2000s, in a top-down mode, with the

THE REGIONAL IMPACT OF CHINESE ECONOMIC ACTIVITY...   119

entrance of Jang Sung-Taek into the core group of the Kim family. Moreover, although Jang Sung-Taek was executed by Kim Jong-un in 2014, his political legacy in the economic reform has been continued by Kim Jong-un, and even enlarged to an advanced level with the support of Chinese economic activities (Adrian, 2018: 237–241).

Chinese economic activities made a breakthrough on the ideological blockade to economic reform through cooperation with Jang Sung-Taek. During the last years of the Kim Jong-il leadership, as the cousin-in-law of the top leader, Jang actually stayed away from the centre stage of North Korean politics for several years until the mid-2000s. As the highest pro-China member of the elite in North Korea, and with no political or military background, it had to be significant for Jang to cooperate with China, and thereby to gain political kudos in order to consolidate his status in the central power. Jang successfully used the visits of Kim Jong-il to China to legitimise and popularise Chinese-style economic reform among the top officials (Gause, 2011: 77–87). Kim Jong-il's real target was to gain aid from Beijing as encouragement to learn the Chinese style of economic reform and to express his concerns about the next leadership of the Kim family in his final years (Lim, 2006). Jang and Jilin provinces together met each other's needs through cooperation in a positive cycle. For Jang, achieving economic cooperation with Jilin province and Yanbian consolidated his status in Pyongyang by demonstrating his ability to attract external funding; at the same time Jilin province resolved its local non-traditional security (NTS) problems. Also, in order to consolidate its cooperation with Jang, Jilin province in return offered training to North Korean officials, practically built a pro-Jang team, and extended Jang's role in North Korea. The cooperation between the two increased again to reach the ultimate cooperation of the mutual management of the Rason SEZ in North Korea, which legitimised the Chinese style of economic reform in the form of inter-state agreements. Thus, to the North Korean economic reform, although Kim Jung-il's stand for Chinese economic reform remained doubtful, to some extent Chinese economic activities managed to break through the ideological opposition of the North Korean elite through cooperation with Jang Sung-Taek.

During Kim Jong-un's period, Chinese economic activities still play two major roles in supporting and extending economic reform in North Korea with some flexibility. Kim Jong-un has a stronger leadership style than his father, which he uses to push through economic reform. The words he used in his early speeches when focusing on economic development and improving normal citizens' living conditions always appeared independently without mentioning the significance of the nuclear programme (Sweeney, 2013: 14–15). Although Jang was executed by Kim Jong-un, this simply meant the transition of reform leadership from Jang to Kim Jong-un, rather than the abandonment of economic reform itself. This can be examined from Pyongyang's criticism of Jang over the sale of national wealth in a cheap way, and the organisation of small private groups with the intention of occupying power (Alton and Chidley, 2013: 8). By contrast, Jang's efforts of pushing through reform in North Korea were not the cause of his execution. North Korean officials still confirm the foundation of thirteen economic cooperative zones in the Sino-DPRK border area with the denial of negative impacts from the death of Jang. Kim Jong-un also visited the many Sino-DPRK joint economic programmes, such as mushroom planting and processing companies. Under this condition, the steady increase of Chinese economic activities in North Korea represents a strong positive response to Kim Jong-un's attitude of implementing a progressive reform on the economic front: limited ideology relaxation; increased external funding, especially from China; larger local economic gains; and larger support to open up (Szalontai and Choi, 2013: 269–291; Piao, 2013: 34–36). By encouraging economic opening up, Kim Jong-un benefits from the ability to distribute huge funds originating mainly from Chinese economic engagements. He promotes the economic gains as a special class in North Korea in order to gain support for ideological relaxation, as described in Pyongyang's propaganda for the development of the economy and nuclear weapons at the same time. The deepened ideological relaxation and the stronger personality of Kim Jong-un can be seen from the introduction of Disney cartoons and NBA basketball into North Korea at the beginning of his era, to the more recent, and key, issue of the disappearance of Kim Il-Sung's and Kim Jong-il's signatures from Kim Jong-un's normal dress.

On the other hand, Chinese economic activities continued in a flexible way, adding to continued ideological change and extension of North Korea's opening up. After the top-down political cleansing of Jang's group, North Korea lost its original team who held Chinese ideological characteristics. However, Kim Jong-un had no choice but to continue the training of his own team to make sure that the mutual management and construction of North Korean SEZs were sustained at the previous level. Thus, the training of North Korean officials continued and represented flexibility. In the past, when Jang was in the top group of Pyongyang, Northeast Chinese governments and universities trained North Korean officials independently, without external support (Zhu and Xu, 2011: 120–130). During Kim Jong-un's period, the previous close individual relationships between Jang and Northeast Chinese officials were collapsed with Kim Jong-un's political cleansing, whereas the training of North Korean officials still continued, mainly in North Korea. The trainees spent limited time in China. After the beginning of mutual management of North Korean SEZs, the training of North Korean officials became a part of Chinese economic engagement with North Korea.

The flexibility of Chinese training is shown through the acceptance to the invitation from the UN Economic and Social Commission for Asia and the Pacific (UN ESCAP) on the joint training of North Korean officials. In other words, with the attendance of some UN ESCAP officials, China offered to train North Korean officials under the auspices of the UN ESCAP. This change was made at the time of frozen Sino-DPRK top level relations and relatively better relations between the UN and North Korea. Indeed, there were criticisms from the UN Security Council over North Korea's missile satellite tests, whereas the UN Security Council did not adopt any new sanctions against Pyongyang in the Kim Jong-un era. The US-ROK military exercises created a major clash in inter-Korean relations when North Korea's nuclear issue met a deadlock with the suspension of Six Party Talks (Jin, 2014). In the connection building between North Korea officials and the UN training team, apart from the traditional economic reform sessions, the Chinese side also selected training programmes in the low-politics field, such as environmental cooperation and animal protection. These measures aim to relax North Korea, reduce their concerns over external ideological influence, and avoid any possibilities of being accused of provocation by the North Korea side. One interviewee from UN ESCAP (Anonymous Interviewee 1, 28 November 2014) admitted that although the economic condition in the North Korea rural area was extremely underdeveloped, the local natural condition is perfect. He admitted that the China-led joint training programme for North Korean officials, especially in balancing the interests of environmental protection and developing tourism, was effective in shortening the psychological distance with North Korean officials and to help them to accept the idea of economic reform:

> In the past, the UN-DPRK relation was a nightmare. Needless to say about the UN troops in the Korean War, several years ago Pyongyang withdrew from the Great Tumen Program under UNDP as a response to UN sanctions against North Korea on its nuclear development and missile tests. Now our relations have improved from another acceptable way for them. Except the top-level diplomats, normal North Korean officials were always nervous in daily communication and interaction with us. However, they were more

friendly after the field trip for environmental and animal protection because their national pride was fulfilled after receiving our praise of their natural environment. Then it was much easier for us to build connections between their original ideas and our economic reform. (Interviewee 9, 2014)

'Dare and Be Able to Reform': Reducing the Concerns of Overdependence on China and Political Instability as a Result of Openness

Although under the cooperation with North Korean top elites, mainly Jang Sung-Taek, in Kim Jong-il's era, and the ideological support of opening up from Kim Jong-un, North Korea's opening up progressed steadily with strengthened acceptance at the top level. However, leaving aside China and South Korea, the existence of external economic actors in North Korea always leads to anxiety in Pyongyang about openness to external sources of information, which could result in domestic political instability (Wei, 2005: 22). The huge economic strength of China also made Pyongyang worry about overdependence on China. Thus, Chinese economic activities reduced these concerns in two major ways.

Firstly, as to the concerns of causing political instability, Chinese economic activities in North Korea followed the rule of self-restraint and non-intervention in North Korea in order to avoid unnecessary negative impacts. For one thing, although the extent of Chinese economic activities in North Korea varies, they remain distant for normal North Korean citizens. Most of the projects in the mineral resources, seafood, and social physical infrastructure are located in the Sino-DPRK border areas and other peripheral regions of North Korea. Even the Chinese tourist guides in joint tourist programmes persuaded Chinese tourists to keep their distance from the North Korean public, a Chinese local government official said (Anonymous Interviewee 2, 12 August 2014). The North Korean labourers in China are also isolated from Chinese society in order to avoid an external impact on them. Thus, it is almost impossible for these economic activities to cause political instability in North Korea. For another, Chinese local-level officials in the mutual management of North Korean SEZs mainly play the role of advisers and trainers, rather than hosts or managers. They mainly monitor Sino-DPRK economic cooperation in the SEZs and also give suggestions to the North Korean side on legislation and the regularisation of law implementation. However, they do not weaken or replace the role of the North Korean side in decision-making, despite the fact that the legislation in Rason SEZ is still under-develop in contrast to China (Sun and Yu, 2012: 47–49; Wang, 2018).

One interviewee said: 'South Korean scholars worry about the transformation of North Korea into a fourth province of Northeast China. They are over-suspicious. We are strongly self-restrained and do not want to take extra responsibilities for North Korea. The legislation of law in North Korea SEZ is developing under a suitable speed which matches the expectations of North Korea' (Anonymous Interviewee 2, 14 September 2012).

The non-intervention principles and self-restraint rules of Chinese economic activities directly reduce Pyongyang's concerns about the potential consequence of economic openness on political stability in the country, and improve its confidence in 'deepening the scales of opening up to external funding'. North Korea not only increased the frequency of the Pyongyang International Expo from once a year during the period from 1994 to 2006 (only in spring) to twice a year from 2007 onwards (both in autumn and in spring), it also enlarged its scale from 12 enterprises in 6 main fields in 1994 to more than 400 enterprises in 50 fields in 2014, and even started a new annual international expo in Rason SEZ from 2010 onwards (Kr-expo, 2014).

By improving its fundamental attractiveness to external investment, Chinese economic activities also made North Korea more confident to accept the short-term rapid increase of those activities. The shortage of necessary physical infrastructure was the most important barrier for North Korea to attract external economic investment. The risk of regional war decreased once tens of thousands of businessmen from China and abroad calmed down over the frequent North Korean nuclear tests. They had warned of the outbreak of war as well as the risks of corresponding UN resolutions and economic sanctions, 'We are scared by the first nuclear test of North Korea. Then we know that from the Kaesong Industrial Zone in 38th parallel to the North Korea SEZs on the Sino-DPRK border, each square metre of North Korea territory is safe. North Korea is only good at threatening enemies by propaganda but will not have a comprehensive war with the South. At the same time, the US and South Korea dare not to attack North Korea because they are anxious about China's response' (Interviewee 8, 2014).

Rason in North Korea aimed to develop itself to become the second Shenzhen in Northeast Asia. Before the beginning of the Chang-Ji-Tu programme and Sino-DPRK mutual governance of Rason in 2011, neither Rason nor other North Korean SEZs had a level of infrastructure construction to match that of Shenzhen. Even Pyongyang, which is not very modernised and faced problems with its power supply in the late 2000s, made a compromise with a Chinese private investor. A businessman from Wenzhou gained the operational rights to the largest shopping mall in Pyongyang in 2007 because part of his investment included the reconstruction of roads and other social facilities in the neighbouring area (Yan, 2012: 70).

In this condition, the construction of physical infrastructure played, and continues to play, a permanent role in attracting foreign funding. In Rason and Pyongyang this has been immediately effective. A large number of companies originating from outside mainland China and South Korea, such as an Australian beef restaurant, a Singaporean supermarket, and a Hong Kong casino, rushed into these two areas. From 2011 to 2014, non-PRC and ROK investments in North Korea increased from eleven to fifty-six (Zou, 2013: 30–31). However, at the general level neither market occupation nor the absolute amount of non-Chinese investments in North Korea could be comparable with China. Also, in contrast to the previous decades, there has been a steady increase in the diversification of sources of investment in North Korea. To Pyongyang, the rapid increase of Chinese investments in the short term, with the construction of physical infrastructure, was less concerning than ever before because the short-term investments in physical infrastructure have brought the long-term attraction of non-Chinese funds. This fit the strategy of Pyongyang to use third-party funds to balance Chinese economic impacts on North Korea. Pyongyang welcomed Chinese investment which funded the country and also paved the way for other countries to invest in DPRK.

To sum up, in the three generations of North Korean leaders, Kim Il-Sung failed to put into practice his ideas for economic reform before his death. Kim Jong-un only followed the previous progress of economic reform in the short length of time he has been in power thus far. The major barriers to Kim Jong-il's economic reform were the concerns about political instability, domestic law, poor infrastructural conditions, and the weak will for economic reform amongst the leadership. Chinese economic activities promoted the attractiveness of North Korea as an investment destination through the improvement of the fundamental physical infrastructure and legal reform. Through the cooperation between Northeast Chinese economic actors and Jang Sung-Taek, Chinese economic activities strengthened the will to open up among the top elites of North Korea through training. The self-restraint principle and non-intervention rule of Chinese economic actors reduced North Korean concerns of political instability due to the injection of external information. Thus, Chinese economic activities indirectly promoted North Korean economic reform and opening up. As the tendency of learning from China's experience of entering the world,

North Korea's economic opening up is what Beijing would like to see. After discussing the role of Chinese economic participation in advancing North Korea's economic reform, the following section discusses the implications of China's economic activities to North Korea's fishery industry and the dispute between China and South Korea.

Implications of the China-South Korean Ieodo Island-Centred Dispute of Economic Zones

Although the section above discusses the positive impacts of promoting North Korea's economic openness by reducing the ideological barrier, building sound physical infrastructure, and avoiding political instability through openness to new ideas and information, Chinese economic activities in North Korea still have negative impacts on inter-state relations in Northeast Asia. This section examines how Chinese economic activities in North Korea in the fishery sector strained Sino-ROK relations by escalating the confrontation around the Ieodo Island dispute. It first outlines the background of the Sino-ROK dispute over Ieodo Island. Then it explains the two factors which made this dispute extremely difficult to resolve, especially the impacts of Chinese economic activities in North Korea on the field of fisheries.

Background

Ieodo Island is located in the northern part of the East China Sea, close to the southern part of the Yellow Sea. It is 147 kilometres away from South Korea's Jeju Island, and 247 kilometres away from Tong Island in Zhoushan, China. Although called an island by South Korea, in fact it is an underwater reef covered by 3 to 4 metres of water. According to the principle of island recognition in UN Ocean Law, an island is the natural land area which is surrounded by water and stays above the water line at high tide (Zhang, 2013; Chung Jae-Ho, 2009: 482).

Before the 2000s, China claimed that Ieodo Island is an extension of China's continental shelf and therefore under Chinese sovereignty. South Korea attempted to legitimise its control of the island by following the principle of exclusive economic zone's middle line, although it does not have continental structure in its southwest territorial direction (Zhang, 2012: 9–10). Although China and South Korea held sixteen rounds of dialogue and negotiation, this dispute has not been resolved. Additionally, even though China and South Korea clarified the status of Ieodo Island as an underwater reef and reached mutual recognition that this dispute was about economic zones rather territory, South Korea still made several small steps to consolidate its control and change the identity of Ieodo Island from a rock to an island (Shi, 2014: 52).

For instance, in 2001, the Korea Institute of Geology formally changed the previous name of the rock to Ieodo Island. Two years later, the South Korea Ocean Research Institute constructed the South Korea Ieodo Island Comprehensive Ocean Scientific Base on Ieodo Island. This base, which is 15 metres above sea level, houses eight permanent research officials, a living area, a helicopter parking zone, a harbour, and a lighthouse. South Korea also uses airplanes and battleships to inspect Ieodo Island. Furthermore, the Jeju local constitute have frequently attempted to establish an official 'Ieodo Island' Day. Seoul also planned to build a battleship fleet called 'Dokdo Island and Ieodo Island' in the Jeju Marine Base in order to maintain its occupation of Dokdo Island and Ieodo Island (Shi, 2014: 53–54). Thus, although South Korea officially claimed that the dispute with China over Ieodo Island was to do with the economic zone rather than being a territorial dispute, South Korea still tried to use the occupy-first policy to strengthen its sovereignty in practice (Xin and Huang, 2013: 419–425).

The Obstacles to Resolving the Dispute

After this introduction to the background behind China-South Korea Ieodo-centred disputes of the economic zone, this section clarifies the real blockades which prevent the resolution of this dispute, especially the role of Chinese economic activities in North Korea in fisheries. It first reduces the number of blockades by denying the significance of the energy factor in the dispute. Then it discusses the other two blockades: the single status in the disputes and the disappearance of the 'buffer zone' between China and South Korea in the sector of fishery under Chinese occupation of North Korean marine territory.

Energy Sector: A Previously Overestimated Blockade in This Dispute
Some articles claim that Ieodo Island is similar to Diaoyu Island in terms of its reserves of underground natural gas and oil. Indeed, the location of Ieodo Island is in the Yellow Sea–East China Sea underground resource area. However, one interviewee denies the potential for exploring energy resources at the same level as Diaoyu Island, and other islands in South China Sea. This interviewee explains that

theoretically Ieodo Island is in the general scope of underground gas and oil, whereas in fact its geographical condition is quite different from other disputed islands. The neighboring geographical condition of other islands, such as Diaoyu Island and Sino-Vietnamese disputed islands, is very flat and in the middle of the resource area. Ieodo Island is at the very edge of this area. The total store of energy resources in the region is huge, but the real amount around Ieodo Island is very limited. I don't think that the amount is larger than the one tenth or even five percent of the estimated amount. Developing Ieodo Island will definitely harm the potential strength of the neighboring area. Meanwhile, in contrast to the flat geographical condition of other disputed islands that are easy for the construction of exploration facilities, Ieodo Island exists at changing locations with huge height distances between its two sides. That's why South Korea could construct the research platform only on the island itself. It is very difficult to find a suitable position to construct the platform, which is much larger than the sum of a living zone and helicopter parking area, and maintain balance, especially when the island is in the moving path of typhoons in the summer. Thus, the exploration activities in Ieodo Island would cost a lot, no matter the use of powerful machines to get the resources dozens of kilometres away, or keeping balance for a group of huge facilities. (Anonymous Interviewee 3, 11 August 2015)

Therefore, it seems that the dispute around Ieodo Island should be easily resolved because it is caused by the competition over fishery resources. However, due to two factors, this dispute is only resolved after dozens of meetings.

The First Blockade (The Single Status Without Dilemma): Occupying and Occupied

Although China and South Korea reached mutual agreement on recognising the dispute over Ieodo Island as a dispute over economic zones, it cannot be denied that the two countries still treat it as a territorial dispute in practice, especially the South Koreans who have taken steps to consolidate their control. The single status of both China and South Korea in other relevant disputes is the first factor. For several decades South Korea has succeeded in implementing the occupy-first policy in disputes with other countries: the Ieodo Island dispute with China and the Dokdo Island dispute with Japan. China is involved in three areas under dispute: Ieodo Island with South Korea, Diaoyu Island with Japan, and islands in South China Sea with many Southeast Asian countries. In all these disputes, China always makes a passive response to the islands being occupied

128   B. GAO

by other countries (although China maintains control of a few islands in the South China Sea, the majority of its claimed islands are occupied by numerous Southeast Asian countries).

The single occupied status of China and the occupying status of South Korea avoids the dilemma of Japan in the dispute. Many scholars, such as Tow (2014: 12–21), stress the importance of the US in restraining Japanese activities in disputes, especially with China. Thus the dispute around Diaoyu Island is in a more balanced status of control for both China and Japan. Practically, Japan controls the island but China also could announce its sovereignty of the disputed island by sending maritime supervision boats into the territorial sea around Diaoyu Island. However, the status of Japan in its territorial disputes created a special dilemma. On the one hand, in its dispute with China, Japan occupied Diaoyu Island, recognised it as historical occupied territory, and denied its status in the Qing-Japan treaties in the late nineteenth century. On the other hand, Japan lost control of Dokdo Island to South Korea after the Second World War. Thus, Japan has a special dilemma in the two disputes: if Japan tries to legitimate its occupation of Diaoyu Island using the occupy-first strategy, it agrees, in practice, with the control of South Korea over Dokdo Island. Meanwhile, if Japan continues the dispute with South Korea by denying the occupy-first policy, it would fail to legitimate its own claim over Diaoyu Island. Clearly, the occupy-first measure cannot be applied by Japan at the same time being denied by Japan in its dispute with South Korea. In contrast to Japan, South Korea and China are single occupier, and single occupied, actors in the dispute. They are not anxious to fall into the dilemma of logic created by Japan's dual roles. When one side insists on the occupy-first strategy, it may lead to rapid confrontation of the issue.

The Second Blockade (No Step Backward): The Reduction of the Sino-ROK Fishery Buffer Zone After the Rapid Increase of Chinese Economic Activities in the North Korean Marine Territory
Besides the single statuses of disputes without the concerns of dilemmas in claiming own rights over the disputed area, the impact of Chinese economic activity in North Korea in the sector of fishery could not be ignored because this created Chinese monopolisation of North Korean marine territory and intensified the Sino-ROK confrontation on fishery resources.

North Korean fishery resources are a natural 'buffer zone' between China and South Korea. Until the early 2000s, there were less than seventy Chinese and South Korean fishing boats in total in North Korean territorial waters without any competition (Li and Leng, 2008: 54–55). However, Chinese economic activities in North Korean marine territory were driven by the huge compromise that China made in the Sino-ROK fishery agreement in 2000. The major victims of this agreement in China were the fishermen from Shandong, Liaoning, and Zhejiang provinces. Apart from a few big companies from these provinces, who chose to build distant fishing fleets to develop fishery business with Latin American countries, especially Chile, most of the fishermen chose North Korea as an alternative because of the low cost (short distance) and local non-polluted ocean environment with huge reserves of diversified stocks of fish and other sea creatures (Xu and Qi, 2013: 14–16). Even though there were incidents of extortion by North Korean militants in the name of inspections for illegal cross-border fishing, the number of Chinese investors and fishing boats in North Korea still increased rapidly from a few dozen (mainly from Dandong and Dalian) to several hundred during the previous decade. Since 2007, fishing licences for North Korea's marine territory can be bought directly from the local Fishery Bureaux. More than ten Chinese fishery enterprises arrived in North Korea to build aquafarms, and freezing and processing plants (Interviewee 3, 2014).

By contrast, South Korean marine economic activities in North Korea met with more difficulties. On the one hand, the tension with North Korea caused by hardliner president Lee Myung-Bak limited the promotion of civil cooperation on fishing between South Korea and North Korea. The number of South Korean boats in North Korea dropped to 100–120 from around 150 in 2005 (Piao, 2013). Although in the era of the Park government relations between Seoul and North Korea improved, the economic marine activities of South Korea in North Korea did not recover under the continuous US-ROK joint marine military exercises and the unresolved dispute over the Northern Limit Line (Wei, 2008: 50). On the other hand, their special identities as South Korean (politically sensitive) also weakened their fishing activities as they became overwhelmed by Chinese fishermen. For instance, Chinese fishermen could use bribery to extend their fishing area, whereas South Korean boats could not use the same strategy because North Korean local officials dare not to take the political risk of accepting bribes. Some Chinese fishing enterprises even benefited by accepting fishing duties from local North Korean firms. Thus, the South Korean fishermen in North Korea increasingly struggle under the actual monopolisation by China of fishery activities in North Korea (Interviewee 4, 2012).

Thus, Chinese fishing engagement in North Korea made up for the loss of numerous fishermen in the Sino-ROK fishery agreement, but it created another front of fishery resource competition in the Yellow Sea with South Korea. The operation of Chinese fishing boats in North Korea also get rid of the further fishery potential of South Korea in the Yellow Sea. Under this condition, although the potential energy reserves of Ieodo Island could not be explored easily due to its special geographical condition, fishery resources became the new focus of competition between China and South Korea. China's single status of being occupied in the dispute, and South Korea's single status of occupier in the dispute, created a direct clash between the two countries, but avoided the dilemma of Japan in dealing with territorial disputes in Northeast Asia. As the only Sino-ROK disputed area with economic zones, neither China nor South Korea would make further compromise to weaken their potential fish supply in the Yellow Sea. In other words, Chinese economic activities in North Korea's fishery sector have a negative impact on China's relationship with South Korea, especially creating barriers to the resolution of disputes over economic zones around Ieodo Island. If the implications of driving North Korea's economic reform in the last section are positive to China's general strategy, the implications in this section indeed go against it.

IMPLICATIONS FOR THE ROLE OF SOUTH KOREA AND US AID IN DENUCLEARISING NORTH KOREA

After outlining the implications of Chinese economic activities for the promotion of North Korea's opening up and economic reform, as well as tightening China-South Korean disputes over exclusive economic zones, including Ieodo Island, in the two sections above, this section discusses the implication of Chinese economic activities in weakening the tactical role of South Korea and US aid in denuclearising North Korea. It will first provide details of South Korean and US aid to North Korea. Then it will compare the funding brought by Chinese economic activities to North Korea with the two aid programmes mentioned above in order to examine how Chinese economic activities in North Korea have weakened the effects of US-ROK aid to North Korea.

THE REGIONAL IMPACT OF CHINESE ECONOMIC ACTIVITY...   131

South Korean Aid to North Korea

This section firstly outlines the aid South Korea provided to North Korea from 2003–2013 under the Roh Moo-hyun (2003–2007) and Lee Myung-Bak (2008–2013) administrations. Then it discusses the changing character of South Korean aid to North Korea.

South Korea Aid to North Korea, 2003–2007

Table 5.1 shows the amount of South Korea aid to North Korea from 2003 to 2007 in billions of won.

Under the continuation of Kim Dae-Jong's Sunshine Policy by Roh Moo-hyun, the aid from South Korea to North Korea from 2003 to 2007 was numerous and diverse. During that time, 1.89 trillion won of aid from South Korea represented 30 per cent to 50 per cent of all the aid to North Korea. Since then South Korea has remained the largest aid supplier to North Korea.

Apart from the aid of strategic products, South Korea also provided humanitarian aid for the victims of natural disasters in North Korea, including 6 billion won in medicines and materials for victims of North Korea's floods in 2004, 1.2 billion won in medical materials to combat influenza in 2005, 80 billion won in anti-disaster materials for floods in 2006, and 4.8 billion won in medical products to combat a forest worm disaster and further disease control in North Korea (Reiss, 2007: 25).

Table 5.1   South Korean aid to North Korea, 2003–2007

	2003	2004	2005	2006	2007
Official aid State level	811	949	1221	2000	1432
Official aid Public level	81	102	120	134	216
Official aid International level	205	262	19	139	225
Agricultural funds	1510	1359	1787	–	1505
Public aid	766	1558	779	709	909
Total	3372	4230	3926	2982	4397

132   B. GAO

South Korea Aid to North Korea, 2008–2012

Following the outline of South Korea's aid to North Korea from 2003 to 2007 in the section above, this section outlines the amount of South Korean aid to North Korea from 2008 to 2012 (billion won).

South Korea changed its aid policy towards North Korea with the coming to power of pro-US president Lee Myung-Bak. The decade of the inter-Korea honeymoon had come to an end. In Lee's era, the total amount of aid from South Korea to North Korea was 239 billion won (1.35 billion RMB). This amounted to 44 per cent of aid under Kim Dae-Jong, and 20 per cent under Roh Moo-Hyum. From 2008 to 2012, the amount of aid from South Korea to North Korea had a steady annual reduction: 116.3 billion won in 2008, 671 million won in 2009, 404 million won in 2010, 196 million won in 2011, and 141 million won in 2012.

The amount of official aid was reduced rapidly and was replaced with public aid, and as a result the content of aid also changed significantly. In the past, Seoul mainly sent food and fertilisers to Pyongyang. After 2008, the public mainly donated medicines and hospital facilities for children through international organisations. For example, in 2008, South Korea supplied North Korea with 13.8 billion won of medicine and children's foods through WHO, and donated a further 166.5 billion won to WHO for buying medicine and relevant facilities for North Korea. In 2008, 2009, and 2011, South Korea also provided 148 billion won in children's products through UNICEF.

The Changing Tendency and Characteristics of South Korea Aid to North Korea from 2003 to 2012

Tables 5.1, 5.2, and 5.3 show that there are two major characteristics of the change in South Korean aid from Roh's era (2003–2007) to Lee's era (2008–2012): 'from strategic to tactic' and 'from effective to less effective for North Korea'.

The long-term strategic role played by South Korea in leading the provision of aid to North Korea changed to a relatively short-term tactic as the price for promoting dialogue in the Six Party Talks. This transition was caused by the replacement of Roh's continuation of the Sunshine Policy by the pro-US hardliner Lee Myung-Bak. This changing tendency is seen in the reduction of official aid, in particular at the state level. On the one hand, Lee chose to implement a pro-US policy towards North Korea. He mainly used the big stick of economic sanctions and military exercises to increase the pressure on North Korea to denuclearise (Wei, 2008: 48–52). In contrast, the small carrot of aid did not require a huge amount to attract North Korea to return to the dialogue. Meanwhile, a hard-line

THE REGIONAL IMPACT OF CHINESE ECONOMIC ACTIVITY... 133

Table 5.2 South Korea official strategic products aid, 2003–2007 (food amount: 1000 tons; value amount: billion won)

	2003	2004	2005	2006	2007
Rice	400	400	500	100	400
Value	151	135.9	178.7	39.4	160
Corn	100	100	0	0	12
Value	19.1	24	0	0	2
Fertilisers	300	300	350	350	300
Value	81.1	94	120.7	120	96.1
Others	0	0	0	0	Fuel 6.2
					Agricultural products 20
Value	0	0	0	0	Unknown

Source: Haggard and Noland (2007), Haggard et al. (2008: 23), Yan (2008a: 20; 2008b: 104–106, 114–116), Zhang (2009: 70–72)

Table 5.3 South Korean aid to North Korea, 2008–2012

	2008	2009	2010	2011	2012
Official aid—state level	0	0	183	0	0
Official aid—public and international level	438	294	21	65	23
Public aid	725	377	200	131	118
Total	1163	671	404	196	141

Source: Alton and Chidley (2013: 110–112), Manyin and Nikitin (2012)

South Korean government must lead to hostility from Pyongyang and a further disconnection in diplomatic relations at the state level, which resulted in almost no official aid to North Korea at the state level.

South Korean aid also became less attractive to North Korea as a result of not only its reduction in amount and value, but also in the change of content. In Roh's era, aid included vast amounts of strategic products such as rice, fertilisers, and corn, which were quite effective in resolving the domestic food shortages and agriculture problems in North Korea. However, the public-dominated aid in Lee's era was mainly children's products and female-care materials, rather than strategic products which were more attractive to North Korea. In addition, the change in the major contributor of aid from the South Korean government to the public confirmed Pyongyang's view of a split in South Korean state-society relations because the South Korean public still chose to donate to North Korea when Seoul stopped its donations (Smith, 2015: 160–170). This strengthened the recognition in North Korea that Seoul's pro-US policy went against public opinion and made it more confident to push through anti-South Korean and anti-US policies and activities.

US Aid to North Korea

After analysing South Korean aid to North Korea, Table 5.4 shows the chronological aid from the US to North Korea from the first nuclear crisis in the Korean Peninsula to the second.

From Table 5.4, it can be seen that the aid offered by the US to North Korea has always been tactical aid for the achievement of short-term targets, such as the attendance of North Korea at the dialogues and negotiations for denuclearisation. During the one and a half decades from the late 1990s, the amount and frequency of aid also reduced significantly. This was a result of the mutual distrust which existed between the US and North Korea following the collapse of the Korean Peninsula Energy Development Organisation (KEDO) as a resolution to the first nuclear crisis in the Korean Peninsula (Xu and Yang, 2012: 31–38). This mutual distrust deepened with several nuclear tests made by North Korea and its frequent withdrawal

Table 5.4 US aid to North Korea, 1996–2009

Date	Form	Target
February 1996	2 million USD food	Encourage North Korea to follow the 1994 Framework
June 1996	6.2 million USD food	Encourage North Korea to join the preparation conference for Four Party Talks
February 1997	10 million USD food	Encourage the attendance of North Korea at the preparation conference of Four Party Talks
April 1997	50,000 tons food	Encourage the attendance of North Korea at the missile proliferation conference
July 1997	100,000 tons food	Encourage the attendance of North Korea at Four Party Talks
February 1998	200,000 tons food	Encourage the attendance of North Korea at the special committee of Four Party Talks
September 1998	300,000 tons food	Encourage the attendance of North Korea at the missile proliferation negotiations
April to May 1999	600,000 tons food, 1000 tons potato	Allow the inspection of nuclear facilities
June 2002	155,000 tons food	Improve the inspection strength of the World Food Programme
January 2003	500,000 tons food	Encourage denuclearisation
December 2005		Stop aid
May 2008 to May 2009	500,000 tons food	Encourage North Korea to return to Six Party Talks

Source: Hanrahan (2009), Kang (2005: 22), Li (2014: 20–22)

THE REGIONAL IMPACT OF CHINESE ECONOMIC ACTIVITY...   135

from NPT and the Six Party Talks. It meant US aid was primarily used to attract North Korea to return to the dialogue, rather than to assist in the security guarantees which North Korea really expected in exchange for denuclearisation (Zhang, 2009: 70). Furthermore, even though North Korea returned to the Six Party Talks and restarted the dialogue, the core deadlock of the Six Party Talks was still not resolved because neither the US nor North Korea agreed to make any compromise first. The US insisted North Korea denuclearise itself completely before agreeing on a security guarantee. Meanwhile, North Korea insisted that the US should provide a guarantee first. In other words, the role of US aid could not be promoted to the same one in KEDO due to this deadlock (Hecker, 2010: 47–50). However, the continuation of the cycle of 'North Korean withdrawal from dialogue/US offer of aid/North Korea return to dialogue' was actually determined by the attractiveness of the US aid to North Korea. In the 1990s, US aid always appealed to Pyongyang because North Korea was in its most difficult economic stage at that time, whereas the condition began to change in the 2000s (Hanrahan, 2009; Yan, 2008b: 104–106). The following section introduces the implications of Chinese economic activities with North Korea to North Korea's withdrawal from the cycle described above.

The Implications of Chinese Economic Activities on the Denuclearisation of North Korea

It is clear from Tables 5.2, 5.3 and 5.4 that aid from both the US and South Korea to North Korea had a tendency of reduction and inefficiency in the denuclearisation of North Korea, but at least these tactics succeeded in making North Korea return to the negotiating table. However, due to the rapid increase in Chinese economic activities in North Korea from 2002, in particular after 2008, the aid from South Korea and the US was no longer sufficient to call for the return of North Korea to the Six Party Talks. For instance, the total amount of Chinese economic activities in the physical infrastructure of Rason Harbor is more than 5 billion USD. This amount is larger than the sum of South Korean aid to North Korea in one decade. In contrast to the short-term tactic and less attractive unofficial aid from South Korea and the US, Chinese economic activities in North Korea can be seen as a source of funding characterised as continuous and therefore attractive. In the Korean Peninsula, China successfully protected its national interest of maintaining regional stability and promoting its own economic development even it made the US unhappy on the failure of denuclearising North

Korea (Roy, 2015: 101–105; Tara, 2016: 56). As one interviewee pointed out, 'the Six Party Talks in fact provided opportunities for South Korea and the US to pay for the dialogue with North Korea and for its further de-nuclearisation. Thus, the game came to an end when the carrots offered by Seoul and Washington were no longer attractive to North Korea who gained much more from others without any extra requirement. Pyongyang became comfortable enough with Chinese economic engagement in North Korea to ignore the limited exchange leverage from the US and South Korea in spite of their consistent support in de-nuclearising North Korea' (Anonymous Interviewee 4, 11 September 2012).

This characteristic means Chinese economic activities in North Korea are developed on the basis of the objective condition of North Korea, such as its huge amount of mineral resource reserves, its non-polluted natural environment, and its special domestic political condition (Dwivedi, 2012: 76–79; Winstanley-Chesters, 2015). These conditions cannot be demolished in a short period unless North Korea subjectively chooses to pollute its natural environment and change its political system overnight. Meanwhile, both regional cooperation in the Tumen River and North Korea's economic opening up remain in the early stage. The development of the Russian Far East also will not be turned over in the future. Thus, Chinese economic activities in North Korea, which have developed for more than a decade from the beginning of the 2000s, will remain active for a long time. This general tendency will not change, although there may be change in specific activities according to the domestic requirements. Meanwhile, as the major investors in North Korea, Chinese economic actors do not meet strong competition in their occupation of the North Korean market, except that Pyongyang may restrain Chinese economic impact by forbidding Chinese investments in specific areas, such as telecommunications. The absence of competitors offers opportunities for Chinese economic actors to sign contracts for long periods, such as fifty years' mining rights or thirty years' fishing rights (Dwivedi, 2012: 80–90). The 'attractive' characteristic means North Korea can benefit from economic cooperation with China. As mentioned above, Chinese economic actors usually sign long-term contracts. These contracts for cooperation over several decades bring an attractive amount of funding to North Korea. Apart from the huge amounts of sustainable funding, Chinese economic actors make construction of the physical infrastructure as a part of their contracts. North Korea benefits by attracting a few foreign companies after removing their concerns about the shortage of physical infrastructure in North Korea, even though their amount and scale cannot match that of Chinese and South Korean companies. According to one interviewee,

> North Korea obtained much more than China. Today we build one road, which can be used by North Korea for one hundred years, as a part of one contract of twenty years' mining mineral resources. After twenty years, we have to satisfy other conditions and leverages to continue the contract. At that time, from the international level, the value of North Korea mineral resources improved with the deepened global resource scarcity. North Korea can ask for a higher price for larger funding. Both of road and resource, they always win. (Anonymous Interviewee 5, 9 September 2012)

Thus, as a long-term and efficient source of funding, in contrast to the aid from the US and South Korea which tends towards reduction and inefficiency, Chinese economic activities in North Korea create long-term uncertainty over the denuclearisation of North Korea because they shift North Korea away from the dialogue and negotiation in the short term by raising the price of making North Korea return to the dialogue and negotiations at a level difficult to reach.

Conclusion

In conclusion, Chinese economic activities have three major impacts on the regional affairs of the Korean Peninsula. These impacts either followed or ran against the general strategy of Beijing. From a positive viewpoint, North Korea's economic reform and opening up were pushed forward by Chinese economic activities with the removal of domestic barriers. Chinese economic participation reduced the awareness of political instability and made North Korean top officials dare to reform, it created conditions for strong leadership in gaining public support for reform and concerns over political instability, and it directly improved the under-developed physical infrastructure and the attractiveness of North Korea to foreign investment. In general, it created a tendency for North Korea's willingness to integrate into the world by learning from China's experience of economic reform and opening up. Thus, Chinese economic participation impacted positively in terms of the general strategy of Beijing to maintain regional security and stability. Apart from the positive impact above, Chinese economic participation in North Korea also runs against the general strategy of Beijing by bringing two negative impacts. The first is the intensification of Sino-ROK competition over fishery resources. The rapid increase of China's economic activities in North Korea's fishery sector, including buying fishing licences and building fishery centres, almost monopolised the North Korean fishery resource and got rid of South Korea's potential. It worsened the bilateral relationship between China and South Korea by preventing the resolution of the Ieodo Island-centred dispute because South Korea strengthened its control of Ieodo Island in order to make up for the loss of fishery resources in North Korea. This effect goes against the generally positive picture of China and South Korea which steadily improved in the 2000s from single partnership to comprehensive strategic partnership. Meanwhile, Chinese economic participation also created a negative impact on denuclearising North Korea and indirectly caused the withdrawal of North Korea from the Six Party Talks. The big contracts brought by Chinese economic actors offered several billion USD to North Korea. To North Korea, its national security is definitely more significant and expensive than natural resources and labour. If the latter have already been exchanged by the billions USD and cooperation programmes for several decades, nuclear weapons and the national security of North Korea should be exchanged at a higher price. In other words, Chinese economic activities play the role of devaluing the aid from the US and South Korea and reducing their effects of calling North Korea back to negotiations where it runs against the will of Beijing on denuclearising North Korea.

REFERENCES

PRIMARY RESOURCE

Anonymous Interviewee 1, Interview with local official, 28 Nov 2014, Seoul, South Korea.

Anonymous Interviewee 2, Interview with local scholar, 14 Sep 2012 Changchun, Jilin province.

Anonymous Interviewee 3, Interview with local scholar, 11 Aug 2015, Beijing.

Anonymous Interviewee 4, Interview with local scholar, 11 Sep 2012 Changchun, Jilin province.

Anonymous Interviewee 5, Interview with local scholar, 9 Sep 2012 Dandong, Liaoning province.

Anonymous Interviewee 6, Interview with local scholar, 11 Sep 2012 Changchun, Jilin province.

THE REGIONAL IMPACT OF CHINESE ECONOMIC ACTIVITY... 139

SECONDARY RESOURCE

Abt, Felix (2014) *Capitalist in North Korea: my seven years in the hermit kingdom.* Tokyo: Tuttle Publishing.

Adrian, Buzo (2018) *Politics and leadership in North Korea: the guerrilla dynasty 2nd ed.* London; New York: Routledge.

Alton, D. and Chidley R. (2013) *Building Bridges: Is there Hope for North Korea?* Oxford: Lion Books.

Bechtol, Bruce E. (2013) *The last days of Kim Jong-il: the North Korean threat in a changing era.* Washington, DC: Potomac Books.

Beck, P. M. North Korea in 2011: The Next Kim Takes the Helm. *Asian Survey,* Vol. 52, No. 1 (January/February 2012), pp. 65–71.

Cha, Victor D. (2013) *The impossible state: North Korea, past and future.* New York: Ecco.

Chung Jae-Ho. China's "Soft" Clash with South Korea: The History War and Beyond. *Asian Survey,* Vol. 49, No. 3 (May/June 2009), pp. 468–483.

Christopher, D. H. Real Reform in North Korea? The Aftermath of the July 2002 Economic Measures. *Asian Survey,* Vol. 45, No. 6 (November/December 2005), pp. 823–842.

Cumings, B. (2005) *Korea's Place in the Sun: A Modern History.* London: W.W. Norton & Co. Ltd.

Dwivedi, Sarita Sangit. North Korea-China Relations: An Asymmetric Alliance. *North Korean Review,* Vol. 8, No. 2 (Fall, 2012), pp. 76–93.

French, P. (2014) *North Korea: state of paranoia.* London: Zed Books.

Gause, E. Ken. (2011) *North Korea under Kim Chong-il: power, politics, and prospects for change.* Santa Barbara, Calif.: Praeger.

Harrold, M. (2004) *Comrades and Strangers: Behind the Closed Doors of North Korea.* West Sussex: John Wiley & Sons Ltd.

Haggard, S. and Noland, Marcus (2007) *Famine in North Korea: markets, aid and reform.* New York: Columbia University Press.

Haggard, S., Noland, M. and Weeks, E. Markets and Famine in North Korea. *Global Asia,* Vol. 3, No. 2 (August 2008), p. 23.

Hanrahan, E. C. International Food Aid Programmes: Background and Issues. *CRS Report R41072* (December 2009).

Hecker, S. Lessons learned from the North Korean nuclear Crises. *Daedalus,* Vol. 139 (Winter, 2010), pp. 47–50.

Jin Qiang-yi (eds.) (2014) Northeast Asia International Cooperation: Dilemma and Resolution. *Paper Collection of Tumen River Forum 2013.* Beijing: Social Science Academic Press Edition.

Kang, J. Policy Dilemma: Food Aid to all Enemy State. *International Studies Review,* Vol. 345, No. 4 (October, 2005), p. 22.

Kr-expo (2014) 'The Introduction of Pyongyang Spring Expo'. http://www.kr-expo.com/cn/chunzhan_jieshao.asp. Retrieved on 7 Sep 2015.

Lankov, A. (2013) *The Real North Korea: life and politics in the failed Stalinist Utopia*. Oxford: Oxford University Press.

Li Dun-qiu. DPRK reform: low voice with focus on efficiency. *World Knowledge (世界知识 Shijie Zhishi)*, No. 10 (2006), pp. 38–41.

Li Fang-Fang and Leng Chuan-hui. North Korea nearby fishery resource and status-quo of economic cooperation. *World Agriculture (世界农业 Shijie Nongye)*, No. 10 (2008), pp. 52–60.

Li Mu. The transition and measure of US Food aid policy to North Korea. *American Research (美国研究 Meiguo Yanjiu)*, No. 1 (2014), pp. 10–39.

Lim, Sung-Hoon. How Beneficial Would the Construction of a Rason-Hunchun Sub-Regional Economic Cooperation Zone in the Northeast Asian Borderlands Be? *North Korean Review*, Vol. 11, No. 1 (2015), pp. 63–81.

Lim Won-Hyuk (February 13, 2006) Kim Jong-il Southern Tour Beijing's Consensus with a North Korean Twist. *A presentation at Korea-China forum on China's economic reform, a model for DPRK*. Washington, DC.

Liu Ming. North Korea economic reform: the exploring of a third way and uncertain future. *World Economy Research (世界经济研究 Shijie Jingji Yanjiu)*, No. 7 (2008), pp. 75–81.

Manyin, E. M. and Nikitin, B. M. Foreign Assistance to North Korea 2012. *Congressional Research Service* (March 10, 2012), p. 13.

Piao Yinzhen (2013) The analysis of the Yellow Sea maritime disputes and its impact on security cooperation between neighboring countries in Northeast Asia. *Master dissertation Collection in China National Knowledge Infrastructure*.

Roy, Denny (2015) The North Korea Crisis in Sino-US Relations. In Simon Shen (ed.) *North Korea and Northeast Asian regional security*. London: Routledge, pp. 101–105.

Reiss, Mitchell B. Hope over Experience. *National Interest*, No. 89 (May/June 2007), p. 25.

Shi Jing-can. Sino-ROK fishery agreement's extension and elimination. *Journal of Gansu Radio & TV University (甘肃广播电视大学学报 Gansu Guangbo Dianshi Daxue xuebao)*, Vol. 24, No. 6 (December 2014), pp. 50–58.

Smith, Hazel (2015) *North Korea: markets and military rule*. University of Central Lancashire. Cambridge: Cambridge University Press.

Sun Xiaoxia, Yu Xiao. Sino-DPRK Cooperation Strategy of Developing Rason Economic Trade zone. *Euro-Asia Economy (欧亚经济 Ouya Jingji)*, No. 4 (2012), pp. 47–49.

Sweeney, J. (2013) *North Korea Undercover: Inside the World's Most Secret State*. London: Bantam Press.

Szalontai, B. and Choi, C. Y. China's Controversial Role in North Korea's Economic Transformation: The Dilemmas of Dependency. *Asian Survey*, Vol. 53, No. 2 (March/April 2013), pp. 269–291.

Tara, O. (2016) *The collapse of North Korea: challenges, planning and geopolitics of unification*. London: Palgrave Macmillan, pp. 17, 56, 72–73.

Tow, T. W. The United States and Asia in 2013: From Primacy to Marginalization? *Asian Survey*, Vol. 54, No. 1, A Survey of Asia in 2013 (January/February 2014), pp. 12–21.

Tudor, D. (2015) *North Korea confidential: private markets, fashion trends, prison camps, dissenters and defectors*. Tokyo; Rutland, Vermont; Singapore: Tuttle Publishing.

Wang Junyou. A Comparative Research of Chang-Ji-Tu and Rason FDI Law System. *Law Expo (法制博览 Fazhi Bolan)*, No. 8 (2018).

Winstanley-Chesters, Robert (2015) *Environment, politics, and ideology in North Korea: landscape as political project*. Lanham, Maryland: Lexington Books.

Wei Houqing. Kaesong Industrial Zone and its impacts to North Korea economic reform. *The Border Economy and Culture (边疆经济与文化 Bianjiang Jingji he Wenhua)*, No. 10 (2005), pp. 21–27.

Wei Zhi-jiang. The transition of Lee Myung-Bak government's policy to North Korea and its implication. *Modern International Relation (现代国际关系 Xiandan Guoji Guanxi)*, No. 8 (2008), pp. 48–52.

Wu Jie and Wang Ping. Investing North Korea: Hot thinking for the cold land. *State-owned Enterprise (国企 Guoqi)*, No. 2 (2013), pp. 58–61.

Xu De-rong and Qi Wei. The problems and strategy of Sino-ROK strategic cooperative partnership. *Journal of China Executive Leadership Academy Pudong*, Vol. 7, No. 2 (March 2013), pp. 26–36.

Xin yuan and Huang Shuo-lin. Sino-ROK Marine Interest Problems Research. *Journal of Shanghai Ocean University (上海海洋大学学报 Shanghai Haiyang Daxue Xuebao)*, Vol. 22, No. 3 (May 2013), pp. 419–425.

Xu Zhengwei and Yang Xiaolong. US Policy on Foreign Economic Aid from the Perspective of Neo-classical Realism—Demonstrated by the Economic Aid to Korea in the Post-Cold War Years. *Pacific Journal*, Vol. 20, No. 8 (August 2012), pp. 31–38.

Vogel, E. F. (2011) *Deng Xiaoping and the transformation of China*. Cambridge, Mass; London: Belknap.

Yan Yi. Kim Jong-un: North Korea speeding up? *Times Figure (时代指数 Shidai Zhishu)* (August 2012), pp. 68–72.

Yan Yu-ye. Post-Cold War US Food Aid to North Korea. *International Information (国际信息 Guoji Xinxi)*, No. 4 (2008a), p. 20.

Yan Yu-ye. Buy Peace: US economic assistance to North Korea after Cold War. *Ph.D. Thesis Collection in China National Knowledge Infrastructure* (2008b), pp. 104–106, 113–116.

Zhang Qing-lei. Ocean dispute and China's peaceful rising—Take example of Sino-ROK Ieodo Island Dispute. *Journal of Changchun University of Science and Technology (Social Science Edition) (长春科技大学学报社科版, Changchun Keji Daxue Xuebao, sheke ban)*, Vol. 25, No. 10 (October 2012), pp. 9–13.

Zhang Huizhi. An Analysis on International Development Aid to North Korea. *Northeast Asia Forum (东北亚论坛, Dongbeiya Luntan)*, Vol. 18, No. 4 (July 2009), pp. 67–75.

Zou Lulu. Exploring North Korea economic reform in the Kim Jong-Il era. *Master Dissertation collection in China National Knowledge Infrastructure* (2013), pp. 12–16, 30–31.

Zhu, Liaoye and Xu, Yong-gen. Exploring the future of North Korea economic reform. *Journal of Eastern Liaoning University (Social Science)*, Vol. 13, No. 5 (October 2011), pp. 130–140.

Zhang Qing-lei (2013) Sino-ROK Ieodo Island dispute Research. *Master dissertation Collection in China National Knowledge Infrastructure.*

CHAPTER 6

Conclusion

Historically, China and North Korea's relationship has been seen as lips and teeth because of their mutual battle against UN troops from 1950 to 1953. The Sino-DPRK honeymoon lasted for four decades until its collapse due to the formal foundation of diplomatic relationships between China and South Korea in 1992. From 1992 to the early 2000s, North Korea and China had no official top-level interaction. From 2002, with the consideration of potential economic reform and opening up in North Korea, Chinese investors entered North Korea and rapidly expanded their activity in the sectors of mineral resources, fishery, light industry, tourism, and labour cooperation. This economic participation commercialised the Sino-DPRK relationship and shifted it from a previously ideological relationship to a military one.

This book attempts to answer four major questions:

1. What drives actors below the state to engage in economic activities in North Korea and how do those motivations differ from the national interests?
2. What is the relationship between Beijing and actors below the state in their economic activities in North Korea after 2002?
3. What is the impact of Chinese economic activity in North Korea on regional security and China's grand strategy in Northeast Asia?
4. What does this mean for the making of China's foreign policy?

© The Author(s) 2019
B. Gao, *China's Economic Engagement in North Korea*,
Palgrave Series in Asia and Pacific Studies,
https://doi.org/10.1007/978-981-13-0887-1_6

143

144   B. GAO

To address these questions, I attempt to examine the commercialisation of the Sino-DPRK relationship as it is driven by a multiplicity of actors below the state, which include governments at the provincial and city levels, local state-owned companies, private enterprises, and social associations. Examples are the Jilin provincial government, Dandong City government, Jilin Tonghua Steel Company, Zhoushan First Ocean Fishery Company, and China's Overseas Fishery Association, who are all economically engaged in North Korea. Their activities both contribute to and occasionally run counter to Beijing's overall objectives of maintaining regional peace and stability in Northeast Asia, and sustaining positive relationships with neighbouring countries. In contrast, the central government in Beijing mainly plays the role of distant management and the provision of necessary institutional support. It rarely directly participates in the economic activities in North Korea, except in affairs relevant to the central state-owned companies. From the point of view of governmental interaction at different levels, the decision-making and implementation of China's foreign economic policy is pluralistic. This can be seen in the decentralisation of Beijing's decision-making authority and the active engagement of actors below the state. Someone may argue that Beijing also concerns the nontraditional security (NTS) problems in China. However, since the opening up in 1978, the classical theoretical approach of each Chinese leader focuses on either ideology (Jiang Zemin's Three Representative Idea and Xi Jinping's Socialism with Chinese Characteristics in New Period) or economic development (Hu Jintao's Scientific Developing Strategy). Beijing always issues the highest priority to economic development in order to legitimise the rule of Chinese Communist Party (CCP). On the contrary, except the air pollution control from 2011 to the recently released 'Three Years' of Blue Sky Protecting Battle Plan' (蓝天保卫战三年行动计划) Beijing rarely directly engaged in resolving NTS problems at the national level. The scale of China might be another barrier. It is so large (9.6 million square kilometres) that some types of NTS problems, such as environmental pollution, diversified in the different regions according to the specific conditions of provinces and cities. The sub-level governments at the province and city level are the key actors of resolving NTS problems. They usually attempt to build connection between resolving NTS problems (usually non-criminal problems) and promoting local economic development because booming local economy is always considered as the largest standard of measuring the one government official's political contribution. Their willingness and effectiveness may not be weakened if resolving NTS problems could be turned into industry of promoting local economic development. To the local state-owned enter-

CONCLUSION 145

prises owned by the regional governments who engage in North Korea economically, they still need to afford social responsibility of resolving NTS problems in their region. Chinese state-owned companies are not famous at making money and creating economic profits but achieving either long-term strategic targets (central state-owned companies and sometimes local state-owned companies also) or short-term tactic targets (local state-owned companies). In this book, there are indeed numerous small and medium enterprises (SMEs) getting involved in North Korea economically, whereas the Pyongyang's totalitarianism on controlling foreign direct investment should not be underestimated. The investing opportunities in North Korea are not directly sent to Chinese SMEs. These cooperation programmes are both approved by North Korea and encouraged selectively by Chinese local authorities who really attempted to address the resolution of local NTS problems. In other words, invisibly, Chinese SMEs are not driven directly by resolving NTS problems but in fact they play a similar role with local state-owned companies on taking social responsibilities.

Chinese economic activities in North Korea present the pluralism of implementing China's foreign policy in the economic field. It includes the pluralism of both designers and drivers at different levels. Although the central government is still important in the primary decision-making regarding China's foreign economic policy, the diversified actors at different levels in the implementation period of that policy could lead to different consequences. Overseas Chinese economic activities may, on the one hand, follow the national strategy, while, on the other hand, they may create divergence. During the commercialisation of the Sino-DPRK relationship, the central government in Beijing remains important in the general foreign policymaking stage. However, in the implementation stage the general policy is influenced by the majority of economic actors at the provincial, city, and individual levels. These sub-state level actors are driven by different reasons which depend on their own conditions. Although these activities, such as the investment in North Korean rare earth minerals, also meet the national interest, most cases are driven by reasons which meet the requirements of actors below the state and which diverge from those national interests. Therefore, the economic activities participated in by the sub-state actors may have unexpected consequences. For instance, the huge funding provided by Chinese economic activities allowed Pyongyang to avoid collapse under the economic sanctions imposed by the US. However, the economic leverage used in the dialogues for denuclearising North Korea in the Six Party Talks is also inefficient. North Korea's nuclear weapons remain and this runs against the national strategy of the denuclearisation of the Korean Peninsula.

146   B. GAO

Although Chinese economic participation in North Korea takes place across several economic sectors, there are three main drivers that motivate Chinese activity in these sectors. They are access to resources, human or material, not available in China or available in limited quantities only; favourable natural conditions; and government regulations, which are less demanding than in China.

Access to the resources not available in China, or available in limited quantities, is the first driver. In the sector of cross-border third industry labour cooperation between North Korea and Jilin and Liaoning provinces, North Korean labour is not available in Northeast China, in particular in Jilin province. Northeast China has lost its attraction for the local population which has resulted in a net population outflow since the economic reforms and the rapid development of Southeast coastal areas. To Jilin province and its ethnic Korean Prefecture, most cheap labour is attracted to work in South Korea. Thus, North Korean workers, who have relatively higher educational background but lower salaries than their counterparts, are a very limited resource in Northeast China. Meanwhile, further cross-border cooperation in the construction of physical infrastructure as a form of Chinese economic participation in the development of North Korea's Rajin Harbor was implemented due to Rajin's special geographical location. It borders Jilin province's closest area to the Sea of Japan so that through such cooperation, Jilin province gains access to the sea via Rajin Harbor, the shortest distance in contrast to Russian harbours or other Chinese domestic harbours dozens of kilometres away. In the sector of the fishery industry, North Korean fishery resources are also available in limited quantities in China. China's fishery resources in the coastal area are very limited due to overfishing and the reduction of fishing areas following the signing of the Sino-ROK fishery agreement. In contrast, North Korean fishery resources are underdeveloped because North Korea's general domestic economic difficulties restrain the daily consumption of fishery products. This is why Chinese governments at city and provincial levels are sending local fishing boats to North Korea. At the same time, in the sector of mineral resources, rare earth, one significant but limited mineral resource in the world, is also under the mutual development of Chinese enterprises and North Korea.

In addition to access to limited resources in China, favourable natural conditions also play an important role in driving Chinese economic actors to engage in North Korea. In the sector of mineral resources, the natural condition of North Korea's coal mines is an ideal one for surface mining compared to the high-risk deep mining in China. Thus, this suitable natural

CONCLUSION   147

condition attracts numerous Chinese enterprises to invest in North Korean coal mines. In the sector of the fishery industry, China's offshore area is very polluted. The Northwest Pacific Ocean near Japan, a previous ocean fishing area for China, is also polluted as a result of the Japanese nuclear accident in Fukushima. In contrast, North Korea's coastal area maintains very clean ocean conditions. Thus, Chinese private enterprises from Shandong province, and local state-owned companies from Dandong, have chosen to establish branches in North Korea's coastal areas in order to benefit from local clean natural conditions and to advance their fishery products in terms of weights and sizes.

The third driver of Chinese economic activities in North Korea is the fewer requirements of government regulation than in China. North Korea is short of many significant issues: foreign funding from economic activities, agricultural technology, and inspection strength in the border area near China. Therefore, Chinese economic activities in North Korea, particularly in its border areas with China, enjoy a relatively relaxed condition of regulation and policy priorities. In the sector of cross-border third industry, different cooperation projects expanded in North Korea very quickly. The number of Chinese cities near the Sino-DPRK border that have developed travel and traffic cooperation with North Korea has increased from two to ten in recent years. Chinese agricultural companies also entered North Korea by building greenhouses for crops and local farms for animals. Chinese official teams are also allowed to join mutual management with North Korea for its border management. Meanwhile, as another important source of foreign currency, North Korea did not have a lot of additional requirement to restrain the investment in the sector of mineral resources such as the scale of companies and the environment protection. Therefore, this leaves room for Chinese SMEs from Shandong, which are unable to compete with local state-owned companies, or even with central state-owned companies in China, to invest in North Korean coal mines to extend their survival. It also reduces the costs of environmental protection to the Liaoning company which invests in rare earth minerals in North Korea because this is a product which involves heavily polluted processing of raw materials.

In the Chinese economic participation in North Korea, the relationship between Beijing and actors below the state is that the actors below the state make up the majority of those who directly participate in North Korea through economic activities. Their activities include direct investments, the construction of physical infrastructure, and technology transfer.

148   B. GAO

At the same time, the central government in Beijing provides both direct and indirect support. Firstly, through institutional support, it signed the general agreement with North Korea on the promotion and protection of trade and investment, and the mutual management of the Rason Special Economic Zone. This is determined by North Korea's political condition as a highly centralised country, which means that Pyongyang is the only actor on the North Korean side with the power to sign agreements with external actors. Actors below the state in North Korea are very few and cannot directly sign agreements with provincial governments in China. Meanwhile, Beijing also provides support to Chinese economic actors as part of its regional development strategy. For example, the Chang-Ji-Tu Plan for Jilin province included cooperation with North Korea on the physical infrastructure involved in the Rajin Harbor project. Beijing upgraded its status from provincial initiative to national strategy in order to strengthen the reputation and attractiveness of this plan, but in fact Beijing did not provide any practical support, such as funding. Secondly, Beijing also offered direct support to China's economic actors in North Korea in a limited number of cases. For instance, it aided North Korea to resolve a deadlock in negotiations between a Liaoning company and its North Korean partner on the investment in a rare earth mine. It also intervened in the cross-border fishery incidents between China and North Korea to protect the safety of the Chinese fishery industry.

Chinese economic activities in North Korea influence the regional order of security in Northeast Asia in three ways. First of all, they advance the economic reform and opening up of North Korea. In fact, in the past, North Korea had several short-term and temporary economic 'openings up'. However, the single aim of such initiatives was to attract foreign investment for the purpose of acquiring foreign currency and without a solid commitment to reform at the top level due to concerns for regime survival. The rapid increase in Chinese economic activities meant North Korea attracted more foreign investment from third countries, such as Egypt, in order to balance the impact of Chinese investment. Meanwhile, in contrast to Western investors who stay out of North Korea because of the underdeveloped physical infrastructure, such as poor electricity and water supplies, some Chinese economic actors actually improved the local physical infrastructure and thereby created better conditions for North Korea to attract external funding. At the same time, Chinese economic actors, from state-owned companies to private operators, rarely added extra political conditions to the economic participation and considered,

CONCLUSION   149

instead, the requirements and special conditions of North Korea. This weakened the concerns of North Korea to China's potential control of its domestic affairs and strengthened its confidence to enlarge the opening up policy.

Another regional impact concerns China's relations with South Korea. Chinese economic activities, particularly in the North Korean fishery sector, have increased the anxiety of South Korea towards China and even complicated the resolution of disputes over territorial waters and exclusive economic zones. Although South Korea benefited from the fishery agreement signed with China under China's huge compromise on fishing areas, its fishery cooperation with North Korea was no longer competitive due to the rapid increase in Chinese fishery participation in North Korea. It stimulated South Korean nationalism towards the protection of its own territory, even the disputed economic zones around Ieodo Island. China and South Korea have held several rounds of negotiations for resolving this dispute; however, all these dialogues failed with the result of a deepened tendency of Chinese monopolisation of North Korea's fishery resources and increasing marginalisation of South Korea's fishery actors in North Korea. Furthermore, by recalling their memory of historical rule by a central empire, the rapid increase of Chinese economic activities in most fields in North Korea led to mounting apprehension in South Korea about DPRK's economic dependence on China, even the possibility of DPRK becoming China's fourth northeastern province.

Thirdly, Chinese economic activities reduced the effects of US economic measures to denuclearise North Korea through the Six Party Talks. The US mainly used either economic sanctions to impose pressure on North Korea or economic leverage in exchange for the denuclearisation of North Korea. However, these two measures achieved little progress due to the Chinese economic participation in North Korea. On the one hand, Chinese economic actors would pay large amounts of funding to North Korea; even the civil fishery cooperation between Dandong and North Korea's coastal area at the city level achieved 24 million RMB. In fact, the total amount of Chinese economic activities in North Korea is more than the value of aid offered by the White House, which amounted to several million tons of food. On the other hand, the economic sanctions imposed by the UN, although mainly by the US, on North Korea were also ineffective because the rapid increase in Chinese economic participation compensated the loss of opportunities for North Korea to trade with other countries resulting from the economic sanctions. Consequently, neither economic sanctions nor economic aid from the US is sufficient to force North Korea to denuclearise, because of the comparatively huge amount of funding resulting from Chinese economic participation in North Korea.

This project contributes to the current academic research at three different levels. First of all, on the topic of Sino-DPRK relations, it explores the domestic drivers behind the commercialisation of Sino-DPRK relations, thereby illustrating the diversified actors in the pluralism of implementing China's foreign economic policy in North Korea. It draws a comprehensive picture of coherence and divergence between the national interest of Beijing and the specific targets of sub-state actors. Moreover, to the study of Northeast Asia, my project shows that NTS issues play an increasingly significant role in building interdependence between states through economic cooperation. At the same time, NTS problems, especially the competition of gaining resources beyond energy, may also lead to conflicts between countries. Finally, to the discipline of international relations, my research confirms the concept of complex interdependence and brings new modes of governance to the multi-level governance theory by applying the characteristics of different modes of multi-level governance in the one case of Chinese economic participation in North Korea.

The argument advanced in this research has important implications for our understanding of China's economic policy towards the outside world. Firstly, it means that China's bilateral economic relations with countries around the world have become commercialised. North Korea is the country which has the most special political relationship with China. The commercialisation of the Sino-DPRK relationship is China's final step towards commercialising its economic relationship with the rest of the world. Meanwhile, China's Going-Out Strategy has shifted. China's national economic champions, that is, central state-owned companies such as China Petrochemical Corporation (SINOPEC) and China National Petroleum Corporation (CNPC), which serve the national interest, especially in the control of resources and energy, are not the major players, even if their funding for purchase is still huge. On the contrary, a number of local state-owned companies and private enterprises have followed and replaced the central state-owned companies, the pioneers of China's Going-Out Strategy, as the major strength of China's overseas direct investment. Their drivers mainly refer to local requirements of social-economic development and their own specific problems, such as the survival of SMEs, rather than the national interests. These economic activities could also be motivated by reasons which actually run against the national interests under some special

CONCLUSION 151

conditions. It is increasingly difficult to politicise the activities of these commercial operators and argue that they are agents of the Chinese state.

Secondly, at the regional level, new forms of bilateral and multilateral cooperation between China and its neighbouring countries have taken place at the provincial and city levels. In the past, this type of case has been rare in cooperation between sub-state actors in China and abroad. The sub-state Sino-Foreign cooperation mainly developed in the form of the 'Friendship-city' concept by sharing cultural and educational resources. Even in the economic sector, previous Sino-Foreign cooperation at the sub-state level has been in the form of domestic special economic zones and industrial parks in China designed by Beijing to attract foreign funding. Different to the previous form of cooperation, in the new form, while called Sino-Foreign, there is little happening at the state level because only central governments take responsibility for signing final agreements in order to provide institutional support. Domestically, the central government also advances the status of regional projects to the national strategy in order to improve the attractiveness of this cooperation, even though the provincial government gets no funding from Beijing. In contrast, regional governments at provincial and city levels practically designed and operated the cooperation, not only in China, but also in the other countries. This new form of cooperation occurs in the current Sino-DPRK economic cooperation. Besides setting up traditional industrial zones for labour cooperation, Jilin provincial government sent its official team to join the mutual administration of the Rason Economic Zone in North Korea and the Sino-Russia-DPRK triangle cross-border tourist zone. These two cases are a completely new form of Sino-Foreign cooperation at the sub-state level in the history of the PRC.

Thirdly, the major role of actors below the state in the implementation of China's foreign economic policy in North Korea means that the effort of the White House to apply pressure on Beijing over the North Korean nuclear problems will not produce the desired result. The US uses this strategy because it considers China as a single unit in the Sino-DPRK relationship and that Beijing controls all activity between China and North Korea. As my book demonstrates, this is not the case. During the second nuclear crisis in North Korea, from the early 2000s, in order to express to the world its will to be a responsible country, Beijing actively engaged in organising the negotiations among the relevant parties from the China-North Korea-US Third Party Talks to the Six Party Talks to resolve the nuclear issue of North Korea. Recently Beijing also supported the economic sanctions made by the

UN over North Korea. However, in Sino-DPRK trade and economic cooperation, Beijing and its central state-owned companies are not the majority actors. At the same time, the economic decentralisation in China makes sub-state actors independent from Beijing on decision-making and the implementation of overseas activities so that they concentrate on their own conditions. Thus, the pressure from the US on Beijing does not influence a change in the condition of the Sino-DPRK economic relationship. In fact, Beijing frequently projects a strong will to denuclearise North Korea, but at the same time continues to fund it through the rapid increase in economic activities.

Furthermore, North Korea will survive longer than the time predicted by many scholars. Scholars from South Korea and the US mainly forecast that the new regime under Kim Jong-un will collapse within a decade due to food shortage, economic collapse, and the large numbers of escapees which result from information leakage and poor border control. However, these three problems may not occur. In the agricultural field, the involvement of Chinese officials in the mutual management of the Rason Economic Zone improves North Korea's agricultural condition in terms of technology. North Korea gains advanced agricultural experience from Northeast China which has previously been the major supplier of agricultural products to the rest of China. Indeed, under the strictest economic sanctions, in the short term Pyongyang meets the problem of external funding through mineral exports for the import of food for the country. In fact, North Korea has also begun its long-term strategy of shifting from an agriculturally self-supporting country as a result of Chinese technology and experience. Meanwhile, the economic collapse of North Korea may not happen in the short term. On the one hand, Chinese economic participation in North Korea is still rapidly increasing. Although the import of several types of minerals is forbidden, there are many other choices in the diversified North Korean mineral reserve. Meanwhile, apart from the mineral resources, other fields of business, such as tourism and labour cooperation, are also encouraged by Pyongyang as alternative funding for mineral export. On the other hand, Chinese economic participation, especially that implemented by the provincial and city governments, at times includes the construction of physical infrastructure. The construction of roads and railway and the supply of electricity and water change the previously negative image of North Korea's investment condition. This is because its shortage of physical infrastructure could attract external funding from third countries, such as occurred in the telecommunications industry when

CONCLUSION   153

an Egyptian company entered the market. Moreover, improved control of the Sino-DPRK border has directly reduced the number of escapees significantly. North Korea's mature nuclear technology requires less funding for further development than at the beginning of its era of nuclearisation. This leaves room for transferring funding to improve economic conditions. These issues strengthen the national confidence of North Korea in its ideological battle with South Korea. In general, North Korea could avoid a short-term collapse caused by food shortages, economic collapse, or refugee waves.

The final implication is an increasingly independent North Korea under the commercialisation of the Sino-DPRK relationship, especially the reduction of aid from China. In the past, China used large amounts of aid in exchange for strong support from North Korea in international affairs, such as that in which North Korea supported China in its ideological debate with the Soviet Union in the late 1950s. On the contrary, the recommencement of nuclear development in North Korea, which actually keeps in step with the commercialised Sino-DPRK relationship, means that Pyongyang absolutely confirms China's deideologised foreign policy after learning the first lesson in 1992 from the foundation of the China-South Korea formal diplomatic relationship. North Korea realises that it has become an ordinary neighbour to Beijing, even though the Sino-DPRK Friendship Treaty, signed after the Korean War, remains effective. Therefore, North Korea has responded with its solid independence and self-interest-centred foreign policy. It does not care about the concerns of Beijing on its nuclearisation, even under the strictest economic sanctions imposed by Beijing. This is because North Korea knows that Beijing cannot completely abandon it when it bonds itself closely with increasingly larger numbers of sub-state actors from China, meets their requirements, and gains funding in return for the continuing development of its nuclear weapons.

My book aims to serve as a starting point for a more full investigation into China's economic relations with North Korea that could be extended, not only to other states in the neighbouring countries of China, but to other geographical and political regions as well.

On 5 August 2017, the UN Security Council imposed the strictest economic sanction on North Korea in the history by banning its export of mineral resources, seafood products, and cheap labour. This economic sanction seriously impacted Sino-DPRK bilateral economic interaction. At the same time, with the official pushing of the Belt & Road Initiative (BRI), North Korea was also increasingly replaced by several member countries of BRI. However, this year, the extended Xi Jinping administration recovered the top-level interaction between Beijing and Pyongyang. In 2018, on 25–28 March, 7–8 May, and 19–20 June, Kim Jong-Un visited China and had a meeting with Xi for three times with the mutual reinforcement of promoting Sino-DPRK traditional friendship. Further research needs to be done to explore the impact of UN sanction on North Korea on Sino-DPRK trade, the status quo of post-sanction economic ties between China and North Korea, and how does BRI offer alternative economic partners and investing opportunities to Chinese businessmen who could no longer develop their business in North Korea.

Appendix A: Introduction

1. Outline of Documents' names

   关于省、市、自治区党政机关机构改革若干问题的通知 Guanyu sheng, shi, zizhiqu, dangzhengjiguan gaige ruogan wenti de tongzhi) in December 1982;

   (关于地市州党政机关改革若干问题的通知 guanyu di shi zhou dangzhengjiguan gaige ruogan wenti de tongzhi) in February 1983;

   (关于县级党政机关改革若干问题的通知 guanyu xianji dangzhengjiguan gaige ruogan wenti de tongzhi), in December 1983;

   (中共中央、国务院关于地方政府机构改革的意见 zhonggong zhongyang, guowuyuan guanyu defang zhengfu jigou gaige de yijian) in January 1991;

   (党政机构改革的方案 dangzheng jigou gaige de fangan) and

   (关于党政机构改革方案的实施意见 guanyu dangzheng jigou gaige fangan de shishi yijian) in July 1993;

   (中共中央关于完善社会主义市场经济体制若干问题的决定. Zhonggongzhongyang guanyu wanshan shehuizhuyi shichangjingjitizhi ruogan wenti de jueding) in 2003.

   To the specific content of document in 2003:

   (合理划分中央和地方经济社会事务的管理权责 heli huafen zhongyang he difang jingji shehui shiwu de guanli quanze), (属于全国性和跨省 (自治区、直辖市)的事务, 由中央管理, 以保证国家法制统一、政令统一和市场统一。属于面向本行政区域的地方性事务, 由地方管理, 以提高工作效率、降低管理成本、增强行政活力,

© The Author(s) 2019

B. Gao, *China's Economic Engagement in North Korea*,
Palgrave Series in Asia and Pacific Studies,
https://doi.org/10.1007/978-981-13-0887-1

shuyu quanguoxing he kuasheng zizhiqu zhixiashi de shiwu, you zhongyang guanli, yi baozheng guojia fazhi tongyi, zhengling tongyi he shichang tongyi, shuyu mianxiang benxingzheng quyu de difangxing shiwu, you defang guanli, yi tigao gongzuo xiaolv, jiangdi guanli chengben, zengqiang xingzheng, huoli).

2. There are six general questions asked to the interviewees during the interview:

- What do you think about the current relationship between China and North Korea? Are there any changes in contrast to the past (according to your individual experience and media report)?
- What role does your organisation play in the economic cooperation between China and North Korea?
- What type of official support do you know/you have already received from the government to the Chinese companies in North Korea? Which level of government?
- Are there any difficulties that you have met/as you know Chinese companies have met in implementing economic activities in North Korea? Is the official support helpful to resolve these problems?
- What factors have motivated your company/Chinese enterprises to develop their business in North Korea? Is there any direct connection between these factors and official support? In other words, apart from the increase of tax to the country, is there any other contribution that your company or Chinese enterprises in North Korea have made so that your or these economic activities are encouraged with official support?
- At the macro level, such as the Sino-DPRK general relationship and the North Korean nuclear problems, what types of potential and indirect impacts that Chinese economic activities in North Korea could or have already created?

Appendix B: China's Economic Activities in the North Korean Mineral Resource Sector

1. This cross-Yalu River oil pipeline started from Jin-Shan bay Oil Store and arrived at North Korea Sinuiju Oil Store. Its length is 30.3 kilometres.

2. In 2006, Shandong province planned to integrate seven big local state-owned coal companies into one Shandong Energy Corporation. These seven companies are Yunzhou Mineral Corp, Zibo Mineral Corp, Zaozhuang Mineral Corp, Xinwen Mineral Corp, Feicheng Mineral Corp, Longkou Mineral Corp, and Linyi Mineral Corp. The Shandong Energy Corp is planned to be founded on 18 December 2010 as the third-largest coal company in China with an expected output of coal over 100 million tons. However, this integration plan was never agreed on by all the seven companies. Although two smaller companies, Feicheng Mineral Corp and Longkou Mineral Corp, agreed on the integration plan, Xinwen Mineral Corp, Zao Zhuang Mineral Corp, and Linyi Mineral Corp maintained neutrality. However, the most powerful one, Yunzhou Mineral Corp, refused to be a listed company in the stock market with complicated stock rights. Another powerful company, Zibo Mineral Corp, also rejected the plan of integration because it did not want to lose financial control and be balanced in the new Corp. Even after the foundation of Shandong Energy Corp was achieved on 23 March 2011 with the absence of Yunzhou Mineral Corp, it still required times to neaten domestic orders (Ding, 2011).

© The Author(s) 2019

B. Gao, *China's Economic Engagement in North Korea*,
Palgrave Series in Asia and Pacific Studies,
https://doi.org/10.1007/978-981-13-0887-1

158 APPENDIX B: CHINA'S ECONOMIC ACTIVITIES IN THE NORTH KOREAN...

3. China's rare earth export quota had a significant reduction in 2010. The export quota of rare earth in 2009 was 50,145.1 tons. In 2010, the quota reduced almost 40 per cent and dropped to 30,259 tons. Since then, China's rare earth export quota always stayed at around 30,000 tons until formal cancellation in 2015.

4. China meets the serious challenge of rare earth loss through smuggling. Smuggling rare earth from China to the foreign countries started from 2006 and rapidly increased every year. From 2008 to 2011, the captured amount of smuggled rare earth reached 16,000 tons. In 2009, the smuggled rare earth reached 20,000 tons, as many as 40 per cent of the 50,000 normal export rare earth. It had a 10 per cent increase of smuggling amount in contrast to the amount of 2008. In 2012, the amount of smuggled rare earth in the largest historical case reached 12,000 tons (China Rare-Earth Association, 2013: 5–6). Although China reduced the rare earth quota from 50,000 tons in 2009 to 30,000 tons in 2010, the smuggled amount of rare earth still supplied the gap of quota (China Rare-Earth Association, 2012).

5. Australia and Brazil are the two major suppliers of iron ore to China and comprise over 80 per cent of China's import of iron ore. From 2003 to 2015, China's import of iron ore increased from 148 million tons to 952 million tons. The corresponding import amount from Australia increased from 21 million tons to 560 million tons (China Custom House, 2015: 25–30).

6. China has been the country with largest vehicle production in the world since 2009 by producing 13.79 million in 2009, 18.26 million in 2010, 18.41 million in 2011, 19.27 million in 2012, 22.11 million in 2013, 23.72 million in 2014, and 24.59 million in 2015 (China Vehicle Association, 2015).

7. These twenty-five programmes are the Jilin parts of the Haerbin-Dalian High-Speed Railway, Jilin-Tumen-Hunchun Custom Railway, Changchun-Tonghua Railway, Helong-Nanping Railway, Tonghua-Guanshui Railway, Songyuan-Taolaizhao Railway, Baicheng-Wulanhaote Railway, Changchun-Baicheng High-Speed Railway, Hunchun-Dongning Railway, Changchun-Changling-Baiyinhushuo Energy transport line, Baihe-Dunhua-Dongjingcheng Railway, Songjianghe-Changbai Railway, Baishan Town-Quanyang Railway, Helong-Nanping Railway, Jingyu-Songjianghe Railway, Liaoyuan-Changchun Railway, Zhengjiatun-Manhanying Railway, Changshuangyan Railway, Baicheng-Jieji Second Railway, Baihe-Helong Railway, Baicheng-Zhenxi Railway, Tongliao-Siping Railway, Changchun-Xibayanhua Railway, and Jilin Railway West Round Line.

Appendix C: China's Economic Activities in the North Korean Fishing Industry

1. North Korean coastal commercial firms are mainly controlled by the North Korean army. Thus, their fishing boats are usually adapted simply from small naval boats. The single-ship trawling skill is a historical, undeveloped fishing method where the fishing boats work alone with nets on one side of the boat. In contrast, the double-ship trawling technology is more advanced with higher requirement for facilities and human control of the fishing boats. It needs two fishing boats to cooperate together by using stronger facilities to attract fish (such as high-powered lights for attracting squid at night), keeping the same (or higher) speed to follow and catch up with fish groups, and finally holding larger nets to catch fish. The fishing catch from double-ship trawling could reach four to five times that of single-ship trawling.
2. The technology transfer, as well as the assistance in helping North Korean local partners to fish, was usually an extra and temporary option in the previous investment in fishing in North Korea in exchange for larger fishing areas. A similar option could also be catching some of the fish for North Korean fishing companies to fulfil their production quotas set by the central government in Pyongyang.
3. The ocean border between China and North Korea near the access to Yalu River is not always very clear. From the late 2000s, in the name of anti-illegal cross-border fishing activities, North Korean local military units were reported to attack and rob Chinese fishing

© The Author(s) 2019
B. Gao, *China's Economic Engagement in North Korea*,
Palgrave Series in Asia and Pacific Studies,
https://doi.org/10.1007/978-981-13-0887-1

boats who had already bought fishing licences from the central government, or who, according to GPS facilities, have not actually crossed the ocean border.

4. Recorded by the Ministry of Commerce of the People's Republic of China (2009), the inter-Korea cooperation in the fishery sector started very early. As early as the 1970s there was inter-government discussion between Pyongyang and Seoul about fishery cooperation. In 1998, in order to resolve the problem of coastal seafood resource decline, the South Korean government planned to develop the marine territory of North Korea as an alternative fishing area; the South Korea Ocean Seafood Department and Research Institution cooperated with North Korea on seafood aquaculture, and research into Yellow Sea seafood resources and environmental research of the East Sea began. South Korea used technology transfer in exchange for the rights of shellfish aquaculture in Hwanghae and Pyongan, and salmon aquaculture in Namdaecheon. Following the summit of the Joint Declaration on the North and South, the discussion and negotiation of inter-Korea economic cooperation began. In 2000, except for the opening of the Kaesong Industrial Zone, North Korea decided to allow South Korean fishermen to enter 2 square kilometres of its east marine territory. South Korea also agreed to negotiate with North Korea on the issue of allowing North Korean fishing boats to enter the disputed sea area between North and South Korea. In 2005, the inter-Korea mutual fishing area in the west sea of the Korean Peninsula was decided in the first meeting of the Inter-Korea Fishery Co-operation Working Conference and an agreement was reached on the further discussion as to specific details, such as the fishing period and number of fishing boats and equipment allowed. In 2007, an inter-Korea agreement was signed allowing South Korean boats to enter North Korean designated marine territory, payment in kind, and the potential construction of mutual fishing areas in the East Sea of the Korean Peninsula.

5. Red tide is a natural disaster occurring with a rapid increase of algae in the river and ocean. It is usually caused by water eutrophication as a direct result of the increase in human pollution. Red tide could cause the mass mortality of fish and other small living creatures in the water.

APPENDIX C: CHINA'S ECONOMIC ACTIVITIES IN THE NORTH KOREAN... 161

6. The eleven major types of seafood production in Bohai Sea are prawns, small yellow fish, big yellow fish, jellyfish, crab, shrimp, megrim, mackerel, squid, codfish, and ribbon fish. Five types which have maintained original output are prawns, megrims, crabs, jellyfish, and squid.

7. North Korea is an underdeveloped country in terms of fishery technology. According to Li (2004: 23–35), due to the lack of advanced fishing technology, in the early 2000s, North Korea only effectively developed half of its ocean territory, which included almost 10 per cent sea area under the DPRK-Japanese agreement for Japanese fishing and Inter-Korea agreement for South Korean fishing in North Korea. Jin (2009: 9–10) states that compared to the Bohai Sea and parts of the Yellow Sea near China, the ocean near North Korea is very clean, compared to the general level of 3.5 (heavily polluted) of the Bohai Sea environment, and level 3 (medium polluted) of the Yellow Sea environment near China, most of the North Korean sea environment achieves level 1 of the international standard for a clean natural environment.

Appendix D: Chinese Cross-Border Economic Activities in North Korea

1. This agreement is the predecessor to the mutual management agreement. The framework formally constructs bilateral cooperation and establishes communication: bilateral meetings are to be held every half year for the exchange of ideas in solving problems; the two sides will create interaction between offices and departments, form corresponding working groups of cooperative areas, and hold relevant meetings of working groups to conduct research on effective strategies for pushing forward bilateral cooperation in order to promote mutual development (Hunchun.gov.cn, 2010; XInhuanet, 2010).

2. The major Chinese representatives were Chen Weigen, vice-head of Jilin province and a member of the standing committee of the Jilin Chinese Communist Party; Zhang An-shun, secretary of the Yanbian Chinese Communist Party and a member of the standing committee of the Jilin Chinese Communist Party; Zhao Zhenghao, chairman of the North Korea Rason People's Committee; Choi Kuang-nam, vice-chairman of the North Korea Rason People's Committee; and a few other important local officials from Yanbian.

3. 'Road-Harbor-District Integration Project' has three major parts: road, harbour, and district.

    The 'Road' includes two parts: railway and highway. The highway means the 48.75 kilometres' road from North Korea Yuanting to Rajin port. The railways are the perspective 218.80 kilometres'

© The Author(s) 2019

B. Gao, *China's Economic Engagement in North Korea*,
Palgrave Series in Asia and Pacific Studies,
https://doi.org/10.1007/978-981-13-0887-1

railway lay in the eastern part of Northeast China from Dongning of Heilongjiang province to Hunchun in Jilin, and the 50 kilometres' special railway from Rajin Harbor to Hunchun Quanhe port which targets to unblock the Rajin Harbor by fast removal of products.

The 'Harbor' comprises three parts: firstly, the existing No. 1–No. 3 port in the Rajin Harbor will be reconstructed; secondly, several new ports will be constructed under the current foundation; thirdly, the custom and products transportation line will be opened from Rajin port to southeast China, Japan, South Korea, and Southeast Asia.

The 'District' means the construction of two big economic zones in Rason area. The first one is the Rajin China Investment and Cooperation District. This district, which is located at Kuan-Gu-dong between Rajin and Xianfeng, with 1.3 square kilometres, will develop the export processing and business service in the future. The other one is the investment, construction, and management of the Harbor neighbouring bonded logistic area. This district is located close to Rajin Harbor with 3.7 square kilometres. As early as March 2006, the local national development and reform commission of Jilin province has formally permitted the project of enlarging the highway between Rajin and Yuanting under the standard of China secondary road.

The project started after the licences of opening and operation of a few projects, which include 'the construction and operation of Rajin Harbor', 'the construction and operation of the railway from Rajin Harbor to Hunchun', and 'Developing mineral mountains have been formally permitted and added into the Sino-North Korea 'Road-Harbor-District Integration project' by the top decision-maker of North Korea. The Rason China Investment and Cooperation District has been put into the plan of Overseas China economic and trade cooperation region by the Department of Commerce.

4. In stage I China invested 3 billion RMB in order to form the transport channel of the Tumen River to significantly improve bilateral trade between China and North Korea. The major cost of China's investment will be used in three parts: 0.3 billion RMB for the enlargement of the road from Rajin Harbor to Yuanting port; 1.2 billion RMB for the construction of a railway from Dongning, in Heilongjiang, to Hunchun, in Jilin; 1.13 billion RMB for the

APPENDIX D: CHINESE CROSS-BORDER ECONOMIC ACTIVITIES IN NORTH... 165

reconstruction of a third port and construction of a new fourth port in Rajin Harbor.

5. It is expected that fifty-one sunshine greenhouses will be built in Rason. In the first three months, seven greenhouses have been built with an investment of 650,000 RMB.

6. One modern chicken farm with 20,000 layers was first built in 2011; this has now increased to a total of 80,000 chickens (30,000 layers and 50,000 broilers).

7. The pig farm was constructed but failed to continue due to environmental problems and difficulties in the selection of a new location.

8. The change of relationship between Cameron's UK government and Beijing can be seen as a suitable case. Cameron's government had a very beneficial beginning for Sino-British relationships in trade and business: in 2010, Cameron visited China and returned with a 3 billion GBP cooperation programme and twelve signed agreements (Xinhuanet, 2010). However, the relationship between China and the UK declined heavily because of Cameron's meeting with the Dalai Lama in May 2012. China punished the UK by stopping the dialogue at the ministerial level with the UK for almost one year. However, after the announcement by Cameron recognising Tibet as a part of China, the relationship between China and the UK in late 2013 normalised with the second official visit of Cameron, which gained 4.5 billion GBP in cooperation programmes and ten signed agreements (Xinhuanet, 2013).

9. The case is the foundation of a new UNHRC (United Nation Human Rights Council) in 2006 to replace the previous UNHRC (United Nation Human Rights Committee). Since 2006, China has successfully been elected three times as a member country of the UNHRC: the first term of office is 2007–2009, the second one is 2010–2012, and the third one is 2014 to 2016 (UNHRC, 2013). The only reason for China's absence in 2013 is that UNHRC rules state that countries can only have one reappointment to UNHRC membership and the new term of office as member must start one year after the end of two previous terms of office. Thus, at the international level, in contrast to the huge leverage of economic power, the human rights issue is no longer an effective tool for increasing pressure on Beijing.

10. Shenyang Consulate Incident.

166 APPENDIX D: CHINESE CROSS-BORDER ECONOMIC ACTIVITIES IN NORTH...

On 8 May 2002, five North escapees attempted to seek political asylum in the Japanese Consulate in Shenyang. They tried to rush into the Consulate. Three of them were blocked by Chinese Security Guards violently but the other two still successfully entered the Consulate. After negotiating with Japanese staff, Chinese policemen took all the five North escapees away from the Consulate. All these five North escapees were sent to Philippines first and then they arrived in Seoul on 22 May 2002.

11. Law of PRC on punishments in public order and security administration: 治安管理处罚法, Zhian Guanli Chufa Fa

    Criminal Law 刑法

    刑法第13条规定, 情节显著轻微, 危害不大的, 不认为是犯罪如果符合以上规定, 就可以不采用刑罚, 而给予治安管理处罚即可......Xingfa di 13 tiao guiding, qingjie xianzhu qingwei, weihai buda de, burenwei shifanzui ruguo fuhe yishang guiding, jiukeyi bu caiyong xingfa, er geiyu zhian guanli chfua jike.

    (第三章:违反治安管理行为和处罚 Di san zhang: Weifan Zhian Guanli Xingwei he Chufa; Chap. 3: Weifan Zhian Guanli Xingwei he Chufa)

    第十九条有下列扰乱公共秩序行为之一, 尚不够刑事处罚的, 处十五日以下拘留、 二百元以下罚款或者警告:

    (一)扰乱机关、 团体、 企业、 事业单位的秩序, 致使工作、 生产、 营业、 医疗、 教学、 科研不能正常进行, 尚未造成严重损失的;

    Di 19 Tiao, you xialie raoluan gonggong zhixu xingwei zhiyi, shang bugou xingshi chufa de, chu 15ri yixia juliu, 200yuan yixia fakuan huo jinggao:

    Raoluan jiguan, tuanti, shiye danwei de zhixu, zhishi gongzuo、 shengchan、 yingye、 yiliao、 jiaoxue、 keyan buneng zhengchang jinxing, shangwei zaocheng yanzhong sunshi de;

    第二十二 条,有下列侵犯他人人身权利行为之一, 尚不够刑事处罚的, 处十五日以下拘留、 二百元以下罚款或者警告:

    (一)殴打他人, 造成轻微伤害的;

    (二)非法限制他人人身自由或者非法侵入他人住宅的;

    Di 22 Tiao, you xialie raoluan gonggong zhixu xingwei zhiyi, shang bugou xingshi chufa de, chu 15ri yixia juliu, 200yuan yixia fakuan huo jinggao:

    (一)Ouda taren, zaocheng qingwei shanghai de;

    (二) Feifa xianzhi taren rensheng ziyou huozhe feifa qinru taren zhuzhai;

APPENDIX D: CHINESE CROSS-BORDER ECONOMIC ACTIVITIES IN NORTH... 167

第二十三条, 有下列侵犯公私财物行为之一, 尚不够刑事处罚的, 处十五日以下拘留或者警告, 可以单处或者并处二百元以下罚款:

(一)偷窃、骗取、抢夺少量公私财物的;

Di 23 Tiao, you xialie qingfan gongsi caiwu xingwei zhiyi, shang bugou xingshi chufa de, chu 15 ri yixia juliu huozhe jinggao, keyi danchu huo bingchu 200 yuan yixia fakuan:

(1) Touqie、pianqu、qiangduo shaoliang gongsi caiwu de;

12. Beijing's reply to Chang-Ji-Tu Initiative

(原则同意《中国图们江区域合作开发规划纲要—以长吉图为开发开放先区》(以下简称纲要), 请认真组织实施 吉林省长春市、吉林市部分区域和延边州(以下简称长吉图)是图们江区域的核心地区)

(Yuanze tongyi <<Zhongguo Tumenjiang quyu hezuo kaifa guihua gangyao—yi Chang-Ji-Tu wei kaifang kaifa xianqu>> (yixia jiancheng gangyao), qing renzhen shishi Jilin

sheng Changchun shi, Jilin shi bufen quyu he Yanbian zhou (yixia jiancheng Chang-Ji-Tu) shi Tumenjiang quyu de hexin diqu).

INDEX

A
Access to clean, 47
Affordable food, 47
Agricultural corporation, 88–89
Agriculture, 40, 49, 73, 74, 81, 85, 88, 97, 103, 133
Australia, 158

B
Baohua Group, 52
Beijing, 1, 3–7, 13, 16, 24, 26, 28, 31–33, 37–41, 48, 49, 56, 57, 60, 64, 74, 84, 85, 89, 97, 104, 111, 119, 125, 137, 138, 143–145, 147, 148, 150–152, 154, 165, 167
   distant governance in Sino-DPRK cross-border cooperation, 99–102
   Ministry of Commerce in, 27
   punishment, and short-term Sino-DPRK relationship, 66–68
   State Council in, 8–9
Beijing Huatong Trade Company, 56

Belt & Road Initiative (BRI), 153
Berlin Wall, 115
Bohai Sea, 11, 161
   environmental pollution in, 58–59
Bonded Company of the Hunchun Border Economic Co-operation Zone, 83
Border security, 74, 76–81
Brazil, 158
Bureau, 29

C
Cambodia, drug trafficking, 74
Cao Guiquan, 8, 9
CCTV, *see* China Central Television
CDFA, *see* China Distant Fishing Association
Central Committee of the Chinese Communist Party (CCP), 7–8
Central government, 9–10, 31
   divergence between actors below the state and, 35–37
Central-local divergence, China's economic activities in, 38–41

© The Author(s) 2019
B. Gao, *China's Economic Engagement in North Korea*,
Palgrave Series in Asia and Pacific Studies,
https://doi.org/10.1007/978-981-13-0887-1

169

170 INDEX

Central SOEs, 25–26
Chang-Ji-Tu, 7, 123, 167
  Plan, 148
  project, 16, 82–85
Changping Corp, Great West Sea
    Programme, 52
Chao, Lv, 65
Chen Deming, 81
Chernobyl accident (1986), 61
Chile, 55
China
  decentralisation in, 8–10
  economic policy of, 3
  Ministry of Commerce, 29, 41
  population in, 11
  rare earth, 158
  Shenhua Group, 32
  urbanisation in, 38
China Central Television (CCTV), 34
China Custom Hall, 89
China Distant Fishing Association
    (CDFA), 49
'China's Detroit,' 39
China's foreign economic policy, 144
China-South Korean Ieodo Island-
    centred dispute
  background, 125–126
  of economic zones, 125
  energy sector, 126–127
  first blockade, occupying and
      occupied, 127–128
  obstacles to resolving, 126
  second blockade, 128–130
China Steel Co Ltd., 29
Chinese cross-border economic
    activities, in North Korea
  agricultural corporation, 88–89
  Beijing's distant governance in
      Sino-DPRK cross-border
      cooperation; cultural decline
      and labour shortage, 101–102;
      illegal immigration, 100–101
  border security, 76–81

Chang-Ji-Tu project, 82–85
  economic security, 75–76
  labour/light industry corporation, 86
  labour shortage and population
      outflow; labour cooperation,
      89–90; North escapees,
      93–100; Road-Harbour
      integration, 90–92; tourism
      cooperation, 92–93
  physical infrastructure cooperation,
      82–85
  Razon Special Economic and Trade
      Zone, mutual management of,
      81–82
  tourism corporation, 86–88
Chinese economic activity, regional
    impact of, 111–138
Chinese government, 2
Choi Yeong-Hee, 56
Choo Jae-woo, 4
Chung-In Moon, 3
Coal liquefaction, 32–33, 35
Coal mines, 27–30, 146, 147
  China's economic activities in,
      32–37
Cold War era, 24
  fishing industry in, 48, 53
  North escapees in, 95
Cooperation and Development
    Strategy of Tumen River
    Region, 85
Cooperation and Mutual Assistance, 1
Criminal Law (China), 79, 80
Cultural Revolution, 1

D
Dafeng International Corporation, 87
Dandong-Sinuiju economic
    cooperation, 3
Dandong Tourism Bureau, 86
Daya High Speed Ocean Transport, 83
Decentralisation, in China, 8–10

INDEX 171

Democratic People's Republic of
Korea (DPRK), 1
economic activities in, 25–26
Deng Xiaoping, 116
Denuclearisation, 4, 6, 16
Department of Commerce (China), 81
Diyuan Industry Corp, 28
'Domestic Seedlings for External
Cultivation 内育外养', 52, 59–60
'Domestic trade with external
transportation: Jilin-Rason
Transport Experiment
Cooperation,' 82
Double-ship trawling technology,
52–53, 159
DPRK, *see* Democratic People's
Republic of Korea
Drug trafficking, 74
Du Ying, 84

E
East China Sea, 11
Economic reform, 2–6, 8, 9, 38, 60,
77, 97, 111–125, 130, 137, 143,
146, 148
Economic security, 75–76
Eleventh Five Year Plan Period of
PRC's National Economy and
Social Development
(2005–2010), 59
Environmental pollution in fishing
area, 58–59
Environmental security problem, 11
Ethnic Shrinking, 75
European Union, 73

F
Feicheng Mineral Corp, 157
Fishery, 12, 16, 23, 48–62, 64–68, 74,
96, 111, 125–130, 138, 143,
144, 146–149, 160, 161

Fishing industry of North Korea,
China's economic activities in,
47–53
clean alternative fishing area,
seeking; environmental
pollution, impacts of, 58–59;
fishing activities in North
Korea, effectiveness
of, 59–61
divergence between central
government and local actors,
64–67; Beijing's punishment,
66–67; fishery incident,
background of, 65–66
Fushikuma nuclear plant accident
(2011), influence of;
background and impact, 61;
fishing to North Korea, 62–64
response to reduction of China's
fishing area, 53–57; difference
between old and new
agreements, 54–57
Fushikuma nuclear plant accident
(2011), 53
background and impact, 61
fishing to North Korea, 62–64

G
Gao Jijun, 91
Gap, definition of, 2–8
Great West Sea Programme, 52

H
Haggard, S., 3
Henan province, 28, 32
Hongyang trade, 28
Hunchun Donglin Economic & Trade
Company, 83
Hunchun Hongfeng Clothes
Company, 86
Hunchun Mineral Corporation, 83

172 INDEX

Hunchun-Rason agricultural cooperation project, 88
Hunchun-Rason Road-Harbor-District integration project, 83
Hunchun Yunda Clothes Corporation, 86
Hundt, D., 3
Hwang Jiang-yep, 77

I

Ikenberry, G., 3
Illegal immigrants, 76
  at local employment, 77–78
  problems on influencing public security, 78–81
Illegal immigration, Beijing's distant governance in Sino-DPRK cross-border cooperation, 99–101
Information security problem, 11
Inter-Korea agreement, 160
Interviewees, 13–14
Iron ore, China's economic activities in, 38–41

J

Jang Sung-Taek, 81, 113, 114, 117
Japanese-Qing War, 115
Jiang Guobing, 8
Jiang Hu-quan, 82
Jiang Ze-min, 116
Jilin Hunchun Dongling Economic Trade Corporation, 83
Jilin Northeast Passenger Transport Corporation, 87
Jilin province, 39, 40
Jilin Telai Clothes Company, 86
Jilin Tonggang Co Ltd., 29
Jilin Yubieer Transport Corporation, 87–88

K

Kim Dae-Jong, 115
Kim Il-Sung, trend of economic reform, 112
Kim Jin Moo, 4
Kim Jong-il, 93, 99, 112, 116–119, 122, 124
  failed economic reform of, 113–114
Kim Jong-un, 117, 119, 154
  economic reform under, 114
Kim Jung-il, 115
Kim Xiuyue, 81, 82
Korean Peninsula Energy Development Organisation (KEDO), 134, 135
KOTRA, 37
Kumgang Mountain Special Tourist Zone, 87

L

Labour cooperation, 89–90
Labour/light industry corporation, 86
Labour shortage
  agricultural programme and supply of food, 97–98
  Beijing's distant governance in Sino-DPRK cross-border cooperation, 101–102
  other activity effects, 97
  physical infrastructure cooperative construction, effects of, 96–97
  Shenzen's experience to Rason, applying, 94–96
  tourism cooperation, 98–99
Laos, drug trafficking, 74
Law of PRC on punishments, 79–80
Lee Myung-Bak doctrine, 115
Level below the state economic activities, 28–31
Liangui, Zhang, 65
Liaoning Equipment Co Ltd., 29

INDEX 173

Liaoning Machine (LIMAC) Corp, 27
Liaoning province, 28
Light industry, 16, 73–75, 78, 81, 86, 89, 90, 114, 143
Li Longxi, 81
Linyi Mineral Corp, 157
Lin Yuejiao, 55
Liu Haiying, 55
Liu Xinrong, 91
Longkou Mineral Corp, 157
Lou Wei, 10

M

Madeli Corporation, 83
Man Haifeng, 3
Mao Zedong, 116
Mineral resource cooperation, 26
Ministry of Agriculture (China), 49
Ministry of Commerce, in Beijing, 27
Ministry of Foreign Affairs (China), 52, 65
Multi-level governance, 56, 74
Mutual Supply of Important Products, 26

N

National Developing and Reform Committee, 85
Ninth Five Year Plan Period of PRC's National Economy and Social Development (1995–2000), 59
Noland, M., 3
Non-traditional security (NTS), 10–12, 23–24, 47, 48, 68, 73, 74, 80, 81, 89–93, 144
Northeast Rejuvenation Plan, 75
North escapees, 79, 80, 166
    labour shortage and population outflow, 93; agricultural programme and supply of food, 97–98; other activity effects, 97;

physical infrastructure cooperative construction, effects of, 96–97; Shenzen's experience to Rason, applying, 94–96; tourism cooperation, 98–99
North Korea
    Chinese cross-border economic activities in, 163–167
    Chinese economic activities in, 2, 12–13, 111–138
    denuclearisation, Chinese economic activities, 135–137
    domestic limitations, economic reform, 117–118
    economic opening up, domestic barriers, 114–118
    economic reform, 112–125
    failed economic reform, history of, 112–114
    political instability, 115, 122–125
    problematic leadership, 116
    promoting economic reform, 118–125
    Six Party Talks, 111
    South Korea aid to, 131–133
    top-down ideological reform, 118–122
    training, external interaction, 118–119
    US aid to, 134–135
North Korea Co-operation Committee, 86
'North Korea Liaofeng Non-ferrous Metals Joint Venture,' 29
North Korean Fishery Association, 49
North Korean fishing industry, China's economic activities in, 159–161
North Korean LongXing Firm, Sea Cucumber Cultivation Base, 52
North Korean mineral resource sector, China's economic activities in, 23–42, 157–158

174   INDEX

North Korean Shangming Trade
 Corporation, 56
North Korean Success Firm, 52
North Korea Rason International
 Linguist Co-management
 Company, 'Road-Harbor-District
 Integration Project,' 83
North Korea Tourist Administration, 88
NTS, *see* Non-traditional security
Nuclear weapons, 12, 111, 112, 120,
 138, 145, 153

O

Ocean Law Treaty of the UN, 54
Ocean pollution, 58

P

Penglai Xingdong Company,
 'Domestic Seedlings for External
 Cultivation 内育外养', 52, 59
Penglai Xingdong Fishing, 52
People's Republic of China (PRC), 1
Physical infrastructure cooperation,
 82–85
Physical infrastructure cooperative
 construction, effects of, 96–97
Political instability, 115
PRC, *see* People's Republic of China
Private companies, 25
Public security, illegal immigrants'
 problems on influencing, 78–81
PwC's China vehicle industry, 39
Pyongyang, 2, 115, 121–124, 145,
 148, 152, 154

R

Railway network, 40, 42
Rajin Harbor, 146
Rare earth, 11, 25, 27, 29–31, 41, 42,
 145–148, 158

China's economic activities in,
 37–38
Rason, 81–85, 87, 88, 91, 92, 94–99,
 103, 113, 116, 117, 119,
 122–124, 135, 148, 151, 152,
 163–165
Rason Economic Zone, 151, 152
Razon Special Economic and Trade
 Zone, mutual management of,
 81–82
Red tide, 186
Regional governments, 9
Regional SOEs, 25
Resource scarcity, 47
'Road-Harbor-District Integration
 Project,' 83, 163–164
Road-Harbour integration, 90–92
Roh Moo-hyun, 115
Ruiyu Mineral Corp, 28

S

SASAC, *see* Supervision and
 Administration Commission of
 the State Council
'Second border' policy, 95
Security
 border, 74, 76–81
 economic, 75–76
 non-traditional, 73, 89–93
'7.1 Reform,' 112
SEZs, *see* Special Economic Zones
Shandong Energy Corp, 157
Shandong Ocean and Fishery
 Department, 60
Shandong province, 28, 32, 33, 36, 157
Shanxi province, 32
Shuguang Industrial Trade Co, 29
SINA, 29
Single-ship trawling, 52
Sino-DPRK Economic and Cultural
 Cooperation Agreement
 of 1953, 48

Sino-DPRK economic relationship, 152
Sino-DPRK Friendship Oil Pipeline, in Dandong, 26
Sino-DPRK Friendship Treaty, 153
Sino-DPRK joint economic programmes, 120
Sino-DPRK relationship, 1–4, 7, 41, 143–145, 150, 153
Sino-DPRK Road-Harbor-District Integration Project, 82
Sino-Foreign cooperation, 151
Sino-North Korean Management Committee, 82
SINO PEC, 35–36
Sino-ROK fishery agreement, 146
 of 2001, 54
 impacts of, 54–55
 implications of, 55–57
Sino-ROK fishery buffer zone, 128–130
Sino-ROK Ieodo Island dispute, 111
Sino-ROK inter-state agreement, 48
Six Party Talks (SPT), 5, 6, 12, 16, 66, 111, 121, 132, 134–136, 145, 149, 151
Small and medium enterprises (SMEs), 24, 145, 147, 150
Small-Island Clothes Corporation, 86
SOEs, *see* State-owned enterprises
South China Sea, 11
South Korea, 113, 115, 128, 149
 in denuclearising North Korea, 130–137
South Korean Exclusive Economic Zone, 12
Special Economic Zone (SEZ), 12, 27, 54, 81, 82, 92, 94, 95, 97–99, 103, 113, 116, 117, 119–123, 148, 151
State-level economic activities, 26–28
State-owned enterprises (SOEs), 32–33
 types of, 25–26

Supervision and Administration Commission of the State Council (SASAC), 26

T
Teng Song-yan, 10
Tenth Five Year Plan Period of PRC's National Economy and Social Development (2000–2005), 59
Tianchi Industrial Trade Co Ltd., 29
Tianjin International Vehicle Expo, 39
Tonghua Iron Corp, 39
Tourism, 2, 12, 16, 73, 74, 77, 81, 85–89, 92–93, 98–99, 111, 121, 143, 152
Tourism corporation, 86–88
 labour shortage and population outflow, 92–93; North escapees, 98–99
Traditional planned economy, 9
Traditional security threats, 10
Treaty of Friendship, 1
Triangulation, 12, 15
Tumen-Namyang-Qibao Mountain Line, 87
Tumen Sino-DPRK Labour Co-operation Zone, 86

U
United Nation Human Rights Council (UNHRC), 165
UN Security Council, 153

V
Vietnam, drug trafficking, 74

W
Walliman, N., 15
Wu Kuang Group Company, 27

176 INDEX

X
Xiao-qing, Wu, 58
Xi Jinping, 153
Xinwen Mineral Corp, 157

Y
Yanbian Ethnic Korean Autonomous
Prefecture, 12, 75, 76, 90, 102
Yanbian Tianyu International Tourism
Group, 87
Yatai Agricultural High-efficiency Test
Zone, 88–89
Yatai Corporation, 88
Yellow Sea, 11, 111

Yide Industry Corp, 28
YiMa Coal Corp, 28
Yunzhou Mineral Corp, 157

Z
Zanhua trade, 28
Zao Zhuang Mineral Corp, 157
Zhang, Feng, 29
Zhejiang province, in Southeast
China, 4
Zhoushan Putuo Distant Fishery
Company, 52
Zhou Zhongshu, 27
Zibo Mineral Corp, 157